COPING WITH CRIME

Volume 124, Sage Library of Social Research

RECENT VOLUMES IN
SAGE LIBRARY OF SOCIAL RESEARCH

COPING
with CRIME

Individual and
Neighborhood Reactions

WESLEY G. SKOGAN
MICHAEL G. MAXFIELD

Volume 124
SAGE LIBRARY OF
SOCIAL RESEARCH

 SAGE PUBLICATIONS   Beverly Hills   London

For information address:

SAGE Publications, Inc.
275 South Beverly Drive
Beverly Hills, California 90212

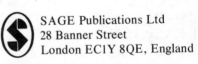

SAGE Publications Ltd
28 Banner Street
London EC1Y 8QE, England

Printed in the United States of America

Library of Congress Cataloging in Publication Data

Skogan, Wesley G:
  Coping with Crime.

  (Sage library of social research ; v. 124)
  Bibliography: p.
  Includes index.
  1. Crime and criminals — United States — Public opinion. 2. Victims of crimes — United States. 3. Crime prevention — United States — Citizen participation. 4. Public opinion — United States. I. Maxfield, Michael G. II. Title. III. Series.
  HV6791.S56   364.4'0973   81-2501
  ISBN 0-8039-1632-9   AACR2
  ISBN 0-8039-1633-7 (pbk.)

FIRST PRINTING

2/82

CONTENTS

ABOUT THE AUTHORS

Michael G. Maxfield is Assistant Professor of Public and Environmental Affairs, and Assistant Professor of Forensic Studies at Indiana University, Bloomington. He received his Ph. D. in political science from Northwestern University in 1979. Dr. Maxfield has conducted research in police discretion, patrol supervision, and urban service delivery. He has published articles in *Journal of Research in Crime and Delinquency, Social Science Quarterly,* and *Victimology.*

Wesley G. Skogan is an Associate Professor of Political Science and Urban Affairs at Northwestern University. He is the editor of *Sample Surveys of the Victims of Crime* and the author of numerous articles and monographs on crime, the police, victimization surveys, and research methodology. He is on the editorial boards of *Evaluation Review, Journal of Criminal Law and Criminology, Journal of Research in Crime and Delinquency, Law and Policy Quarterly,* and several other professional journals. He is completing a policy-analytic book on the politics of crime, examining in detail the issue of crime and the elderly.

ACKNOWLEDGMENTS

This volume is based on a great deal of labor by many persons, and a great deal of tolerance by a few more. It stems from a larger project conceived of and organized by Fred DuBow and managed for many years by Dan A. Lewis. Without either of them there would have been no Reactions to Crime Project. We received a great deal of advice and assistance from colleagues at the National Institute of Justice, including Winifred Reed, Richard T. Barnes, Fred Heinzelmann, Lois Mock, and Richard Rau. They held their administrative reins loosely. Our activities have been reviewed on occasion by Gerald Suttles, Peter Manning, Richard Taub, Jack Fowler, Victor Rouse, and Gilbert Geis. Their comments were always taken seriously, and occasionally to heart. Other research projects at Northwestern have contributed generously to this volume. Margaret T. Gordon and Stephanie Riger supported some of our survey work, and Paul J. Lavrakas made available his data on the Chicago metropolitan area. Robert Kidder, Louise Kidder, and Ellen Cohn made great intellectual contributions at the time when our research plans were being drawn up. Terry Baumer got the work done. Final preparation of this volume was supervised by Marlene B. Simon, and Sandy Levin did the graphics. A number of dedicated people have typed its various versions, but Kumi K. Choe, Martha Malley, and Kathryn McCord produced the final copy.

The tolerance was contributed by our families, who survived the days when this report was being written. In their various ways Barbara, Susan, Mary, and Molly made it worth doing.

This volume was prepared under Grant 78-NI-AX-0057 from the National Institute of Law Enforcement and Criminal Justice, Law Enforcement Assistance Administration, U.S. Department of Justice. The principal survey reported upon in this volume also was supported in part by Grant R01MH29629-01 from the National Institute of Mental Health. The Chicago Metropolitan Area Survey used here was conducted by Dr. Paul J. Lavrakas, supported by Grant 78-NI-AX-0111 from LEAA. Points of view or opinions in this volume are those of the authors and do not necessarily represent the official position or policies of the U.S. Department of Justice.

PART I

VICTIMIZATION AND FEAR

Chapter 1

THE PROBLEM AND THE CITIES

Introduction

This volume is concerned with how city dwellers cope with the problems of crime and fear of crime. Crime and fear are related problems, but they do not always go together. The research upon which this volume is based began as an effort to understand several apparent paradoxes. The first was that more people are fearful of crime than report being victimized. Another was that people who are least likely to be victimized are among the most likely to report being fearful. Finally, we also observed that during a time when levels of crime and fear were both climbing, governments were spending large sums of money funding efforts to encourage people to do something to protect themselves. While many explanations for these apparent contradictions come to mind, these inconsistencies have led some to question whether or not levels of fear of crime in American cities are at all "realistic."

The central message of our research is that fear is indeed a consequence of crime, but that most consequences of crime — including fear — are indirect. While victims of crime are more fearful as a result of their experiences, many more people have indirect contact with crime. The sources of this vicarious experience include the media, personal conversations with victims and others, and observations of neighborhood conditions. These convey a great deal of information about crime, and most urban dwellers cannot get through a day without being touched by it in one way or another. The less distant or abstract the message, the greater its consequences for fear. Fear in turn plays a substantial role in shaping some forms of coping behavior. The frequency with which urbanites expose themselves to risk of personal attack and the extent to which they strategically alter their on-street behavior to minimize those risks when they must face them were strongly related to fear and assessments of neighborhood conditions.

On the other hand, our research exposed a few new paradoxes to be unraveled. First, while this investigation documents anew the tremendous emphasis on crime and violence in the media, we could find no particular consequences of exposure to those messages, either for fear or behavior. Second, we found many of the most important measures people could take against crime were not being taken by those who most needed to do so. Rather, these measures were either taken more frequently by those who least needed protection, or they were irrelevant to crime and fear entirely.

We learned all of this studying conditions and events in three American cities — Chicago, Philadelphia, and San Francisco. In each city we interviewed thousands of people, probing their assessments of crime and gathering reports of what they had done about it. The Census Bureau has also conducted surveys in these jurisdictions, and we used their data as well. Field observers were stationed in selected neighborhoods in each city. They attended meetings, interviewed community leaders and local officials, and kept an eye on things that took place there. In addition, coders read and systematically recorded crime news in the daily newspapers serving these cities, in order to understand what our informants were seeing over breakfast. This volume uses information from all of these sources to probe the relationships among crime, fear, and reactions to crime.

Crime, Fear, and Reactions to Crime

A review of the research literature on these issues underscores the fact that, despite their importance, relatively little is known about the relationships among crime, fear, and things that people do in response to crime. There is considerable uncertainty even about how much crime there is, and exactly who its victims are. Until recently, official police records filed with the FBI constituted the only broad-based information available on the incidence of crime. While they tell a great deal about the kind of crime that police departments record, these figures are known to rise and fall for reasons having little to do with the true rate of victimization. Numerous contingencies of citizen reporting of crime to the police and official recording of those complaints cloud the picture of the actual distribution of crimes and victims. With the development of more reliable techniques for measuring many kinds of crime through victimization survey interviews, more is now known about who is a victim of what, and what the consequences of victimization are.

According to victimization surveys, crime is extraordinarily common. Each year government pollsters question thousands of Americans about their experiences with crime, and returns indicate that over 40 million major, nonhomicidal criminal incidents took place in 1977 (U.S. Department of Justice, 1978a). Official police reports include many more kinds of crime, things not asked about in the surveys, and they point to similarly large totals. These figures have been climbing since the early 1960's. After accelerating at a tremendous rate for more than a decade, however, both the police reports and the victim surveys indicate the increase in crime has slacked off since the 1974-1975 period, and rates for serious offenses have stabilized at about the levels for those years (Skogan, 1979a). These figures remain at an extremely high level in comparison to other Western industrial countries, even though those nations have ridden the same social roller coaster with respect to crime (Gurr, 1977b).

Opinion measures of fear of crime parallel these trends. On occasion the Gallup organization (American Institute of Public Opinion Research, monthly) and the National Opinion Research Center (1978) have asked Americans if there is a place in their neighborhoods "where you would be afraid to walk alone at night." These surveys have given us readings of the state of public opinion since 1965. They point to a steady increase in fear, from a low of 31% "yes" to a high of 45% "yes." However, reports of fear increased primarily during the 1967-1974 period, and they, too, have remained at virtually the same level since then (Baumer and DuBow, 1977). The surveys indicate that people consider crime primarily a local problem, and crime and disorder peaked as the nation's number-one problem during the big-city riots of the mid 1960s (Smith, 1979).

There is no comparable data on what people *do* about crime, which presumably would be the best barometer of its impact upon their lives. There is an ample supply of anecdotal and media accounts of the debilitating impact of crime on the quality of life. People of all races and regions are reputed to stay behind locked doors, to avoid using public transportation, to shun shopping downtown, to decline to go out on the town for entertainment, and to avoid involvement with strangers, even when they are in need of help. While these consequences for daily living are only indirect indicators of the effect of crime upon the quality of life in America, they reflect its impact upon some of the most fundamental human values, including freedom of movement and affiliation with others, freedom from fear and anxiety, and the quest for community based on mutual trust and dependence.

However, the relation between rates of crime and this behavior is not a simple one. Crime rates for areas do not always correspond with what people who live there report doing. Furstenberg (1972) found that, even in very high crime areas of Baltimore, one-quarter of his respondents reported taking no particular precautions against crime, while in the safest areas about one-quarter did a great deal in their neighborhoods to avoid being victimized. Wilson (1976) found that in Portland people who lived in the lowest crime areas were the ones who reported spending the most on security. One could conclude from this either they were not acting rationally, or that those measures were extremely effective! In any event, residents of high crime areas were not the ones who were fortifying their homes. Surveys indicate that in general there is little relation between most forms of household protection and measures of fear, or perceived risk of victimization (Scarr et al., 1973; Maxfield, 1977; Sundeen and Mathieu, 1976a). There is some evidence that people who have been victims of personal crimes are more likely to do things to protect themselves than those who have not fallen victim, but few of them report taking drastic steps or reducing their exposure to risk dramatically.

The same surveys, however, have confirmed that the relationship between crime and fear also is problematic. As we noted, many more people are fearful than have had any recent experience with crime. While victims are more afraid than nonvictims, the bulk of those wary of walking the streets have not been victimized. Moreover, many of the most fearful fall into social categories that enjoy the lowest rates of victimization. Women and the elderly evidence the highest levels of concern about crime, but relatively few in these categories fall victim to violent crime or even theft. In many cases it is necessary to look beyond people's direct and personal experiences to understand what they think about crime and what they do in response. High levels of fear expressed in many communities do not always square with what people do about crime. In particular, the rate at which victims report incidents to the police is surprisingly low, even in major crime categories. Many people are careless with regard to their person and property; for example, a large proportion of the burglaries recorded in victimization surveys are carried out without need of forcible entry, through unlocked doors or windows (U.S. Department of Justice, 1979).

The problems of crime and fear seem to be worse in cities. Crime rates certainly are higher there. In fact, there is evidence that in all parts of the world, and for most of this century, crime has been more frequent in great cities than in the surrounding countryside (Archer et al., 1978). Serious assaultive violence, handgun use, and robbery are so heavily concentrated in the big cities of this country that the overall national violent crime rate is highly contingent upon events and conditions there (Skogan, 1979a). The same opinion surveys that track fear of crime over time also indicate that fear is more pervasive in large cities among all social groups. Anxiety increases with city size at almost every step, although there is a substantial jump in levels of fear in places with populations above 100,000. Changes in offense rates in big cities have mirrored the rate at which people have moved out of them into the suburbs. Since World War II, metropolitan sprawl has grown around central cities, with the largest increases in inner-city crime, and suburbanization is most extensive outside of those cities reporting the highest levels of violence (Skogan, 1977a).

This Research

Our work began with the central constructs of crime, fear, and behavior, but we quickly began to expand the list of things about which we needed to know. Several more factors seemed important for understanding what people did about crime, and why.

First, it is clear certain people are more vulnerable to crime than others. Some are less open to attack due to their size, strength, and capacity to resist the predations. Others are vulnerable because generally they live in close proximity to potential offenders. These are factors that are generally related to both fear and behavior, and that people often cannot do very much about.

We also were interested in conditions and events which characterize people's immediate environment. By almost any standard, some places are "good places" and others are "bad places," and that should make a significant difference in what the residents of an area think and do.

Another "environmental" factor, albeit a more abstract one, is the pattern of media coverage of crime in a community. There is always a great deal of speculation about the impact of television and newspapers on people's perceptions of crime and estimates of risk. Two issues are important in this regard: the content of those media messages, and who was attentive to them.

Other forms of communication are less impersonal than the media, and their content may have greater immediacy. The frequency of personal conversations about crime and with whom those discussions took place were major topics in this research.

The survey we conducted probed people's knowledge of crimes and their images of victims. In addition to media and conversation, another form of experience with crime is contact with its victims. When victims are from one's own neighborhood the contact should be even more relevant for understanding fear. Proximity to victims can be identificational as well as spatial, so we gauged the "social distance" between people and their images of victims in the community.

These factors made up the core of a working model of why people act as they do in response to crime. A very general sketch of the relationship between these factors and crime response is presented in Figure 1.1, as the "crime-related" segment (on the left-hand side) of this operating model. Some of these constructs are more causally distant from fear and behavior than the others. There undoubtedly are important linkages among the components of the model as well.

The list of crime-related behaviors to be investigated grew to four. They were:

(1) Personal precaution. These are things people can do to protect themselves from personal attack.

(2) Household protection. This category contains a number of specific measures households can take to prevent burglary and property theft.

(3) Community involvement. There is substantial interest among policy makers in factors encouraging participation in collective efforts to reduce crime.

(4) Flight to the suburbs. Politically and economically this may be the most significant reaction to crime.

The operating model sketched in Figure 1.1 includes several "non-crime" components, depicted on the right-hand side. People are caught up in institutional and organizational matrices which limit the range of choices they have about what they do, how they live, and where they live, and affect their selections among those alternatives. Role constraints limit people's freedom of choice with regard to personal behavior. Resources families have to affect changes in their lives in response to crime, and the investments they have to protect from the threat of crime, determine many household decisions. Decisions organizations make about which issues to place on the agenda guide the involvement of their membership in specific programs. Market and nonmarket forces steer people to particular environments, and may imprison them there.

This analytic guide is thus a cognitive and volitional model of human behavior that is tempered by the recognition of significant exogenous forces. On the left-hand side it highlights the importance

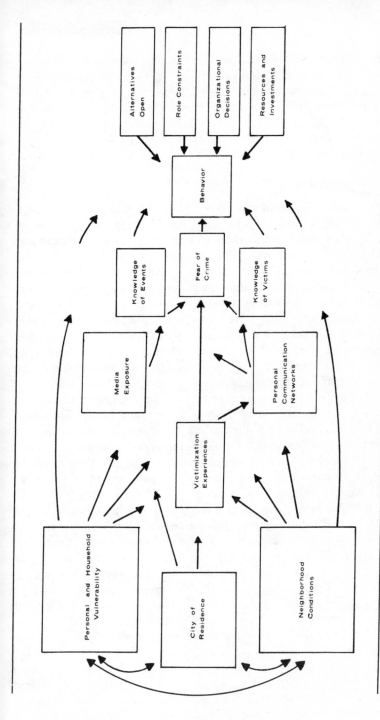

Figure 1.1 The Operating Model

17

of environmental conditions, personal qualities, direct and vicarious experience, the media, and perceptions of threat in understanding what people do about crime. This model assumes that people gather cues from their environment, assess its risks and rewards, and tend to act accordingly. On the right-hand side the model highlights limits on freedom of choice, factors which consciously or unconsciously re-shape that goal-directed behavior.

DATA COLLECTION

A variety of kinds of data were collected to address the research questions implied by the operating model. Field representatives were placed in ten study neighborhoods. They observed events there and conducted structured and informal interviews with citizens, local businessmen, police officers, and community leaders. The field re-ports were collected and examined in detail. A content analysis was conducted of citywide newspapers serving these communities. Stories concerning crime were noted, and details about those stories and the newspapers were systematically recorded. Finally, opinion surveys were conducted in each of the three cities. All of these types of data will be employed in the chapters which follow to elucidate the nature of fear and the antecedents of crime-related behavior.[1]

The field observers were graduate and undergraduate students in sociology and anthropology. They were recruited locally and super-vised by a full-time field director stationed in each city. Observers were trained in their task by senior researchers in the project. They were instructed to attend all important meetings in their assigned sites, to keep track of events there, and to make and maintain exten-sive contacts with people in the community. Much of the field work-ers' time, however, was spent interviewing specific types of people (such as real estate agents), finding answers to specific questions posed by the senior research staff. The interviews were open-ended, but the same questions were pursued for a particular category of informant in each of the research sites. Field workers set aside a substantial amount of time each week to review their notes and tape recordings. Their field reports transcribed as directly as possible what they saw and heard. There were almost 10,000 pages of field reports. This volume makes extensive use of those notes to illustrate key points and to bring to life our quantitative data.

The content analysis of newspapers serving the three cities was a major research effort.[2] This volume examines patterns of violent crime coverage in the nine metropolitan daily newspapers, although community newspapers and those with more limited circulation were examined as well. The data were recorded by coders who examined every story in each issue of those newspapers, from November 1977 through April 1978. They noted 11,475 crime-related stories concerning violence during that period. The coders transcribed information about the content of each story and measured the total size of each story, the size of headlines, and the total amount of space in each issue devoted to news of any kind. The coding was supervised carefully and the reliability of the data was continually monitored.

In this volume the data are used to characterize what newspapers in each study city were saying during the months our survey interviews were being conducted. They describe one aspect of the "crime environment" around the respondents at the time. In addition, the data enable us to compare the substantive content of newspaper crime coverage with the image of crime people hold.

The survey data which form the basis for most of the volume were collected during the last months of 1977.[3] Interviews were conducted by telephone from field offices located in each community. The survey employed a technique known as Random Digit Dialing (see Tuchfarber and Klecka, 1976) to ensure that residents who recently had moved or had unlisted telephone numbers were adequately represented in the data. Numbers were generated randomly by a computer, and each working telephone in a city had an equal chance of being called. Calls reaching group quarters, businesses, and other nonresidential places were politely terminated. Each citywide survey included interviews with 540 adults, while each of the neighborhoods was represented by a sample ranging in size from 200 to 450 respondents. The size of these samples was lowered somewhat by the need to down-weight respondents from households with more than one telephone number (they were more likely to be sampled), and to correct the sample for a slight overrepresentation of women. The citywide surveys had a total effective sample size of 1,389 when these corrections were made. In every case those questioned were randomly selected from among the adults who lived in the household we reached by phone. Telephone numbers which went unanswered or gave a busy signal were recalled several times in an attempt to contact residents there. Respondents to the citywide surveys were contacted using all of the three-digit residential telephone exchanges serving the legal boundaries of the central city. In order to contact residents of specific neighborhoods within the city, numbers were called at random only for telephone exchanges which served those areas, and each answering household was quizzed to make sure that it lay within the correct boundaries. Spanish-language interviewers were available in each city, and every effort was made to complete interviews before another randomly generated telephone number was substituted for the "refusing" household. The response rate for the survey was 61%.

Two other surveys are employed in this volume. One was conducted by the Census Bureau in each of these cities to gauge the extent of criminal victimization. The other is a survey of the Chicago metropolitan area, the only data source which includes views of suburbanites as well as residents of central cities. Extensive use is made of this survey in Chapter 14 in examining flight to the suburbs.

CITY AND NEIGHBORHOOD SITES

These operations were conducted in Chicago, Philadelphia, and San Francisco. Although one of these cities is eastern, one midwestern, and the other located on the West Coast, they all have a great deal in common. All are old cities, plagued with racial conflict, physical decay, and economic crisis. Each is ringed by growing, prosperous suburbs, while they are losing population, jobs, and housing at a marked rate. All had crime problems of considerable magnitude.

In the mid 1970s, Philadelphians enjoyed the lowest crime rate of the three cities. Official statistics and victimization surveys both placed it below Chicago, and well below San Francisco, on most indicators. It followed the national trend of stable and declining crime rates. However, the tumultuous mayor of the city, Frank Rizzo, battled crime in the headlines whenever he could get it there. Still, compared to those in the other two cities, Philadelphia newspapers devoted the least attention to crime issues. As the next chapter indicates, crime in Philadelphia was overconcentrated (even when compared to other big cities) in Black neighborhoods. This enabled city hall and the metropolitan media to discount crime's significance, and the police to fail to record much of it.

Chicago fell between Philadelphia and San Francisco on both police and survey measures of crime. Official rates in Chicago were also in a decline during the period in which the field investigations and surveys were under way. The town's three major newspapers were very competitive, and devoted a great deal of attention to crime. However, as Podolefsky et al. (1980) perceptively note, the political structure and neighborhood orientation of the city served to defuse crime as an issue by "localizing" it. The political machine in Chicago effectively kept crime (and most social issues) off the governmental agenda. Concomitantly, the large size and particularistic ethnic orientation of the city's neighborhoods encouraged most residents to see crime as a problem "somewhere else."

Little of the above applied to San Francisco in the mid 1970s. The city had the highest official crime toll and the highest victimization survey rate of the three. In San Francisco the official crime rate was 2.5 times that of Philadelphia. The Bay City did not share the apparent good fortune of the others in terms of crime trends, for throughout the study period official statistics there continued to climb. Newspapers in San Francisco devoted more text space and more headline attention to crime than did the newspapers in other cities, and focused heavily on violent crime. Crime was a hot political issue in San Francisco, with the liberal troika of Mayor Moscone, Chief of Police Gain, and Sheriff Hongisto sharing the political flack for the facts noted above.

While these cities differed to some extent in each detail, for their residents the consequences of crime were quite similar. As the next chapter documents, the burden of crime was borne mainly by the same groups everywhere. Blacks and the poor generally ended up on the bottom of the heap with respect to crime. In categories of offenses in which they did not, the distribution of victimization followed a similar pattern in each city. Significantly, residents of these three cities also reported strikingly similar levels of fear of crime.

The best comparative reading of levels of fear in American cities comes from a series of sample surveys which were conducted for the Law Enforcement Assistance Administration by the U.S. Census Bureau during the 1972-1974 period. Those surveys were designed to produce estimates of rates of victimization for residents of 26 major cities, including the 3 under scrutiny here. Interviews were conducted with almost 10,000 persons aged 16 or older in each city. (For more details about these surveys, see Garofalo, 1977b.) Respondents were asked:

> How safe do you feel, or would you feel, being out alone in your neighborhood at night? Very safe, reasonably safe, somewhat unsafe, or very unsafe?

The results of these surveys for this question are presented in Figure 1.2. Depicted are the proportion of respondents who indicated they felt either "somewhat" or "very unsafe" in each city.

These figures indicate that the three study cities were quite similar with regard to levels of fear. They cluster together just above the average for all 26 cities. Because the percentages of Figure 1.2 are based on survey samples, the differences among the three are of little substantive significance. They are, for all intents and purposes, "the same." Further, if one trims from the list the city with the most deviant score, San Diego, our cities all fall very near the overall city

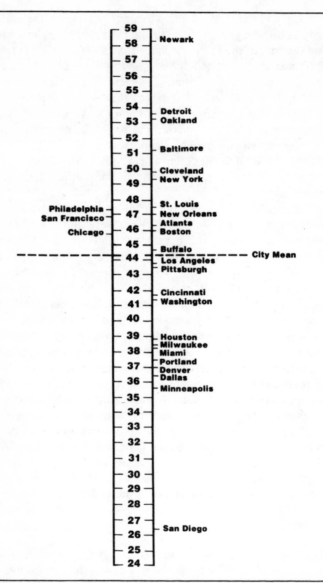

Figure 1.2 Percentage "Somewhat" or "Very" Unsafe, for 26 Cities Surveyed for LEAA

NOTE: Cities surveyed 1972-1974.
SOURCE: Unpublished Census Bureau tabulations.

mean for fear. In this sense they are typical of large cities, and the findings which are reported in this volume *may* be generalizable to other places. On the other hand, the fact that these study cities were so similar may lead us to doubt prematurely the generalizability of those findings. In the main, we found few important city-level differences to report in this volume. Almost all of the differences between cities which the survey revealed disappeared when we controlled for simple racial and social differences in the composition of their populations. If this study had been conducted in a more heterogeneous set of places that might not have been true.

If these cities were similar in some important respects, the neighborhoods within them which were chosen for intensive investigation certainly were not. Generally, differences among these areas could not be explained by simple differences in their population make-up. Rather, they varied in many interesting and fundamental respects. Briefly, those neighborhoods were:

PREDOMINANTLY BLACK NEIGHBORHOODS

Woodlawn. Woodlawn is almost a classic ghetto slum, lacking only large blocks of public housing to complete the picture. It is located on the south side of Chicago. Woodlawn is the poorest of the study neighborhoods. While there are scattered, often well-maintained, single-family homes in the area, the bulk of the people in Woodlawn live in multiple-unit apartment buildings. The housing stock is very deteriorated, the streets run-down. Commercial areas in Woodlawn are dominated by taverns, exploitive stores, and boarded-up buildings. Since 1970 the population of the area has declined considerably, due to abandonment and demolition of buildings and a serious epidemic of arson. Incomes are low and unemployment high in Woodlawn, and many families are headed by women. It is a high crime area, but enjoys a substantial degree of formal community organization.

West Philadelphia. This is a working-class Black neighborhood. The area is made up predominantly of single-family homes. Public housing developments located in West Philadelphia are of the low-rise and scatter-site variety. A large proportion of the residents of the community are homeowners, and perceive renters and project dwellers to be the primary source of trouble in the neighborhood. The most important local issues are housing and economic development. Vacant lots and spots of irregular land use dot the area.

Logan. Logan is located in central Philadelphia. It is ethnically quite diverse, housing a substantial number of whites and Asians.

The community has undergone tremendous racial change during the past decade. Many of the remaining whites are older, and often do not get along with younger, Black residents of the area. Whites trace many of the neighborhood's problems to that racial transition. Logan has relatively few long-term residents. On the other hand, most housing is single-family row-style, and a large proportion of families own their homes. Family incomes are low in this area, and there is a substantial amount of unemployment.

HETEROGENEOUS NEIGHBORHOODS

The Mission. The Mission District lies immediately south of downtown San Francisco. Formerly a white ethnic area, it is undergoing rapid population change. A large number of Hispanics live in the Mission, many of whom reside in large apartments or large old homes which have been cut up into small flats. Black residents of the neighborhood are concentrated in public housing projects. While this is a low-income neighborhood, the in-town location is attracting middle-class rehabilitation efforts. Based on our survey, the median length of residence in the Mission was only 2.8 years. Housing and disruption of the community, caused by the construction of a subway through it, seem to be the most significant issues here.

Wicker Park. Wicker Park is located in the near northwestern quadrant of Chicago. The population of the area is changing rapidly, contributing to a substantial degree of social disorganization. The current population is about one-third Black, one-third Hispanic, and one-third white. The latter group is older and predominantly Polish. Newcomers are young, and there are many children in the area. The housing stock is badly deteriorated. Building abandonment and arson are serious problems in Wicker Park. Unemployment and poverty stalk the area.

Visitacion Valley. Located in southernmost San Francisco, this is a moderate-income homeowning area, housing a diverse congerie of whites, Blacks, Asians, and Hispanics. The ethnic mix seems to be stable, and there are relatively few short-term residents of the area. A substantial proportion of the Black population of the Valley lives in two large low-income housing projects. True multiethnic residential integration exists throughout the area, however. The remainder of the population lives in single-family homes. Residents of Visitacion Valley have a long history of political organization, with high levels of participation in public affairs. At the time of our study crime was perhaps the community's most important issue.

PREDOMINANTLY WHITE NEIGHBORHOODS

South Philadelphia. This is Philadelphia's large, working-class Italian community. It is the home of former mayor Frank Rizzo and Hollywood's contribution to boxing, Rocky Balboa. In addition to being large, the area is quite diverse. While most of the area is neat and prosperous, some parts are deteriorated. Scattered through South Philadelphia are enclaves of Blacks, who made up 16% of our survey respondents. The Black tracts cluster around public housing projects. Boundaries between white and Black areas are widely known and strictly observed. Despite rampant racial paranoia among whites in South Philadelphia, community pride abounds. Most families in the area are low- to moderate-income, and live in small, connected row houses.

Back-of-the-Yards. Located on Chicago's near south side, this is a highly organized (the original turf of Saul Alinsky) Irish and Eastern European working-class neighborhood. There is a mix of tidy single-family homes and low-rise apartment buildings in the area. While many people are homeowners, property values have been declining (in real dollars) for some time. This, in part, accounts for stability in the area — families cannot afford to move. The southern end of this area is undergoing racial transition, but the bulk of respondents to our survey indicated that little fundamental change is taking place in the neighborhood.

Lincoln Park. The study area is on the western fringe of this middle-class "in-town" neighborhood on Chicago's north side. It was by far the most affluent area surveyed. Residents are white and young. Many are employed professionally, and relatively few have children. Most rent apartments in multiple-unit buildings. There is also a great deal of housing rehabilitation and "gentrification" taking place in the vicinity. The chief problems of the area are traffic congestion and unwanted commercial development. This is one of the city's principal entertainment and refreshment areas. The official crime rate in Lincoln Park is very high in several categories.

Sunset. Sunset is a white, middle-class, homeowner neighborhood lying immediately to the south of Golden Gate Park in San Francisco. Many city employees live in the area, a place where there are many older residents who have raised their families. Of all the communities we studied, Sunset had the most long-term residents, the lowest unemployment rate, and — with Lincoln Park — the highest income and educational levels. When asked about neighborhood changes in the past few years, Sunset residents were the most likely to indicate that things were "the same." On all of our measures this was the most "civil" study neighborhood, reporting the least concern about crime and enjoying the lowest official crime rate.

The chapters which follow evaluate in detail our operating model of the antecedents of action against crime. The chapters in Part I describe patterns of victimization and fear, and the crucial role of vulnerability in both crime and its consequences. Part II sets fear of crime in its community context. It explores the effects of three key neighborhood characteristics: the extent of crime problems, signs of disorder, and neighborhood integration. Part III turns to the processes by which individuals learn about crime. The crime content of the mass media, attentiveness to the media, and the development of informal neighborhood conversational networks are detailed there, along with the impact that information which is acquired in this way has upon fear. Part IV is devoted to individual and household behavior. Four chapters in this section examine in turn the frequency of personal precaution, household protection, community involvement, and flight to the suburbs. In the final chapter we summarize our key findings and reformulate the operating model with which we began.

NOTES

1. For a detailed review of the data sources which were exploited here, see Maxfield and Hunter, 1980.
2. For a detailed review of the content analysis project, see Gordon et al., 1979.
3. For a detailed review of the survey, see Skogan, 1978a.

Chapter 2

CRIMES AND VICTIMS

Introduction

Our investigation of the problems of crime and fear began during the third quarter of the 1970s, a period of some stability with regard to these issues. During the decade between 1965 and 1974, crime resembled a tidal wave. In that span the number of property crimes recorded by the FBI rose by a factor of 4, and the violent crime rate rose 336%. Then those rates of increase slowed dramatically. Nationally, most categories of reported crime peaked in 1974 and 1975, and they remained stable — although at a high level — during the remainder of the 1970s. This pattern obtains even if we examine the results of national victimization surveys rather than FBI figures; both depict the same trend during the period following 1972 for which both sets of estimates are available (Skogan, 1979a).

Official figures for our three study cities largely parallel these trends. In Chicago and Philadelphia most major crimes peaked during 1974 and 1975, and they have been dropping somewhat since that mid-decade watershed. Crime peaked one year later in San Francisco, in 1976. Our surveys in these three cities were conducted during the fall of 1977, when these downturns — if they truly reflected the experiences of residents of these communities — should have been most visible in Chicago and Philadelphia, and perhaps should have gained some attention in San Francisco.

Crime rates in these three cities are extremely high in comparison to national totals. This does not particularly distinguish Chicago, Philadelphia, or San Francisco; rather, it reflects the apparently universal concentration of crime in urban places (Archer et al., 1978). In the United States this concentration reached its peak in 1970, when the nation's 32 largest cities, which housed 17% of its population, recorded 65% of its robbery (Skogan, 1979a).

The concentration of crime in America's great cities simply means that it is a feature of the urban environment, something to be dealt with by residents of big cities almost on a daily basis. Crime certainly is not the only problem overconcentrated there, and the city environment can present stressful problems for anyone attempting to negotiate it. Like traffic jams, fires, and the housing shortage, crime challenges the "coping capacity" of many people.

In this chapter we will examine patterns of crime in our three study cities. We will focus upon those who have had the most direct experience with that problem, victims. As we shall see in later chapters, criminals may have many *indirect* victims, and the consequences spread far beyond the scene. First, however, we will examine "who has been a victim of what," and how frequently, with an eye toward understanding what they try to do about it.

Crime in Three Cities

Police reports from these cities indicate that all of them experienced rates of crime which were substantially higher than those of the nation as a whole. In the latter half of the 1970s they were faced with crime problems of considerable magnitude. The homicide rate in Philadelphia stood at twice the national level, and Chicago's was half again higher; the official rape rate in San Francisco was three times the national average, as was the frequency of assault. Rates of robbery and burglary reported to the police were twice the national figure in the least troubled of these communities. The robbery rate in San Francisco was one-third higher than that of Chicago, and more than twice that of Philadelphia.

This does not mean that the *actual* rate of crime was distributed in this way across the cities. There are a number of factors which confound the relationship between the public's experiences and official accounts of crime. Official measures of the level of crime do not reflect very accurately the actual amount of criminal activity. Many victims do not notify the authorities; in major crime categories, perhaps 50% of all incidents are not reported to the police (Skogan, 1976a). Further, the police do not necessarily record all of the incidents which citizens bring to their attention, and the rate at which they do so may change. The reasons for this nonrecording are diverse, and include command decisions, department rules, police estimations of the seriousness of events and the motives of the parties involved, and their need to keep the official crime rate under control (Black, 1970; Seidman and Couzens, 1974). It seems that the readiness of the police to record citizen complaints varies considerably from community to community. One analysis concluded that the police in Chicago recorded about 64% of all robbery and 39% of all burglary complaints, while in San Francisco the figures were 51% and 59%, and in Philadelphia, 38% and 35%, respectively (Skogan, 1976b).

Because of the rather substantial impact of reporting and recording practices upon official crime statistics, it is necessary to bypass them in order to gather many kinds of useful data about crimes and victims. In effect, victimization data gathered through population surveys is "the other side of the story" told by official figures. For this reason, the Law Enforcement Assistance Administration (LEAA) sponsored victimization surveys in each of our three cities. These surveys provide data both on the frequency of criminal incidents in these communities and on the personal attributes of victims, as compared to those who were not victimized.

The victimization data reported here were gathered in surveys conducted in Chicago and Philadelphia early in 1975, and in the San Francisco survey of 1974. In each case the survey was used to gather reports of victimization for the previous year. As a result, the most up-to-date victimization data available for our cities is for the 1973-1974 period. However, there appears to be considerable stability in the findings of these surveys from year to year (see Cook et al., forthcoming), as well as great similarity of the *relationships* between crime and other factors over time and across surveys (Garofalo, 1977a). Therefore, we will employ the general patterns these surveys describe for the three cities to augment the analysis of our own 1977 surveys.

In the victimization surveys, people were asked about crimes against themselves and their households. When they recalled an incident, detailed information was gathered about the nature of the offense, the attributes of offenders, and the consequences of the crime. The data vary in quality. Methodological investigations suggest that victims' reports of robbery (defined by the use of force or threat of force to take something) and burglary (which involves tresspass of home or garage) are quite reliable. The survey data on rape is somewhat less so, and that on assault generally is suspicious. In the case of rape and assault, one factor clouding the data is the relationship between the parties involved in such incidents. The surveys appear to substantially undercount violent encounters between acquaintances and family members; not surprisingly, those involved in such disputes often fail to recall them in interviews conducted by government representatives (Turner, 1972). For this rea-

TABLE 2.1   Victimization Rates for Cities

City	Personal Theft	Stranger Assault	Household Burglary	Rape (Females)	Property Theft
San Francisco	52	31	115	5.0	191
Chicago	46	20	112	4.4	160
Philadelphia	33	22	91	2.3	154

NOTE: Rates are per thousand persons 12 years old and older and residential households. Chicago and Philadelphia data are for 1974, San Francisco for 1973. "Personal Theft" category combines robbery and personal larceny with contact (primarily purse snatching). "Property Theft" category combines rates for personal larceny without contact and household larceny. Rape rates are for females only. Burglary and property theft rates are per thousand households.

SOURCE: U.S Department of Justice, 1976: Tables 2, 3, 4 and 18 (Chicago and Philadelphia); U.S. Department of Justice, 1975: Tables 2, 3, 4 (San Francisco).

son, in the telephone survey we asked only about assaults by strangers; for example, "being attacked or beaten up by strangers."

As part of our questioning we asked respondents about such matters as the extent of crime in their neighborhoods and their estimates of their risk of being victimized, and we did not want to probe subjects in which survey data are known to be unreliable.

Table 2.1 presents data on victimization rates for major crime types in categories comparable to those employed in our own data-gathering efforts. In all personal crime categories these surveys show San Francisco to have been the highest crime city during the 1973-1974 period. The stranger assault rate there was 50% higher than in Chicago, and the personal theft rate in the West Coast community was 13% above Chicago's count. Only for household burglary did Chicago outstrip San Francisco, and then the difference between the cities was only 6 percentage points. In almost every category Philadelphians reported the lowest crime rate among the three cities.

The relatively high level of crime in San Francisco did not go unnoticed. Political leaders there knew of the problem and pondered its consequences. In an interview,[1] Councilman John Barbagelata noted that the crime rate had increased and that his constituents thought that crime was the city's number-one problem. He indicated that he knew that this was not the trend of other cities:

> People are upset. They haven't been told the truth. They think "San Francisco is no different from other cities." But this situation is unique. Other cities are reducing their crime rate.

He also noted that this was not good for the image of the city.

To run a city, you've got to compete with other cities. We have to compare with Seattle, Los Angeles, Sacramento, San Diego, Oakland. We shouldn't be the most liberal. We don't want to attract lazy, good-for-nothing people. We should press crime at least as much as these other cities.

Council member Dorothy von Beroldingen read the consequences of the crime rate in her observations of street life:

Tourism is being driven out. People are afraid to go out. Merchants lock their doors. This is happening right now on Grant Avenue in the Financial District. But these are just realistic responses to what is happening now.

Mayor George Moscone apparently had a higher threshold of acceptance of crime than others. In an interview in the San Francisco *Examiner* in January 1977, he noted that "crime is an overhead you have to pay if you want to live in the city." The mayor, to be sure, was being held responsible by some councilmen for the increasing crime rate, for he had cut the uniformed patrol force by 10% in his 1976 budget, at a time when the rising crime rate was apparent. Chief of Police Charles Gain thought these attacks constituted a "political crime wave," for hostile council members were using the figures to criticize his administration of the police department. Councilwoman von Beroldingen:

I would get the best Chief I could find, and put him on probation. Someone who could reorganize the Department's morale, and who would be in favor of foot patrolmen. I'd try to get someone who could reassure the citizens that crime wasn't taking over.

A few concrete policies emerged from the city's administration as a result of concern over the increasing crime rate. A highly publicized Street Crime Unit was created to combat robbery; the mayor and the chief supported a citywide public safety program, attended many community meetings, and met with neighborhood leaders about crime problems.

In Philadelphia, law-and-order politics also was prominent, despite the relatively low rates of victimization recorded there. Political discussion there was dominated by the get-tough stance of Mayor Frank Rizzo; James Tate ran a winning mayoral campaign in 1967 on the promise to name Rizzo chief of police, and Rizzo capitalized on his reputation to capture the mayorship in 1971. Although the crime rate continued to increase during most of his first term, his sheer presence in office defused the issue as a source of leverage by the "outs" against the "ins." Whenever the irony of rising reports of crime was brought up during his stay in office, Rizzo would turn the criticism against other elements of the criminal justice system (especially judges) who were his political enemies. Also, as we shall see, surveys in Philadelphia have revealed that victimization rates there were relatively low for whites, and high for Blacks. Because Rizzo's strategy for building a winning electoral coalition was based upon ostentatiously excluding Black residents from participation in policy making, a substantial component of the crime rate in Philadelphia could be discounted politically at a very low figure. This enabled Rizzo to "talk tough," while bankrupting the city to his own advantage.[2]

The data presented in Table 2.1 also present a useful picture of the relative importance of each kind of crime, based upon its frequency. By far the most common types of crime involve threats to property rather than to life and limb. Simple thefts, those which do not involve breaking into a home or a street confrontation between victim and perpetrator, were by far the most frequent offenses. They were followed closely by burglary, a more serious crime because it involves the illegal entry of a home. Far less common were thefts which involved confrontations between the offending and aggrieved parties. Crimes in this category included robberies (which involve the use of force) and purse snatching (which do not) — for example, the predatory street crimes popularly known as "muggings." Assaults by strangers were somewhat less common than personal theft, while the rape rates generated by these victimization surveys were quite low.

Not only do property crimes substantially outnumber more serious personal offenses in each of these cities, but in general the gravity of an offense is inversely proportional to its frequency. As we shall see in Chapter 4, simple thefts are ranked quite low in seriousness by the general public, who gives successively greater weight to crimes involving breaking and entering, physical violence, forcible theft, and sexual assault. The latter, for example, ranks second only to murder in terms of the seriousness with which it is viewed by the public. This inverse relationship between the frequency and seriousness of crime may serve to blunt the impact of the seemingly vast (perhaps 37,000,000 incidents per year) crime problem. Chapter 4 explores the relationship between victimization and fear, and documents the effect of common events upon victims' fears.

The Victims of Crime

In addition to facilitating intercity comparisons of crime rates, LEAA's surveys reveal a great deal about patterns of victimization at the individual level. In this they differ greatly from official statistics on crime, which tell us very little about victims. This analysis of the victimization problems facing key population groups indicates that there are some important differences among the experiences of the males, young people, the poor and high-income groups, and Blacks. Consistent with the city-level comparisons, the surveys show that within most groups the residents of San Francisco were the most victimized, followed by those from Chicago and then Philadelphia. However, people's fears were not always directly related to these objective risks. While some highly victimized groups evidence a great deal of fear of crime, others seem to fall near the bottom of the scale.

While the victimization surveys gathered a great deal of background information on crime victims, this chapter focuses upon four fundamental demographic factors which will prove important throughout this volume: race, age, sex, and income. It will examine in detail only three crimes: personal thefts (robbery and purse snatching), serious ("aggravated") assault, and burglary. These crimes were chosen because they involve most of the elements which provoke fear and concern in the minds of victims, and because they are problems probed in detail in the survey of reactions to crime. All are frequent enough (unlike rape) to be measured relatively accurately in the city victimization surveys, and methodological investigations suggest that the victimization surveys gather relatively reliable reports of these types of experiences (unlike, for example, attempted or minor violence) from their victims.

Figure 2.1 depicts the relationship between family income and victimization rates for personal theft and serious assault. This figure illustrates both the city-level *average* victimization rate for each income group and the *range* (the highest and lowest city rates) around that average. While the mean generalizes about people's experiences, the range tells how accurately that mean describes this set of cities. Rates for both types of crime declined steadily with income. The decline was most precipitous from the lowest income category to about the $10,000 per year mark. Personal theft in particular was largely a lower- and working-class problem. Predatory theft rates varied among the communities in the general fashion indicated by

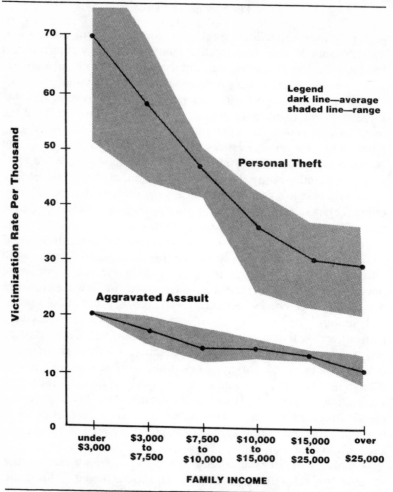

Figure 2.1 Income and Victimization Rates for Personal Theft and Aggravated Assault

NOTE: Averaged across rates for three cities. Personal theft category includes robbery and personal larceny with contact between victim and offender.
SOURCE: U.S. Department of Justice, 1976: Table 8 (Chicago and Philadelphia); U.S. Department of Justice, 1977a: Table 20 (San Francisco).

official crime statistics: San Franciscans outranked Chicagoans, who in turn outpaced Philadelphians in every income category.

The relationship between serious assault and wealth was less clear-cut. While victimization rates generally declined with increasing income, those at the top of the financial ladder are not as isolated from risk as those at the bottom when assault is contrasted to personal theft. Violence strikes surprisingly widely in the social structure. On the other hand, serious assaults were much less common than street muggings for every income group.

Figure 2.2 illustrates the relationship between age and victimization rates for personal crimes. Note that we have excluded data on victimization of younger persons (the victim surveys included those as young as 12 years of age) to maximize the comparability of these data with our own. Rates for assault fit the expected distribution: In all three cities, they dropped very sharply with age, and all but vanished among those over 65. The bulk of assaultive violence struck those under 35, a figure quite comparable with national data.

Robbery and purse snatching also matched the national pattern, albeit with a distinctive emphasis on the victimization of the elderly in San Francisco. In general, purse snatching is the only crime measured in the victim surveys which strikes the elderly with any frequency. When it is combined with robbery, nationwide rates for personal theft among the elderly are about as high as those for others over 35 years of age (Antunes et al., 1977). This pattern was clear in the victim survey data for Chicago and Philadelphia. In San Francisco, on the other hand, there was a substantial upturn in personal theft among the elderly, due largely to the frequency of purse snatching there. Robbery rates, which include incidents involving force or the threat of force, were about the same for all adult groups in San Francisco. However, 43 of every thousand elderly were afflicted by purse snatching, while the comparable rate was 27 per thousand in the 50-64 age group.

Figures 2.3 and 2.4 present victimization rates for personal crimes against men and women. The data illustrated there match national patterns: In each city, males suffered substantially higher rates of victimization, especially from assault. Men far outstripped women in the robbery component of the personal theft figures, but the gap was largely closed by purse snatching. In general the cities ranked as expected within each sex category. However, the high rate of victimization in San Francisco meant that women there experienced more personal theft than men living in Philadelphia, and women in Chicago slightly outstripped Philadelphia males. In short, for personal theft, city differences were as important as sex differences in describing aggregate rates of victimization.

Assault, as measured in the city victimization surveys, was related to race about as we would expect based upon national figures. As we see in Figure 2.5, Blacks reported victimization rates which

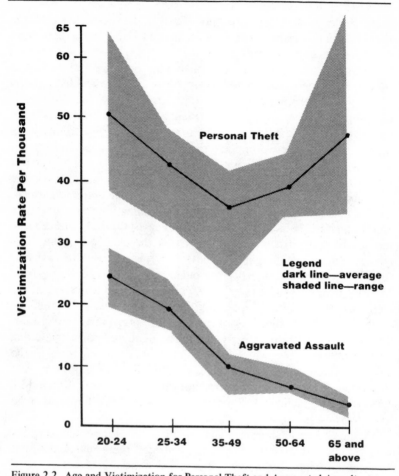

Figure 2.2 Age and Victimization for Personal Theft and Aggravated Assault

NOTE: Averaged across rates for three cities. Personal theft category includes robbery and personal larceny with contact between victim and offender.
SOURCE: U.S Department of Justice, 1976: Table 6 (Chicago and Philadelphia); U.S. Department of Justice, 1977a: Table 18 (San Francisco).

were slightly higher than those for whites — with the exception of San Francisco. There, victimization rates for whites were higher than those for Blacks. The same pattern was apparent in data for personal thefts in San Francisco, as illustrated in Figure 2.6. Again, Blacks in San Francisco were victimized by robbery and purse snatching at a rate of about 20 per thousand less than whites — a dramatic difference. This is quite contrary to the national norm. In the other cities,

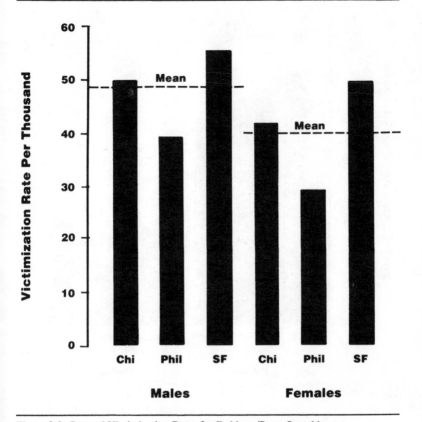

Figure 2.3 Sex and Victimization Rates for Robbery/Purse Snatching
SOURCE: U.S. Department of Justice, 1976: Table 4 (Chicago and Philadelphia);
U.S. Department of Justice, 1977a: Table 11 (San Francisco).

Blacks were far more likely to be victimized than were whites, as national data would lead us to expect. Victimization rates for personal theft among whites in San Francisco were so high that whites there and Blacks in Chicago were plundered with approximately the same frequency.

An examination of patterns of victimization from property crime modifies only a few of the conclusions illustrated thus far. We focus here upon burglary, perhaps the most serious and fear-provoking of the property offenses examined in the victimization surveys. For that

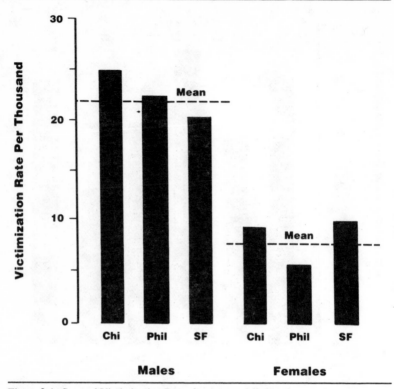

Figure 2.4 Sex and Victimization Rates for Aggravated Assault
SOURCE: U.S. Department of Justice, 1976: Table 4 (Chicago and Philadelphia);
U.S. Department of Justice, 1977a: Table 17 (San Francisco).

offense, those 65 and older (in this case we examine the data by the age of heads of households) continued to enjoy the lowest rates of victimization. Across all cities burglary rates dropped steadily with age, and those in the oldest age category were victimized only one-fourth as frequently as households headed by younger adults.

Like violent crime, burglary struck Black households far more frequently. Examining the data again by the characteristics of heads of households in our three cities, Figure 2.8 depicts the great gulf between the races in this regard. In each case, residents of San Francisco were more likely than others to be victimized, while Philadelphians came off best.

The most important way in which burglary differed from violent crime involved the relationship between victimization and wealth. In the national crime panel monitored by the Census Bureau, burglary

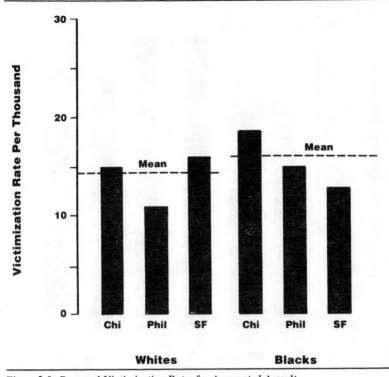

Figure 2.5 Race and Victimization Rates for Aggravated Assault
SOURCE: U.S. Department of Justice, 1976: Table 5 (Chicago and Philadelphia);
U.S. Department of Justice, 1977a: Table 19 (San Francisco).

rates are highest for those at the top *and* bottom of the financial ladder, and lowest for those in moderate income categories. Robbery, purse snatching, and assault, on the other hand, generally plague the poor. But in the case of burglary, the wealthy face risks as substantial as those bedeviling the less well-to-do. The city victimization surveys generally reflect this pattern. As Figure 2.9 illustrates, burglary victimization rates bottomed out among those in the $15,000 income category. They were somewhat higher among the very poor, and much higher among the most wealthy. However, the data were far from uniformly curvilinear with regard to family income. While San Francisco and Philadelphia charted the expected course, Chicago middle-income families suffered high rates of victimization as well. As a result, the most accurate generalization from our data about the distribution of burglary would be that it is widespread, striking with some frequency at every rung on the income ladder. Unlike personal

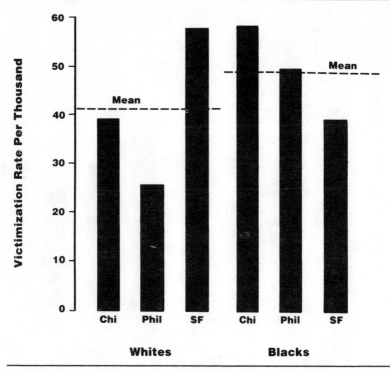

Figure 2.6   Race and Victimization Rates for Robbery/Purse Snatching
SOURCE: U.S. Department of Justice, 1976: Table 5 (Chicago and Philadelphia);
U.S. Department of Justice, 1977a: Table 17 (San Francisco).

predatory and assaultive crimes, burglary threatens the well-to-do
and the urban middle class. Elsewhere it has been argued (Skogan and
Klecka, 1977) that this is the result of contrary forces representing the
differential desirability of potential targets (favoring the rich) and
differences in their availability to potential offenders (weighted in the
direction of the poor). High-income households offer more lucrative
possibilities for gain, and often professional burglars will travel long
distances to exploit those opportunities (Reppetto, 1974). On the
other hand, most burglaries are not carried out by professionals, but
rather by youths who act more spontaneously and tend to select
targets close to home. The result is to "democratize" the category of
victim somewhat, spreading a great deal of relatively serious crime
throughout the city.

In sum, these data on patterns of victimization identify some
special population groups who face more serious problems with major

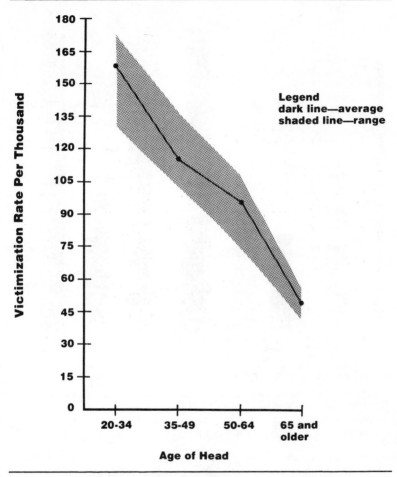

Figure 2.7 Age and Victimization Rates for Burglary

NOTE: Age is that of head of household. Households headed by persons under 20 years of age are excluded.
SOURCE: U.S. Department of Justice, 1976: Table 13 (Chicago and Philadelphia); U.S. Department of Justice, 1977a: Table 61 (San Francisco).

crime than most. As we have seen, the most consistently victimized group is young adults, those under 35 (and especially under 25). They bear a disproportionate share of the assaultive violence, predatory personal crime, and household burglary plaguing these cities and others. Men rather than women are most frequently victimized by all of the crimes considered in detail here, with the exception of the purse snatching component of our personal theft category. Black residents are especially prone to burglary and personal theft, and outdistance

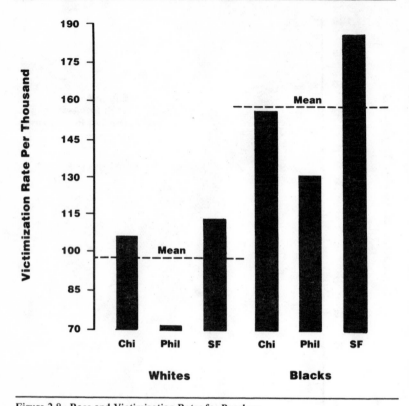

Figure 2.8   Race and Victimization Rates for Burglary
SOURCE: U.S. Department of Justice, 1976: Table 12 (Chicago and Philadelphia);
U.S. Department of Justice, 1977a: Table 62 (San Francisco).

whites in terms of assaultive violence in two of the three cities. The
elderly generally are victimized less frequently than others, but
(especially in San Francisco) they are often singled out in street
robberies and purse snatchings. Similarly, the well-to-do largely are
insulated from most of these crimes, but frequently fall victim to
burglary (and property theft generally), even in comparison to those
in the lowest income groups.

Chapter 5 examines the relationship between these key demographic characteristics and fear of crime. The findings illustrate one of
the more prominent puzzles in victimization research, the often inverse relationship between victimization rates and fear of crime
among certain groups in the population. While Blacks and the poor do
register higher levels of concern about crime, so do women and the

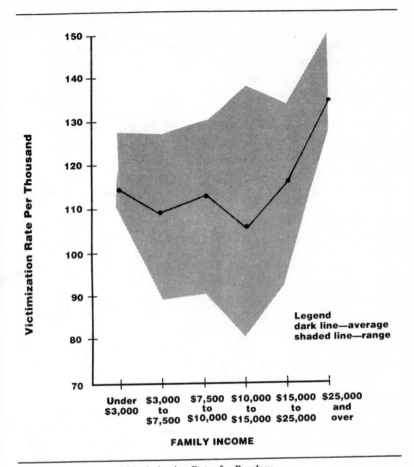

Figure 2.9 Income and Victimization Rates for Burglary
SOURCE: U.S. Department of Justice, 1976: Table 14 (Chicago and Philadelphia);
U.S. Department of Justice, 1977a: Table 63 (San Francisco).

elderly, groups which we have seen generally enjoy low rates of
victimization from crimes considered here. Rather than objective
risk, we speculate that several kinds of special vulnerabilities play an
important role in shaping people's psychological reactions to crime,
and that these vulnerabilities reflect their personal physical and social
make-up.

Crime as a Rare Event

Because they are based upon interviews with individuals, victimization surveys shift the basis on which data on crime are evaluated.

Traditionally, official crime counts have been combined with population data for the jurisdiction from which they are reported, to compute rates of victimization for every 1,000 or 100,000 residents. Crime rates are a limited analytic tool because they do not relate characteristics of victims to their experiences. Those reports typically combine offenses against individuals and households with those affecting businesses and organizations, and the relative mix of personal versus institutional crime in cities varies considerably (Skogan, 1978b). As a result, those data are best employed for a very limited purpose — to describe the volume of crime in a jurisdiction.

Published reports based upon the victimization surveys likewise adopted a rate basis for analyzing the data, albeit describing the aggregated experiences of social groups (like "the elderly") rather than jurisdictions. Those reports were the source of the data analyzed in Figures 2.1 through 2.9, and contain such information as the "burglary victimization rate per thousand households" (91.0 in Philadelphia), and the "robbery rate per thousand persons twelve years of age and older" (28.8 in Chicago). While lending us a great deal of analytic power, these figures continue to disguise a very important social fact, the distribution of the status of "victim." In many cases analytic models would be more powerful if one could classify city residents as "victims" or "nonvictims," and explore the consequences of that experience for the perceptions and behaviors of the individuals involved.

When analyzed in this fashion (as in Chapter 4) data from LEAA's surveys document one of the most significant facts about victimization: Recent and personal experiences with crime are relatively infrequent. Even in cities, most adults are not victimized in any way in the course of a year, and in many households none of those questioned had any information about crime to pass on to the interviewer. While far too many offenses are committed each year, in an analytic sense, serious crime — and especially personal victimization — is a "rare event."

The infrequency of recent victimization is illustrated by the data collected for these three cities in 1974 and 1975. (Here we examine only persons 18 years of age and older, to maximize the comparability of the figures with those from our own surveys.) In those surveys, 5.5% of all respondents indicated that they had been robbed in the previous year; for assaults of all kinds that figure stood at 7%, while for purse snatching and pocket picking together the total was only 4%. About 0.8% of the women interviewed indicated that they had been sexually assaulted. The frequency of being a victim was much greater, of course, when we examine property rather than personal crimes. In the same surveys, 22.9% of all persons lived in a household which had been burglarized, 9.5% were associated with automobile theft, and fully 49.6% had some of their property taken or lived in a household where some jointly enjoyed article of value had been stolen. On the other hand, a very considerable proportion of incidents in both the personal and property categories were described by their victims as "attempts." In Chicago, for example, these accounted for 45% of rapes, 35% of assaults, 28% of burglaries, and 37% of auto thefts (U.S. Department of Justice, 1976: Tables 2 and 11). Also, some victims were struck more than once in the preceeding year, upping the incident total but not the number of victims. For robbery, multiple victims contributed 0.6 percentage points to the "5.5 % victimized" count. Further, many property crimes which were successful involved very small financial losses.

As a consequence, the bulk of the crimes being examined here seriously affected only a very small number of people, even in these great cities. Overall, only 5.7% of the adult residents of these cities actually were attacked by anyone in any personal crime, only 3.2% reported any injury, and only 1.7% were injured in a crime to such an extent that they had to seek medical attention.

The difficulty is that these low frequencies are not in accord with many of the apparent consequences of crime, including fear and the adoption of precautionary strategies to avoid victimization. In the same surveys that gathered this victimization data, 66% thought that their chances of being victimized by personal crime had risen in the past two years, 47% thought that crime had gone up in their immediate neighborhoods, and 48% indicated that they would feel unsafe alone on the streets of their neighborhoods at night. Concern about crime clearly was of much greater proportion than was recent personal experience with crime. As Chapter 4 indicates, victims of crime are more fearful than those who have not been victimized. However, the bulk of those who are fearful have not been victims, and we will have to search elsewhere for the roots of their anxiety about crime.

NOTES

1. These interviews are documented in "Reactions to Crime Working Document M-28F," by Armin Rosencranz. They were conducted in the spring of 1977.

2. This analysis of events in Philadelphia is drawn from a detailed report by Stephen Brooks (1980).

Chapter 3

FEAR OF CRIME

Introduction

Soundings of public opinion indicate that crime is one of the major concerns of Americans. Since 1964 crime has been an amazingly persistent issue; its place on the public's agenda consistently has been high, although its exact ranking has been affected by the appearance and disappearance of other issues competing for attention. Since 1965 Gallup, Harris, and other polling organizations have been quizzing people about their personal reactions to crime, including whether or not they "feel more uneasy" or "fear to walk the streets at night." While the way these questions were worded affected the exact figures they obtained, the evidence suggests that levels of fear of crime rose significantly between 1965 and the mid 1970s, and that since then they have remained stationary (Baumer and DuBow, 1977). Interestingly, this matches closely the course of the "crime wave" of the latter half of the 1960s and early 1970s, which seems to have leveled off as well (Skogan, 1979a; Fox, 1978).

Fear of crime is particularly an urban problem. While in small towns less than 30% of all residents report being afraid to walk somewhere nearby at night, in large cities this figure exceeds 60%. Among selected subgroups in the urban population this figure climbs even higher; among the urban elderly, for example, fully 75% indicate that they are afraid to walk the streets at night (Cook et al., forthcoming).

It is thus in cities that the costs of fear of crime may be greatest. For individuals those costs come in the form of opportunities forfeited or lost, while for the polity they involve changes in urban structure which do not bode well for the future.

Individuals pay the price of fear when they pass up chances to employ and enjoy the opportunities created by urban life because of

47

crime: when they stay at home or out of parks, when they avoid public transportation or the use of public facilities, and when they invest large sums (both financial and psychological) in fortifying their homes and places of work. Likewise, when concern about crime forces restaurants to close, subways and stores to limit their hours of operation, and designers to substitute brick for plate glass on shopping streets, the potential consumers of those services pay a penalty as well.

The impact of crime on daily life was described in these terms by a Black woman interviewed in South Philadelphia.

> People used to sit on their steps in the evening, doors were open. Now the streets are deserted early in the morning and after dark. My mother used to go to church every morning — she stopped doing it — she is afraid of having her purse snatched. Many church and social activities here have stopped — people won't go out at night [South Philadelphia, November 10, 1976].

The social system pays the price of fear in the same concrete terms. Fear of crime stimulates the movement of jobs from central cities to sprawling suburbs, undermines the economic vitality of central business districts, and thus erodes the inner-city tax base. Fear also may eat away at the cohesiveness of neighborhoods, undermining their capacity to act autonomously to solve their problems.

While it is not strictly true that "all we have to fear is fear itself," we may need to focus upon the dynamics of fear as a distinct object of policy analysis. As we shall see, fear of crime does not always parallel the risk of victimization for individuals, and it is affected by forces quite proximate to neighborhood and family life. These may offer sources of program leverage in dealing with the problem that can be applied with realistic expectations of some success. Fear of crime may present a more tractable target than do offense rates. While it is not an insoluble problem, crime presents grave difficulties for those who would attack it directly. There are many kinds of crime and many kinds of criminals, all moved by different forces to attempt various wrongs. The opportunistic street mugger, the skilled safe cracker, and the besotted spouse abuser have little in common except that they all have run afoul of legislative intent. The "root causes" of these things lie in individual, family, and neighborhood pathologies which are very difficult for governments to do anything about (Wilson, 1975). Poverty, housing segregation, prenatal malnutrition, and alcohol abuse are problems that have evaded solution for longer than crime has been high on the national agenda.

Fear, on the other hand, may be a problem with sources of policy leverage that offer some realistic expectation of success. Fear may be alleviated by participation in efforts to make it difficult for crime to pay, by reducing opportunities for victimization, and by decreasing vulnerability. Fear may be reduced by activities organized by neighborhood groups and organizations which increase community security by encouraging surveillance. This may not only discourage offenders, but it may lend a sense that "someone is watching" and would intervene in a risky situation. To the extent to which fear of crime is a function of individual feelings of vulnerability, helplessness, or a collective decline in recognition, trust, and solidarity, such efforts may attack that problem independently of their effect upon crime (see Henig and Maxfield, 1978).

What is Fear of Crime?

It may seem unusual that there is uncertainty about just what "fear of crime" is, for fear is one of our most elemental emotions. Fear is both a physiological state and an expressed attitude. The physiological state is triggered by learned associations with fear-provoking stimuli. The physical manifestations of fear include a rapid heartbeat, a narrowed field of vision, high blood pressure, enhanced reaction time, an increased flow of blood to the large muscles, and endocrinic changes — such as the release of adrenalin into the blood stream — which prepare us for "fight or flight." But while these physiological reactions are well known, they are difficult to measure in sample surveys. Fear is also an expressed attitude, however. We can ask people if they are afraid of various conditions or events, an operational task closer to our capabilities.

Controversy over the measurement of fear arises from differences in the way in which "afraid" and "of what" can be operationalized. A variety of synonyms have been put forward as candidates for the proper phrasing of the emotion, including "anxious," "worried," and "concerned." Others have stretched for the presumed determinants of those emotions and operationalized fear in terms of perceived risk of falling victim or estimates of the amount of crime. We settled upon "safety" (or the lack of it) to operationalize fear, asking people, "How safe do you feel?"

Operationalizing the stimulus, the object of the attitude, is more problematic. It is clear that people have a variety of fears depending upon the crimes, circumstances, persons, occurrences, and potential consequences involved. All of these can differ markedly from incident to incident, and there is no reason to suspect that people feel "safe" or "unsafe" from all crimes in the same degree. However, a survey question measuring fear must pose a situation-specific stimulus component which at least implies specific kinds of risks and potential consequences. There has been relatively little systematic investigation of the issue of what crimes, situations, and so on, people fear most, or which incidents elicit the most general and widespread concern. It has been assumed that citizens are most fearful of crimes which potentially may lead to physical violence. These are "personal contact" crimes which involve a confrontation between victim and offender. That violence may in turn result in injury or death. The Crime Commission also concluded (but neither investigated nor demonstrated) that people are afraid of strangers. (Note that this sidesteps "fear of domestic violence," which probably constitutes the bulk of adult agression.) Skogan's (1977a) interpretation of the stranger issue emphasized that strangers are feared because they are unpredictable; we do not understand their motives and thus cannot forecast what they may do. Our fear-of-crime measure reflects anxiety about these problems, for we phrased its stimulus component in terms of "being out alone in your neighborhood at night." This points to a specific kind of personal attack, one likely to be perpetrated by people from outside the household but roving the immediate vicinity.

This rather narrowly defined context for assessing fear has both advantages and disadvantages. Its major disadvantage is that it misses entirely one emotion-arousing crime, burglary. While burglary is a property crime, DuBow (1979) suggests that it has a strong "fear component" because victims are conscious that there *could* have been a physical confrontation within the intimate setting of their household. As a result, burglary victims reputedly are afraid of being home alone and often fear the invader's return. Silberman (1978) also notes the dismay that people feel when their most private refuge is violated, evidencing their vulnerability. Our chosen context for assessing fear does not measure concern about the loss of valued and perhaps irreplaceable property and the often considerable financial strain that can be imposed by property crime.

On the other hand, defining fear in terms of street crime in the neighborhood at night has several advantages. First, and perhaps most convincing, is the fact that those incidents are the most important in the eyes of the public. We can see this in the results of Wolfgang's recent (1978) research on the seriousness of crime. In a large national survey he asked people to estimate (using any numerical value they wanted) the magnitude of the seriousness of various incidents which were described to them. They were to use as the basis for this scoring a value of ten for the theft of a bicycle from the street. Scores were accumulated for several hundred types of incidents through more than 60,000 interviews. They were then transformed into additive scales which can be used to score the relative serious- ness of various components of criminal incidents. Wolfgang finds that physical injury and the use of a weapon by far overshadow virtually all levels of financial loss when people evaluate crimes in this fashion. The loss of $100 thus translates into an increment of 3.6 in the seriousness score of an incident, while robbery with a weapon scores 7.3 regardless of any other increment granted for financial loss or injury. As a result, a crime described as "the theft of $10 from outside a building" receives a score of 1.7, while a robbery of the same amount at gunpoint scores 9.4, a physical attack in the course of a $10 robbery which leads to a substantial injury scores 14.6, and a forcible rape scores 25.8.

By fixing our interest on street crime in a neighborhood context, we also focus upon what Stinchcombe et al. (1978) argue are the distinctive attributes of crime as a fear-provoking stimulus object: its concentration in space, its association with signs of danger, and our inability to do much about it. Crime excites our emotions, they argue, because "there are certain times and certain places in which the risk is much higher. People who are hardly conscious of crime most of the time are occasionally sharply reminded of being in a fearful situation" (pp. 2-3). They are so reminded because people associate the risk of victimization with "signs of danger." Fear "requires that we be able to recognize that we have entered a high risk situation so that we can be afraid in advance, not just when the danger suddenly appears" (pp. 2-4). We do so by recognizing patterns of street activity, the character of land use, the incidence of vandalism, the nature of persons we see on the street, and other cues that we have come to associate with danger.

Personal violence also is fear-provoking because it is seemingly random; what happens is out of our control. "The potential damage in street crime is also very serious. When one is the victim of street crime one may be seriously injured or even killed, and there is little one can do to control the situation. . . . One can do very little to avoid being the victim of a crime, and one cannot do very much to lessen the potential damage once one has been chosen as a victim" (Stin- chcombe et al., 1978: 2-7). There is a great deal of experimental evidence (summarized in Cohn, 1978) that a feeling of control over events or conditions is strongly related to the anxiety or concern that they provoke, in a negative direction. The effects of all of these aspects of concern are magnified by the persistence of danger. For most people exposure to such conditions is episodic, and they develop routines which enable them to avoid those risky situations. Thus, when in our surveys we find that people characterize their immediate neighborhoods as potentially dangerous, we should find that such conditions are very related to our measure of fear.

A young woman we interviewed at a community meeting in San Francisco's Visitacion Valley testified to the power of this concern:

> You know, all of these other problems exist around here, it's true. . . . I'm really not that worried about burglaries. . . . I mean I can always get my stuff back, or replace it. That's not my main concern. Mine is that *I am physically threatened* right here in my own neighborhood!!! I feel unsafe just walking the two feet from my car to my front door. I won't go into my house after dark these days!!! I would never dream of using the car port that was assigned to me . . . not because I'm afraid my car might get wrecked . . . but because I'm afraid *I* might be harmed walking back around and into my own house!!! [She was very passionate and upset.] Just the other night, a friend of mine was leaving my house. He went outside, and found out that his car had been stolen. As he was standing there, some guy came up to him and said that he'd help him find his car or whatever . . . then the guy mugged my friend and took off with his wallet!!! Now I called the police right away. They came in 15 minutes, but that seems like years when something like that has just happened!!! And the reason that it took them that long was because at that very same time, they said that *two* other incidents had just taken place right in the Terraces!!! One was a stabbing and one was a robbery. Now I'm a female . . . I feel very helpless and don't know what can be done about all of this [Visitacion Valley, March 31, 1977].

Parenthetically, these arguments and illustrations do not mean that we think that fear of violent attack is the most significant factor shaping people's lives, even in big cities. There is evidence that other concerns may be as important, if not more so. In a Portland survey, Yaden et al. (1973) found, when they asked "how much personal danger" people felt from various untoward events, that fear of auto accidents overshadowed fear of crime. Garofalo (1977a) reports that residents of eight large cities ranked "environmental problems" including trash, noise, overcrowding, and the like, higher than crime on a list of things that they might not like about their neighborhoods. The Census Bureau's annual survey of housing asks nationwide samples of people to evaluate problems in their neighborhoods, and typically they find that crime is cited less often than "street noise," "heavy traffic," "poor street lighting," and other environmental and land-use issues. Virtually the same ranking obtains in central cities (U.S. Bureau of the Census, 1978a). Finally, Skogan's (1978b) report on the use of victimization data compared *objective* measures of the risks people face from crime and other happenstances. He found that robbery was about as frequent as death from heart disease, that serious assault was about one-half as frequent as unemployment, and that unmarried women were five times more likely to bear an illegitimate child than to report being robbed or raped. While we do not discount the importance of the issue of crime on people's lists of things to worry about, it is important to understand the context of that concern.

Levels of Fear

Based upon our telephone surveys late in 1977, fear of crime stood at a moderate level in our three study cities. In those surveys we asked:

> How safe do you feel, or would you feel, being out alone in your neighborhood *at night* — very safe, somewhat safe, somewhat unsafe, or very unsafe?[1]

The question was repeated to ask about "during the day" as well. The bulk of our respondents indicated that they felt either "very safe" or "somewhat safe," with only about one in three placing themselves in either of the "unsafe" categories. As we expected, very few (about 5%) reported that they felt at all unsafe during the day.

Like previous surveys, we found few significant differences between residents of our three cities on our safety measures. Chicagoans on the average were the most fearful and San Franciscans the least fearful, but the contrasts were slight and more people in San Francisco than in Chicago put themselves in the "very unsafe" category (but more said they felt "very safe" as well). These slim city differences parallel the findings of the Census Bureau's earlier surveys, for they too found few differences between these communities in terms of fear of crime. The difficulty may be that the most substantial spatial correlate of fear of crime is size of place. Fear levels are extremely low in rural and small-town America, and they begin to climb with a vengeance in places over about 100,000 in population (Cook et al., forthcoming). By those standards, these three cities are all at the top of the scale, despite their large differences in population.

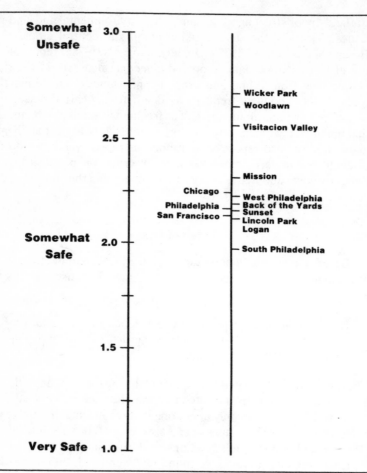

Figure 3.1 Fear Levels for Cities and Neighborhoods
SOURCE: Computed from citywide surveys and ten neighborhood-level surveys.

There are more important differences in levels of fear *within* these cities than between them. Black neighborhoods and white neighborhoods, settled areas and disorganized areas, all have little in common with each other with respect to fear of crime. This is illustrated in Figure 3.1, which charts average fear-at-night scores for our three citywide samples and for our ten special neighborhood surveys.

While these scores are subject to some sampling variation, when that is taken into account differences in fear among the ten neighborhoods are highly significant statistically, while the city-level scores are

virtually identical. Three neighborhoods emerge as particularly troubled places: Woodlawn and Wicker Park in Chicago and Visitacion
Valley in San Francisco. These three localities all were plagued with
serious crime problems. Woodlawn is a black and poor community on
Chicago's south side, while Wicker Park and Visitacion Valley both
are extremely heterogeneous and ethnically changing neighborhoods.
At the bottom of the fear ladder, on the other hand, is a stable, white
ethnic community, South Philadelphia.

Is This Fear of Crime?

Our measure of fear of crime is a relatively narrow and simple one.
Our survey question does not even ask about "crime" at all, but
rather about feelings of safety while walking alone in the nearby
community. It is important to demonstrate the *validity* of this measure
— to present at least indirect evidence that it indeed measures "fear of
crime." That a survey indicator of a concept "measures what it is
supposed to" is an assertion that always must be questioned, especially when we have only a single item purporting to represent it in any
given set of data.

One difficulty is that the fear of crime may not be an independent
trait of individuals. Rather, the concern registered in public opinion
polls may be merely another manifestation of other fundamental
predispositions, including distrust, suspicion, and anxiety about
change. Because urban dwellers have many good reasons to evidence
these predispositions, they may register "high" on their reactions to
crime-related items as well. Also, any discussion of the validity of
fear of crime measures must deal with the question of race. It is
widely argued that among whites discussions of crime are in fact
covert conversations about their fear of Black Americans.

If any of these counter hypotheses are true, we should reject most
arguments about the "fear of crime." In practical terms, for example,
the discovery that expressions of concern about crime really reflect
other matters would imply that many crime-related programs would
have little effect on levels of fear. In our view, an important attitudinal
domain is one that is relatively independent of other, related predispositions. In measurement terms, this argues that measures of fear of
crime should pass tests of their "discriminant validity."

Discriminant validation involves evaluating the relationship between potentially similar constructs. Following Campbell and Fiske
(1959), the utility of a hypothesized trait can be rejected if measures of
it have high correlations with indicators measuring something else,

suggesting the proposed trait is not distinct from others already well known and more generally useful. In this case, our measure of fear should be relatively unrelated to indicators tapping suspicion, distrust, anxiety about social change, and racial fears among whites.

An appropriate vehicle for testing the discriminant validity of a fear of crime item similar to our own is the General Social Survey. In this survey program respondents were asked: "Is there any area right around here — that is, within a mile — where you would be afraid to walk alone at night?" Note that this question very closely resembles the item employed in our survey. This question was used in four national surveys of public opinion between 1973 and 1977. Note that the term "crime" is not used, an omission that should favor the null hypothesis that the item is not independent of other concerns and fears.

The General Social Survey also has included a number of related indicators tapping the domains of social trust and anomie. Over the years the survey has been conducted, all of these questions have been asked of some 2800 persons. Table 3.1 reports their interrelationships, and their association with "fear of crime" in this survey.

In Table 3.1 are reported the multiple correlations between each attitude measure and each of the six remaining indicators. These correlations indicate the extent of the "overlap" between responses to the survey items. In general, responses to measures of trust, suspicion, and dissatisfaction with social change are mildly related to one another; the multiple R^2s for those items average about .30. The fear-of-crime item included in the survey clearly passes this test of its discriminant validity, however. It is correlated only about .02 with the remaining six measures.

We can use the same approach to explore the extent to which crime is "a code word for race" among white Americans as well. The data on racial attitudes of whites collected in the General Social Survey illustrate the magnitude of simple forms of racial intolerance. We employed responses to five questions to measure that prejudice: two inquire about interracial marriage (concerning whether it should be legal, and how the respondent would feel about it occurring in his/her family), one about the right of whites to keep Blacks out of their neighborhoods, one asking if Blacks should "push where they are not wanted," and the proverbial question about a Black person "coming to dinner." Of this nationwide sample of whites, one-third felt that the law should not allow interracial marriage and 46% felt they would be "very uneasy" if a relative of theirs married a Black person. If a Black were to come to dinner, 13% stated they would

TABLE 3.1 Fear of Crime and Related Attitudes

Survey Questions	Multiple R^2 With All Other Items
Is there any area right around here — that is, within 1 mile — where you would be afraid to walk alone at night?	.02
Generally speaking, would you say that most people can be trusted or that you can't be too careful in dealing with people?	.34
Would you say that most of the time people try to be helpful, or that they are mostly just looking out for themselves?	.34
Do you think most people would try to take advantage of you if they got a chance, or would they try to be fair?	.31
In spite of what some people say, the lot of the average man is getting worse, not better.	.18
Most people don't really care what happens to the next fellow.	.34
These days a person doesn't really know whom he can count on.	.24
(Number of Cases)	(2807)

SOURCE: Computed by the authors from the cumulative General Social Survey.

object "strongly," 22% definitely thought that whites should have the right to keep Blacks out of their neighborhoods, and 44% agreed "very strongly" that "Blacks should not push where they are not wanted." Responses to these questions were substantially intercorrelated (an average r of +.40), and form an additive scale with a reliability of .75.

The correlation between our summary measure of racial tolerance and fear of crime was only −.05. There was no significant tendency for whites who were less tolerant to be more likely than others to report concern about walking in their neighborhoods although the data tended very weakly in that direction.

It is often argued that reports of concern about crime are colored by other more general social concerns. For example, Skogan (1977b: 14) saw fear of crime as a "diffuse construct affected by other aspects of urban life." Garofalo and Laub (1978) argued that expressions of fear in fact reflected generalized concern about unwelcome neighborhood change and a decline in the quality of community life. These data suggest that they were wrong. At least for these measures of social trust, anxiety about change, and racial intolerance, concern about one's personal safety is a quite independent issue.

In addition to his validation study, another methodological investigation indicates that our fear-of-crime question is a useful one. This project employed a panel of citizens who were quizzed on a repeated basis over a six-month period. The question used in our survey to measure fear evidenced the highest stability in responses over time of all those included in the panel study. The over-time reliability of the item was .73, and it was among the most consistent correlates of other attributes of the respondents who were questioned repeatedly (Bielby and Berk, 1980).

In the next chapters we will examine in detail the correlates of this fear of crime. We will explore the relationship between victimization and fear, and the fear-provoking consequences of media attentiveness and personal communication about crime. We will explore the implications of physical and social vulnerability for fear, and the impact of neighborhood conditions on people's willingness to walk the streets there after dark. Then we will detail the crucial role of fear in "summarizing" all of these factors and shaping how people deal with crime in their communities.

NOTE

1. The phrase "or *would* you feel" was added to forestall replies along the lines of, "But I never go out." We did not want to confuse the issue of fear with that of behavior, which is quite distinct. Note that this question is a very slight variant of that employed in LEAA's city victimization surveys.

Chapter 4

VICTIMIZATION AND FEAR

Introduction

In this chapter we consider the impact of personal experience with crime on fear. We will examine the effects of criminal incidents which involved our respondents (in personal crimes like robbery or assault) or their households (including burglaries and property thefts). The data on these incidents were gathered for our three cities by the Census Bureau, as part of their city survey program. The victimization data for Chicago and Philadelphia describe the situation there in 1974, while in San Francisco they refer to calendar 1973. We use these data to classify people as "victims" or "nonvictims" of various types of crimes during the year, and to examine levels of fear of crime in these contrasting groups.

We find the data help clarify the relatively limited role that such experiences can play in explaining the overall level of fear of crime in these communities. We argued above that concern about crime appears to be higher for personal than for property offenses, but even in central cities those crimes occur relatively infrequently. Among different types of personal crimes, those which are rated by the public as being most serious are even less frequent in occurrence. In truth, many victimization experiences are not very traumatic. Also, because many more people report being afraid than report being victimized, personal experience with crime simply cannot explain much of the current level of fear in these cities. While victims are more fearful than those who have not fallen prey, most of the fearful have not recently been attacked.

In contrast, burglary plays an important role in instigating fear because it is far more frequent in occurrence than any personal crime. Its effect on fear of crime individually is less than that of personal victimization, but societally its impact is aggregated over a far greater number of persons. We also find that the relationship between reports of victimization and expressions of fear is muted by the confounding effects of sex and age, two powerful correlates of each. Youths and males are more likely to report being afraid. Controlling for the personal attributes of victims and nonvictims clarifies (and strengthens) the connection between victimization and fear.

The Frequency of Victimization and Fear

In victimization surveys respondents are quizzed about their experiences "during the past year." They are asked about a number of events (such as "being hit with a rock or bottle") which could signal the occurrence of a crime, and they are questioned in detail about each incident to determine if it was criminal in nature. These surveys indicate that victimization is a relatively infrequent event. As we saw in Chapter 2, no more than about 6% of the population of these cities reported experiencing any particular type of violent crime during the 1973-1974 period, and more than 90% did not report *any* victimizations in this category. That figure rose somewhat for serious property crimes, and losing a minor piece of property was quite common. However, the latter seems to have little effect upon the fears and concerns at issue here.

The frequency of victimization is thus quite disproportionate to the number of persons in these cities who indicated that they were fearful of personal attack in their neighborhoods. At the time the victimization surveys were conducted, over 30% of those questioned reported that they felt "very unsafe" or "somewhat unsafe," more than three times the proportion involved in personal crime during the previous year. The substantial disparity between the two frequencies guarantees that direct personal victimization cannot account for much of the overall variation in levels of fear in the general population, although it certainly may be linked to the fears of those who were directly victimized (see Skogan, 1977b).

Table 4.1 illustrates this point, relating robbery victimization to expressions of fear by residents of the three cities. Two points can be observed there. First, victims were more likely than nonvictims to report feeling "very unsafe," and they were the less likely of the two groups to report feeling "very safe." Second, of the 7151 (6637 plus 514) persons who reported feeling "very unsafe," only 7% had been robbed in the past year. While robbery victims were more fearful than others, most of the fearful were not robbery victims.

TABLE 4.1   Robbery Victimization and Fear

| | Victimization | |
Fear	Robbery Nonvictims	Robbery Victims
Feel very safe	13.5% (3,854)	10.1% (165)
Feel reasonably safe	38.6 (10,996)	35.4 (576)
Feel somewhat unsafe	24.5 (6,985)	23.0 (374)
Feel very unsafe	23.3 (6,637)	31.5 (514)
Total	99.9 (28,472)	100 (1,629)
Percentage of total	94.6	5.4

SOURCE: Computed from combined 10% random samples of Census Bureau city vicitimization surveys.

The same disparities can be observed for each of the personal crimes measured in the victimization surveys and, as we shall see below, the enhanced fears of victims can be clarified by controlling for some confounding demographic correlates of victimization and fear. In every case, however, recent personal victimization simply is too infrequent to explain why most people report being afraid. For non-victims that fear can, at best, only be anticipatory. Part of this could be an artifact of victimization-survey methodology. Such surveys can reliably measure only recent events, and it may be that our group of "nonvictims" were, in fact, victimized in the past. However, the one-year reference period for the survey questions measuring victimization was employed because of a strong tendency of victims of crimes more distant in the past to neglect to recall them, and it is likely that the impact of such incidents on current perceptions of crime would be greatly attenuated.

In their studies for the Crime Commission, Biderman et al. (1967) asked Washington, D.C. residents to recall "the worst crime that has ever happened to you." They recalled a total of 260 incidents, only 108 of which occurred more than two years previously, and only 60 of which happened six or more years in the past. People's memories of crime seem to be recent ones. While we have no evidence of the *lifetime* probability of being victimized, unpublished research (Sko-

TABLE 4.2   Fear Among Victims and Nonvictims

Type of Victimization	Percentage Feel "Very Unsafe"	Ratio of Victim to Nonvictim Fear	Percentage of Sample[b]
Rape[a]	50.0	1.5:1	0.7
Nonvictim	34.0		99.3
Robbery	31.5	1.3:1	5.4
Nonvictim	23.3		94.6
Purse snatch[a]	48.3	1.4:1	5.2
Nonvictim	33.3		94.8
Physical attack	29.7	1.3:1	5.7
Nonvictim	23.4		94.3
Physical injury	33.3	1.4:1	3.4
Nonvictim	23.5		96.6
Physical injury medical care required	38.6	1.6:1	1.7
Nonvictim	23.5		98.3

SOURCE: Computed from Census Bureau three-city victimization surveys.

   a. Females only.
   b. Total weighted sample size 30,102; female sample size 15,917.

gan, n.d.) using victimization-survey estimates of age-specific rates and some simple assumptions about future trends suggests that, for robbery, the probability still will fall below 50%, and that among our respondents — who at the median were in their mid 30s — the sum of their past experiences would be significantly less.

There are, of course, differences among crimes in the extent to which they seem to stimulate fear on the part of their victims. Wolfgang (1978) reports that attributes of crime, like the display of a weapon, physical assault, and injury, all contribute to people's estimations of their seriousness, and we find that the relationship between victimization and fear is greater for some crimes than for others.

Table 4.2 illustrates how the specific character of various victimization experiences relates in different fashion to levels of fear. For example, for these cities as a whole, the greatest difference in fear between victims and nonvictims is found when we contrast victims who were injured and needed medical care to everyone else.[1] Because parametric correlations are inappropriate for describing the widely differing proportions of victims and nonvictims in Table 4.2, we report simply the ratio of victims who say they feel "very unsafe" to nonvictims who make the same claim, as our measures of "impact."

The difference in fear between rape victims and nonvictims is about the same as that found for the injured victims contrast. Among women, rape victims are about one and one-half times as fearful as nonvictims, a substantial difference in light of their already high level of fear. The simple presence of a weapon, on the other hand, does not seem to have much of an effect when victims of those crimes are contrasted with the remainder of the population (not shown in table).

Although certain subcategories of criminal incidents with specific attributes seem to be more fear-provoking than run-of-the-mill personal crimes, an analysis of victimization rates for those more significant predations indicates that they are of exceptionally low frequency. Table 4.2 indicates the proportion of persons who are presented in each victim and nonvictim category, and victimization seems in general to be the least frequent for the most fear-provoking types of crime. Note, for example, the relatively low frequency of rape and of crimes requiring medical attention, in contrast to crimes with smaller "fearfulness ratios."

This matter is explored more systematically in Table 4.3, which relates Wolfgang's most recent (1978) seriousness scores for selected incidents to the frequency with which events of that type occur. To construct this table we searched Wolfgang's 200-odd offense descriptions to find incidents which best matched definitions of the major categories of crime measured in the victimization surveys. Thus the table combines data from two different sources, doubtless with some error.

Table 4.3 strongly suggests that *the most serious crimes are quite infrequent,* even relative to other types of victimization. The most frequent crimes presented in Table 4.3, those which hit more than one in a hundred in the United States, all score in the lower reaches of the seriousness scale. Some less frequent crimes also are not serious, including pocket picking (reputedly a dying art), but no truly serious crime is very frequent, based upon these figures.

All of this points to the relatively limited role that recent direct victimization can play in explaining fear of crime. While victims are more fearful than nonvictims, most fearful persons have not recently been victimized. Among victims, those who suffered from the most heinous crimes are even fewer in number than victims of lesser crimes, those who were *not* assaulted, injured, or threatened with a gun. Further, a large proportion of those categorized as "victims" were involved in unsuccessful, attempted crimes. This does not mean that "crime does not make a difference." Rather, it suggests that the locus of fear for most big-city dwellers is to be found elsewhere, in their vulnerability to crime, in concern about its potential conse-

TABLE 4.3 Frequency and Relative Seriousness of Crimes

Type of Victimization[a]	Rate per Thousand[a]	Seriousness Score[b]	Wolfgang Offense Description[b]
Household larceny under $50	74.7	1.7	A person steals property worth $10 from outside a building.
Burglary-forcible entry	30.4	3.2	A person breaks into a building and steals property worth $10.
Burglary-attempted forcible entry of a home	20.8	4.2	A person attempts to break into a home, but runs away when a police car approaches.
Simple assault without injury	11.4	1.5	A person intentionally shoves or pushes a victim. No medical treatment is required.
Attempted vehicle theft	6.3	3.6	A person attempts to break into a parked car, but runs away when police car approaches.
Simple assault with injury	4.0	7.3	A person beats a victim with his fists. The victim is hurt, but does not require medical treatment.
Robbery with weapon without injury	2.1	7.3	A person threatens a victim with a weapon unless the victim gives him money. The victim gives him $10 and is not injured.
Pocket Picking	2.0	3.3	A person picks a victim's pocket of $10.
Robbery with serious injury	1.0	14.6	A person, using force, robs a victim of $10. The victim is hurt and requires hospitalization.
Robbery with a gun	1.0	9.4	A person robs a victim of $10 at gunpoint. No physical harm occurs.
Purse snatching	0.9	4.9	A person snatches a handbag containing $10 from a victim on the street.
Forcible rape	0.8	25.8	A man forcibly rapes a woman. No other physical injury occurs.
Homicide	0.1	35.6	A person intentionally injures a victim. As a result, the victim dies.

SOURCE: a. U.S. Department of Justice, 1977c: Tables 1, 8, 17, and 18. Rates for homicide calculated from Federal Bureau of Investigation, *Uniform Crime Report 1976.* b. Marvin E. Wolfgang, "National Survey of Crime Severity: Final National Level Geometric Means and Ratio Scores." Philadelphia: Center for Studies in Criminology and Criminal Law, University of Pennsylvania, 1978.

quences, in things that happen to their friends and neighbors, in what they hear is happening in their neighborhoods, and in other vicarious sources of crime information.

The Impact of Victimization Clarified

Although Table 4.1 indicated that victims of robbery in our three cities reported higher levels of fear than those who were not victimized in that way, the relatively small differences between the two groups — especially in light of the seriousness of the crime — may have been surprising. One would expect these differences to be more dramatic. Part of the difficulty lies in the fact that the relationship between victimization and fear is confounded by the propensity of groups in the population who are more likely to be involved in personal crimes also to express less fear of walking in their neighborhoods at night. Some of this may be laid to their unwillingness to express those fears to interviewers, and part (as we shall argue in the next chapter) may be related to their perceived invulnerability to such happenstances, despite their relative frequency. In particular, the tendency of males and younger persons to (a) be more frequently involved in violent episodes, and (b) to express more confidence in their after-dark safety, serves to mask the relationship between victimization and fear of crime. When the personal attributes of individuals are partialed out, that relationship is substantially stronger.

Figure 4.1 gives some indication of the magnitude of the impact of victimization on fear, once confounding relationships with age, sex, race, and income of individuals independently affecting their levels of fear have been removed. Average fear levels for victims before and after such controls have been introduced are graphed relative to the average score for the adult population as a whole. In each case the relationship between victimization and fear is sharper once those confounding relationships have been clarified. The starkest effect of introducing such controls is found in the case of weapon use; guns, clubs, and knives are used almost exclusively in crimes involving male victims. Victims of weapon crimes thus are actually *below* the population mean in terms of fear before this is taken into account. Most crimes against women are "strong-arm" affairs in which (mostly male) offenders rely on strength and and numbers. Physical attacks are more common among youths, men, and the poor; patterns for stranger assault are similar, and, in addition, such crimes strike more frequently among Blacks. In every case these patterns of victimization are confounded with the general correlates of fear, masking in part the effect of such experiences.

In addition to the personal crimes analyzed in Table 4.2 and Figure 4.1, there was evidence in the victimization surveys in our three cities that experience with one property crime, burglary, was related to fear. Although the effect did not appear to be strong (the ratio of victims to nonvictim fear comparable to those presented in Table 4.2 was 1.1 to 1), it increased substantially when we controlled for characteristics of victims which also are related to fear. As we indicated at the outset, our measure of fear is tied to a narrow set of crimes which threaten only in specific circumstances. There is no question that the threat of burglary engenders fear, and that in particular it raised the possibility of a personal confrontation between victim and offender in an intimate context (Bard and Sangrey, 1979). Consider this experience reported by a woman who was interviewed in San Francisco:

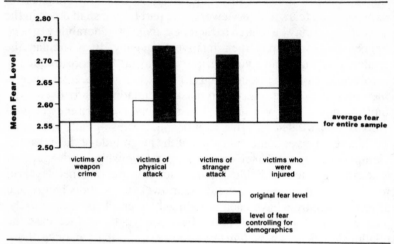

Figure 4.1 Fear Levels Among Victims
SOURCE: Computed from combined city victimization surveys. Fear levels estimated controlling for age, race, sex, and income; calculated using multiple regression.

> We heard noises, so I went out onto the patio and started looking and listening, though I couldn't hear or see a thing. Well next thing I know, I see these pairs of legs coming down over the fence . . . so I dash inside quietly and run upstairs and look out the upstairs window, and sure enough these guys had jumped down onto our patio and were coming in through the sliding doors which I had left open [Visitacion Valley, August 1976].

This form of home invasion is not a situation raised in our specific operationalization of fear, and we can only interpret this persistent relationship as evidence of the generalizability of burglary victimization experiences into other areas of concern.

The work of Tyler (1978) and others (Scarr et al., 1973; Sparks et al., 1977) indicates that people generalize from specific crime experiences in several ways. Direct experiences with crime affect estimates of their own risk of victimization, judgments about their future vulnerability, and (through the latter judgments) their behavior. In addition, direct experience with crime affects judgments about the level or rate of crime, and other general assessments of the environment. Based on this research, there is ample reason to expect that people who have been burglarized will think that their neighborhood is a risky place, and that this should be reflected in our measure of fear.

In our three survey cities about 15% of the households we contacted reported being burglarized during the previous year; in the victim surveys conducted in these cities a few years earlier (using much better measures), 23% of the households had been involved in a burglary. On the other hand, only 5% reported being robbed, 5% (of women) reported having their purses snatched, and 4% reported being assaulted by a stranger during the same period. Although the individual effect of personal crime may be the highest, the aggregate effect of burglary may well outstrip it due to these differences in frequency.

In addition, burglary strikes more widely across American society. While assaults and predatory crime tend to weigh most heavily on those at the bottom of the social and economic ladder, burglary victimization rates for the very rich are as high as rates for the very poor. In many suburban areas burglary is about the only crime problem, and burglary is an exception to the general rule that rates of serious crime are the highest in the largest cities. In the Census Bureau's victimization surveys, burglary rates in the smallest central cities are higher than those in places over one million in population, and rates in those cities are lower than burglary counts in their suburbs (U.S. Department of Justice, 1977b: Table 27). As a result, to the extent that burglary stimulates fear of personal violence, it provokes it in places where crimes other than burglary rarely occur. Remember as well that burglary is extraordinarily frequent. In these three cities LEAA's victimization surveys uncovered about 219,000 household burglaries in a one-year period. Burglary, then, may account in part for the diffusion of fear of crime throughout American society.

In summary, we have seen that personal experience with crime can play only a limited role in explaining the general incidence of fear of crime even in large cities. For those who are involved personally such experiences can be traumatizing. A woman in San Francisco related the following incident, a "typical" street robbery:

> My husband and I were walking to Safeway one day. There were a couple of big Black guys up ahead of us. They were coming towards us and as they got closer, they stopped as if they were going to ask us a question. We looked up once we got to them, and they sprayed our eyes and asked us for money. Fortunately, neither of us had a lot of money with us. Next thing I know, we were taken to the hospital where they fixed up our eyes. It was scarey [Visitacion Valley, July 1976].

However, while victims are more fearful than nonvictims, few people have been victimized in any recent period of time. The relationship between victimization and fear is stronger than is apparent at first blush, for personal crimes strike young males more frequently than any other population group, and they are generally *less* likely than anyone else to express concern about crime. Further, the crimes which seem to produce the most fear in their victims are among the least frequent, and they are heavily concentrated at the bottom of the social and economic hierarchy. Burglary is the most egalitarian offense, but it is more weakly related to fear of crime. We speculate that burglary affects levels of fear because people generalize from it to form impressions of neighborhood conditions.

NOTE

1. Note that "everyone else" includes all *other* kinds of victims as well as "complete nonvictims."

Chapter 5

VULNERABILITY AND FEAR

Introduction

Some of the most consistent findings of survey research on crime problems concern the relationship between fear of crime and demographic indicators of vulnerability to personal attack. From city to city and survey to survey we find that women, the elderly, Blacks, and those at the bottom of the education and income ladder report more fear of crime than their counterparts (Baumer, 1979). Even the details of these relationships (including their relative importance and even the magnitude of their regression coefficients) do not vary from study to study (Cook et al., forthcoming). This further suggests that these demographic features point in some way to the fundamental causes of fear. We suspect that these attributes reflect two underlying dimensions from which people assess their environments and develop accommodations with the risks they perceive there: physical and social vulnerability.

The Concept of Vulnerability

In our view, there are two independent dimensions of personal vulnerability to crime, one physical and the other social. By physical vulnerability we mean openness to attack, powerlessness to resist attack, and exposure to traumatic physical (and probably emotional) consequences if attacked. Women and the elderly often are unable to resist attack because the modal threat for almost all personal and property crime in the United States is young and male, often acting in a group. Based upon arrest statistics, perhaps 55% of all perpetrators of violent crimes are males under the age of 25, a figure that does not change much if we examine the victims' reports of offenders in sample surveys (Hindelang, 1978; U.S. Department of Justice, 1977b). In those surveys about 52% of all robberies were carried out by two or more criminals acting in concert, as were about 42% of all assaults by strangers (U.S. Department of Justice, 1977b: Table 53).

A young woman who was interviewed by a field observer in the Mission District in San Francisco was confronted by just this set of circumstances, and was unable to do much about her plight.

> I was walking down 24th over there and there were five boys walking down the street towards me. They were spread out the length of the sidewalk so I had to walk through them. I thought maybe I should walk across the street or something but I figured that would just attract their attention, so I just kept walking. Well, they separated when I walked past but one of them all of a sudden reached out and grabbed my breast [Mission, December 1976].

Because of the youth and vigor of many offenders, others in the population — most notably women and the elderly — often find it difficult to resist their predations. Indeed, we found that when asked about how to deal with sexual assault, most women in our survey did not recommend strategies like "fighting back against their attackers" (31% did), or "carrying weapons for protection" (24%). More endorsed precautions like "not going out alone" (73%), and "refusing to talk to strangers" (52%). Riger and Gordon (1979) suggest that the issue is one of the ability of individuals to resist, rather than of the motives of attackers. They found no significant differences between men and women in response to the question, " Do you ever feel afraid that someone might deliberately harm you?"; on the other hand, they found large differences by sex in the proportion who felt that they could successfully defend themselves against attack.

Survey data on differences among women suggest that variations in physical vulnerability are at work in these male-female distinctions, for women themselves vary in this regard. Riger and Gordon (1978) asked women to describe themselves in terms of their strength and speed. They found that those who saw themselves as physically vulnerable were significantly more fearful of crime. Further, most of their female respondents ranked themselves "below average" in terms of strength and speed. As Stinchcombe et al. (1978) note, women's lesser defensive capacity also reflects their socialization to patterns of less aggressive behavior. Their early training stresses passivity and dependency. This may be altered: in a before-and-after study of the effects of a self-defense training course for women (using a control group of psychology students), three researchers found that "women who have enrolled in the course felt more control over their bodies and less worry (or fear) about crime" (Cohn et al., 1978: 293).

Change along this control dimension probably was a key component in this reduction in fear. Stinchcombe and his associates (1978: 2-6) argue that one important characteristic of the risk of criminal victimization, as opposed to other (often more frequent) risks, is that we seemingly cannot do much to reduce them.

> It is generally not the victim's fault that the criminal has picked him or her, so there is nothing much a victim can do to avoid such risk. The very fact that a crime is being committed implies that the criminal thinks the victim lacks the means to control the situation. . . . [F]ear involves the perception of high risk of serious danger which a person cannot reduce or control.

While we are less certain that people cannot do anything to reduce their risk of victimization, there is doubtless substantial individual variation in the extent to which they think that this is the case. If this belief covaried with their physical attributes it would serve as a psychological mechanism linking physical vulnerability and fear of crime. Whatever the mechanism, crime seems to be a persistent concern among women. In their sample of urban dwellers, Gordon et al. (1980) found that 48% of women reported "thinking about their safety" either "all of the time" or "most of the time." The comparable figure for men was 25%.

The elderly also are often not very agile, and may more easily fall victim to vigorous young males. In addition, they may suffer physical disabilities or a general reduction in acuity which makes it difficult for them to evade attack or fend off those who would harass them (Singer, 1977). In the victim surveys, both female victims and those over 65 who were assaulted were less likely than their counterparts to report taking any self-protective actions during the course of the incident (U.S. Department of Justice, 1977b: Table 58). For both women and the elderly, physical vulnerability is an instance of what Dussich (1976) has termed "passive vulnerability." Active vulnerability, in his scheme, reflects opportunities for victimization that individuals create by their own lack of caution, inattention to their environment, or by their own aggressiveness, in provoking disputes. These include many offenses which Wolfgang (1957) dubbed "victim precipitated." Passive vulnerability, on the other hand, is due to the physical condition of individuals and recognition by potential offenders that they can be exploited. Because those conditions usually cannot be altered, that potential for exploitation is an enduring feature of their lives, and it should not be surprising if it greatly affects their assessments of the risks of their environment and their subsequent accommodations to those potential risks.

In addition to their openness to attack by vigorous young males, women and the elderly also may be more subject to the most extreme consequences of criminal assault, including physical injury and sexual violation. Fear can reflect anticipation of the consequences of attack. The elderly are more frail than the bulk of the population, and they may have special difficulty recovering from broken bones and other serious injuries. Conklin (1976: 107) argues that the elderly "think they are less likely to survive an assault or a robbery without severe injury; the young may feel they can better take care of themselves in such situations." In fact, older victims face the prospect of never recovering at all. One of our field interviewers talked to an elderly Black woman from Woodlawn, in Chicago, who had been victimized:

> She had had her purse snatched one time when she was walking on 67th Street and some young kids came by and grabbed her purse and knocked her down. She then told me that she had been layed up in the hospital for over two months because of that incident. Because when she fell, she had broken her hip. I noticed as she was walking that she was still walking with a limp [Woodlawn, July 1977].

In addition, the limited social support offered many elderly persons magnifies the potential consequences of victimization. Many elderly persons — and especially women — live alone; this is the fastest-changing demographic characteristic of the elderly population, and in older age categories it exceeds 50% of the population (see Cook et al., forthcoming). Many of them have no one to take care of them if they are injured, foreshadowing their perhaps permanent institutionalization if the worst should befall them.

While, as a group, women are more vigorous than the elderly, they still can be physically pummelled more easily than their male counterparts. Victimization surveys indicate that women are slightly more likely than men to report being injured in the course of both robberies and (nonsexual) assaults (U.S. Department of Justice, 1977b: Table 61). In addition, sexual assaults very often involve further physical injury. Hindelang et al. (1978) report that proportionately more rape victims were otherwise injured (48%) than those involved in any other type of personal attack.

In attempting to account for high levels of fear among women, Riger and Gordon (1979) stress the important role of threat of sexual assault. That special concern accompanies the potential for injury or death and the routine indignities attendant to every robbery or violent personal encounter. Empirically that risk is significant. If we sum together police figures on female homicide victims and victimization survey counts of female victims of rape, robbery, assault, and purse snatching, it appears that, for the United States as a whole, rapes and rape-murders account for about 5.5% of those violent encounters. This is certainly a large enough figure to justify concern, and when the seriousness of these crimes is taken into account their frequency becomes even more troublesome. Wolfgang's (1978) recent research indicates that the general public rates rape second only to murder in terms of the seriousness of the crime. In violent encounters, women have more to lose.

In this chapter and the following we use sex and age (often measured as being under or over fifty) as our primary indicators of the physical vulnerability of our respondents. If we had had measures of the height, weight, and vigor of our respondents, they would have been useful as well.

The second aspect of the concept of vulnerability is its *social* dimension. People are socially vulnerable to crime when they are frequently exposed to the threat of victimization because of who they are, and when the social and economic consequences of victimization weigh more heavily upon them. We measure social vulnerability by the actual risks faced by population groups, and by their resources for dealing with the consequences of crime.

Among major population groups, the risk of victimization by violent crime is disproportionately borne by Blacks and the poor. On a nationwide basis, rape and robbery rates for Blacks are about 2.5 times the comparable figures for whites, while people in the lowest income category reported rates for these crimes which were 3 times those for people in the upper reaches of the income distribution (U.S. Department of Justice, 1977b: Tables 56 and 12). This doubtless reflects the way in which the social and economic system determines where people live, work, and play. In the main, Blacks and poor people of all races live in greater propinquity to places where criminals live and do their work (crime being an extraordinarily close-to-home vocation). This is reflected in the plight of middle-class Blacks, who suffers substantially higher rates of victimization than their white counterparts, in part because they cannot so easily shift their places of residence to safer parts of the metropolitan area. In American cities, Blacks and the poor are more likely to be bound to the less desirable inner zones of the community, where crime rates are always high, regardless of who happens to be inhabiting them (see Shaw and McKay, 1942).

Race and income also are related to the resources and facilities which may be available to help individuals deal with the consequences of victimization. In part this is a direct function of income, for people with little money simply cannot easily afford to replace stolen items or repair damage to their property. They also may find that time lost from work as a result of efforts to restore their equilibrium in the aftermath of victimization directly affects their pocketbooks. Private insurance does not help them much, for they are among the least likely to be insured. Finally, survey measures of perceptions of the efficiency and efficacy of public services, including the police, indicate that Blacks and the poor are less satisfied than their counterparts with those services (Skogan, 1979b, 1975).

In this chapter we use race (combining Asians and whites in one group, and Blacks and American Indians in another) and income (often measured as a family income of under or over $10,000) to represent our respondents' social vulnerability to crime. Like Hindelang et al. (1978), Baumer (1980), and others, we interpret these primarily as surrogates for area of residence, reflecting patterns of racial and economic segregation which confine Blacks and the poor in less desirable and higher risk areas of the city.

Vulnerability and Fear of Crime

Age, race, sex, and income are among the most consistent correlates of all measures of fear of crime, reflecting (we argue) the underlying dimensions of physical and social vulnerability to crime. In rough order of the strength of those correlations, females are more fearful than males, older persons are more fearful than young people, Blacks are more fearful than whites, and poor people are more fearful than the relatively well-to-do. Further, these effects are generally linear and additive; fear "accumulates" among successively more vulnerable groups, but without significant interaction effects. Thus, simple multiple regression can adequately capture their independent significance and cumulative importance as predictors of fear of crime.

A simple portrait of the relationship between these personal attributes and our measures of fear of crime is presented in Table 5.1. It reports the proportion in each group who indicated that they felt "very unsafe" if alone on the streets of their neighborhoods at night.

As Table 5.1 illustrates, the strongest bivariate association between these measures of personal vulnerability and fear is that for

TABLE 5.1   Fear Among Major Population Groups

Demographic Group	Percentage "Very Unsafe"	(N)
SEX		
Males	6.4	(643)
Females	22.8	(693)
AGE		
18-20	7.1	(71)
21-26	6.3	(256)
27-32	6.3	(263)
33-39	9.3	(174)
40-49	10.6	(149)
50-59	22.2	(152)
60 plus	40.7	(179)
FAMILY INCOME		
Under $6,000	27.4	(215)
$6-10,000	17.0	(203)
$10-15,000	10.2	(255)
$15-20,000	6.5	(184)
$20-25,000	7.0	(81)
$25,000 plus	10.9	(95)
RACE		
Whites	12.6	(857)
Blacks	20.1	(368)

SOURCE: Computed from combined citywide surveys.

sex. Women were almost 3.5 times as likely as males to place themselves in the "very unsafe" category. Age was related to fear in
slightly curvilinear fashion, but the effect was not significant enough
to lead us to take this into account in our statistical analyses. Below
the 50-59-year-old category, fear levels generally rose slowly with age,
discounting the slight "jump" in fear in the under-20 group (who were
few in number in this survey). There was a substantial discontinuity
between those below 50 years of age and those just older than them,
and a similar doubling in the proportion in the highest fear category
when we compare those in their 50s to those over 60. Categories of
family income also evidenced a bit of curvilinearity in their relationship with fear, but again not significantly so. In general, fear levels
decrease steadily with increasing family income, discounting a slight
upturn in fear among those reporting incomes of more than $25,000 a
year. Finally, Blacks were about 1.5 times as likely as whites to place
themselves in the most fearful category.

One feature of these measures is that, in the main, the two dimensions of vulnerability are independent. Race, for example, is virtually uncorrelated with sex. The data do reflect the major features of the American social system, and in these cities women and Blacks report lower incomes, and women and whites live longer. However, none of the indicators are so substantially intercorrelated that the bivariate relationships suggested in Table 5.1 are confounded by that colinearity.

In addition to being uncorrelated, there also was no interaction between these measures that affected their relationship to fear. In an analysis of variance, all of the main effects (the four indicators) but none of their potential interaction terms were significant predictors of fear. This indicates that the fear levels of particular groups can best be described by their main components, and that there is no "additional" effect of being more vulnerable on two or three dimensions at the same time. For example, older women are simply as fearful as their sex and age, taken separately, would lead us to predict. The linear and additive character of the data enables us to generate estimates, like those given in Table 5.2, of the cumulative effect of age, race, sex, and income on fear of crime.

Table 5.2 presents estimates of the average fear of crime scores for each of sixteen population groups defined by the four indicators. Fear of crime was lowest in the young, white, male, moderate-income group (they had a mean score of 1.63 on the one-to-four scale), and highest among older, Black, female, poor respondents (with a mean score of 3.28, double the bottom figure).

Careful inspection of the figures reported in Table 5.2 reveals that, while each "increment of vulnerability" characterizing a population group contributes to its average level of fear, some of those attributes count more heavily than do others. Numerically, the greatest difference between any two groups can be laid to age; those under 50 were, on the average (controlling for all the other factors), .09 units below the overall population mean for these three cities (which was 2.14). Those 50 and older were .57 units above that figure. The impact of advancing age on fear is so strong that, of these sixteen population subgroups, all but one of the top half include persons in their 50s or older. Only white males in the higher-income group scored in the less fearful half of the population even though they were older. Closely following age were gender differences, with an overall distance of .46 scale units separating the sexes. The four most fearful groups in our three cities were composed of women of all races and income categories. Then followed groups which, we argue, were socially

TABLE 5.2   Fear Among Detailed Population Subgroups

| | Demographic Indicators of: | | | Estimated |
| Physical Vulnerability | | | Social Vulnerability | Average |
Age	Sex	Race	Income	Fear Score
older	female	black	poor	3.28
older	female	black	moderate	3.07
older	female	white	poor	3.02
older	female	white	moderate	2.81
older	male	black	poor	2.76
younger	female	black	poor	2.62
older	male	black	moderate	2.55
older	male	white	poor	2.50
younger	female	black	moderate	2.41
younger	female	white	poor	2.36
older	male	white	moderate	2.29
younger	female	white	moderate	2.15
younger	male	black	poor	2.10
younger	male	black	moderate	1.89
younger	male	white	poor	1.84
younger	male	white	moderate	1.63
			Population Average	2.14

SOURCE: Computed from combined citywide surveys. Estimates based on multiple regression using dichotomous independent variables. The "poor" were those reporting incomes under $10,000; "older" persons were those 50 and above.

rather than physically vulnerable. Blacks were .26 units above whites on the fear scale, and those with low family incomes were .21 units above the well-to-do. The most fearful group were older, Black, poor women, of whom 64% felt "very unsafe" in their neighborhoods at night.

These data argue for the relative primacy of physical over social forms of vulnerability. The indicators are so independent of one another that simple multiple regression can be used to gauge their relative impact. The two measures of physical vulnerability were almost 2.5 times as important for statistically explaining fear as were our two measures of social vulnerability. Together the four measures explained 20% of the variance (R = .45) in fear of crime.

The Paradox:
Vulnerability, Victimization, and Fear

In this chapter we have discussed in detail the concept of vulnerability to personal crime. We argued that there are two aspects of vulnerability, one physical and the other social. The former concerns

openness to attack, powerlessness to resist, and exposure to significant physical and emotional consequences if attacked. Social vulnerability involves daily exposure to the threat of victimization and limited
means for coping with the medical and economic consequences of
victimization.

We have seen that fear of crime is strongly related to each dimension of personal vulnerability. These relationships are among the most
consistent empirical findings of survey research on crime. From place
to place and from time to time throughout the 1970s, persons in more
vulnerable categories have reported higher levels of fear.

It should be apparent, therefore, that the findings of this chapter
and the one preceding it present us with somewhat of a paradox.
Among our indicators, those reflecting physical vulnerability were by
far the strong correlates of fear. On the other hand, those indicators
also were the most consistent correlates of *low* rates of victimization.
Across all major crime categories, women and the elderly were less
likely than their counterparts to report being victimized. This too is
one of the most consistent empirical findings of well-conducted victimization surveys. *Within* each group, the relationship between victimization and fear is consistent with our earlier findings; when they
are victimized, women and the elderly are more frightened as a
consequence. However, relatively few of them have experiences of
that sort to report.

Among other things, this has raised the question of whether or not
the fears of many in these "objectively low-risk" groups are indeed
irrational. It might be argued that they reflect concerns of a symbolic
or emotive nature, rather than concrete probabilities. However, we
saw in Chapter 3 that fear of crime is at least independent of other
common measures of distrust or suspicion, and the same can be said
among women and the elderly as groups. Further, as we shall see in
Chapters 11 and 12, we are not sure that low rates of victimization and
low risk of attack necessarily go together. We shall demonstrate that
physical vulnerability is strongly related to the frequency with which
people adopt protective tactics which limit their exposure to risk and
reduce their chances of being victimized. These behavioral adaptations to crime thus may explain the high-vulnerability/low-
victimization status of certain groups. The fears of those in this
category stem not from direct experience or statistical expectations,
but rather from what *could* happen to them and the potential consequences of criminal attack.

PART II

CRIME AND FEAR IN COMMUNITY CONTEXT

In this section we examine the influence of community-related factors upon fear. In Chapter 6 we first explore the extent to which people are plagued by problems with major crimes, then turn to more indirect signs that a community is troubled. We examine such neighborhood conditions as building abandonment, teenage trouble-making, drug use, and vandalism. Finally, we detail the degree of community integration, or cohesion, that characterizes our respondents and the neighborhoods in which they live. After describing these factors in some detail, we turn, in Chapter 7, to their impact upon fear.

Chapter 6

NEIGHBORHOOD PROBLEMS AND POTENTIALS

Introduction

We have seen in the previous section how individual experiences with victimization and vulnerability to crime powerfully affect fear. Now we turn to the influence of environmental conditions on fear and the effects of the linkages between people and their surrounding community. An important component of any analysis of how people understand and attempt to deal with crime must be their assessment of the risks which surround them. Neighborhoods are important if for no other reason than that they circumscribe people's lifespace for a significant fraction of the nonworking day. Events and conditions there should have an important effect on one's daily behavior. In addition, there are a variety of factors that tie one's personal fate to that of one's local community. People who own their homes, or have children enrolled in a local school, or enjoy relatives or close friends in the vicinity share more than a passing interest in neighborhood conditions, regardless of their personal experiences or sense of vulnerability to crime. The more closely their fates are tied to the community the more sensitive they may be to local conditions, and the more likely they may be to respond actively to them as individuals or in concert with others. Finally, neighborhoods form an important locus for action. Crime problems of the type we are considering here share the important attribute that they happen in a *place;* these victimizations and related conditions have a location. Strategies for dealing with them have an important locational, or "turf-based" component. Their perceptions of how much of a problem crime and disorder is in their area, as well as their commitment to it, should play an important role in determining what people think and do about the problem.

In this chapter we examine three important dimensions along which neighborhoods vary considerably and across which there are substantial differences among urban dwellers. These are crime, disorder, and integration. The first two are crime-related conditions, while the third is a neighborhood factor which plays an important role in theories of criminogenesis.

We examine here neighborhood problems with crimes like burglary, assault, rape, and personal theft. This chapter also investigates the extent of what we call "signs of disorder," including building abandonment, drug use, teenage impropriety, and vandalism. The neighborhoods which were surveyed varied in the degree to which these events and conditions were problems there, and these neighborhood factors were systematically related to the personal characteristics of our respondents as well. In later chapters we examine the role that these crime-related factors play in generating fear and shaping individual reactions to crime.

The third of our neighborhood factors, integration, is, in theory, intimately linked to the extent of crime and disorder problems. Two measures of integration will be employed here, one gauging the extent of residential ties among our respondents and the other the extent of their social ties. Our data confirm the strong negative relation between integration and disorganization. We also found that the extent to which persons are socially and residentially tied to their communities plays an important role in shaping the flow of information about neighborhood crime, and in facilitating efforts to prevent victimization and reduce the crime rate.

Extent of Crime Problems

Many older residents in our study communities expressed a great deal of nostalgia for "the good old days," and doubt about the future. One Black man in his sixties recalled his version of the past in Woodlawn:

> He said he had lived in Woodlawn for a long time, that he had lived in Woodlawn when there were no gangs and when he considered it (as he called it) "a real pretty little paradise." He said he remembered a time when everybody could walk the streets without their being assaulted or mugged or anything like that. That the neighborhood was well kept. That there wasn't any writing on the walls and garbage in the streets. You know, there wasn't no abandoned buildings. He said that Woodlawn really looked like a nice area before that time [Woodlawn, July 1977].

Our surveys also indicated that there was a substantial degree of pessimism about neighborhood conditions among residents of our three cities, especially those in Chicago and Philadelphia. In order to gauge their perceptions of general neighborhood trends, we asked each of our respondents:

> Would you say that your neighborhood has changed for the better, or for the worse, in the past couple of years, or has it stayed about the same?

Overall, about half of them indicated that things had stayed the same during that period, and the remainder split (27% to 21%) in the direction of things "getting worse." Differences among the cities in this regard were quite significant, however. By far the most optimistic were residents of San Francisco, where only 20% thought that things had gotten worse; in Chicago that figure stood at 31%, with Philadelphians not far behind. Thus nearly one-third of all Chicagoans thought that things around them had been getting worse, while only 19% thought that they had improved to any degree.

In light of this, we were not surprised to find that for some residents of these cities crime constituted a serious neighborhood problem. In order to assess local crime conditions we asked each respondent how much of a "problem" various kinds of crime were in their neighborhoods. The crimes were burglary, personal theft, stranger assault, and rape. In each case they were asked if the kind of crime described was "a big problem," "some problem," or "almost no problem." In all, at most 25% of our respondents indicated that some type of crime was a big problem for people in their neighborhood, but the three-city averages were all below 20%. Burglary was a big local problem to 19%, 18% felt the same about personal theft, while for stranger assault the figure was only 8%, and for rape, 6%. City-by-city totals are given in Table 6.1.

While these figures may seem high, they do not suggest that residents of these cities were incapacitated by concern about crime. For most of them crime was not a serious neighborhood problem. Because crime problems tend to cluster geographically (as we shall see in detail below), there is a great deal of overlap in these responses, and 70% of our respondents reported that *none* of these problems constituted a source of serious concern in their immediate areas.

Rankings of neighborhood problems were not even in the most general accord with the distribution of victimization in these cities. Burglary was greatly underrepresented in the universe of neighborhood problems. Based upon official reports, the burglary rate was 7

TABLE 6.1   Crime Problems in the Neighborhood

| City | *Percentage Responding "A Big Problem"* | | | | |
	Burglary	Personal Theft	Stranger Assault	Rape	(N)
Chicago	20	25	10	7	(390)
San Francisco	20	17	8	6	(446)
Philadelphia	16	14	6	5	(424)
(Significance of differences)	(.53)	(.01+)	(.27)	(.57)	
Average	19	18	8	6	(1260)

NOTE: Number of cases varies slightly from crime to crime; averages are given here.
SOURCE: Computed from citywide surveys.

times the robbery rate in these cities, while it was 11 times the assault rate and 69 times the rape rate. By that measure all of these personal crimes (and especially robbery) were overrepresented as problems, or burglary was massively undervalued. In either case, the mix of neighborhood problems as seen by residents overemphasizes personal crimes — especially personal theft — and thus "tilts the scale" in the direction of more fear-provoking incidents. This suggests that people's "problem" rankings took into account elements other than the frequency of crime, and included estimates of the seriousness of incidents, or their potential consequences, as well as risk.

In addition, we cannot discount our respondents' concern about the impact of crime upon others significant in their lives when they assessed neighborhood conditions. There is some evidence about the magnitude of people's concern for the safety of relatives. In a study of Black and white mothers in Philadelphia, Savitz et al. (1977) found that many were more worried about their children's safety than they were about their own. Springer (1974) found that policemen in Seattle were fearful of their wives using a certain park that they thought to be safe enough for most people. By extension, we could surmise that people take into account the experiences of friends and neighbors when they assess conditions in their immediate vicinities. We shall see in later chapters that reports of crime conditions are related to such things as the extent of personal contact with crime victims, and that contact contributes to fear.

Our data on perceptions of crime as a neighborhood problem are not in accord with the general distribution of crime across these three cities. The distinctively high rates of victimization for personal theft,

TABLE 6.2   Crime Problems Measures at the Individual and
            Neighborhood Levels

| Below Diagonal Individual-Level Correlations | *Above Diagonal Neighborhood-Level Correlations* | | | |
	Burglary	Personal Theft	Stranger Assault	Rape
Burglary		.60	.73	.84
Personal Theft	.37		.81	.65
Stranger Assault	.35	.44		.82
Rape	.26	.31	.36	

NOTE: Number of cases above diagonal was ten, the number of neighborhood surveys. Neighborhood scores were percentages indicating crime was a "big problem." Those scores were based upon responses by 200 to 450 residents in each area. Number of cases below diagonal was approximately 1200, the number of respondents to our citywide surveys. All correlations are Pearson's r.

stranger assault, and rape that we found in San Francisco were not well-represented in the data on neighborhood problems. The most notable discrepancy was the high ranking that Chicagoans gave to robbery and purse snatching, despite the fact that both the victimization surveys and the *Uniform Crime Report* placed them below San Francisco in that regard. In fact, we found a general *lack* of difference between the cities with respect to these crime problems. This is in accord with the nature of crime, which in large places like these tends to be a neighborhood rather than citywide phenomenon. As we noted, crimes tend to "go together" in space, clustering jointly with various well-known social and economic aspects of community areas. (This is the foundation, of course, of at least one "school" of sociology.) As a result, for cities of vaguely similar size there generally is more variation in crime rates (and presumably "crime problems") within them than between them. This has important consequences for our analysis, for to the extent to which neighborhood conditions have important consequences for how people perceive and respond to crime they should serve to obliterate inter*city* differences in these phenomena. While victimization rates vary in frequency to some degree from city to city, the characteristic crime problems facing our respondents on a day-to-day basis do not, which should weaken any expectations for strong intercity differences in reactions to crime.

Table 6.2 documents the consistency with which problems with crime plague some neighborhoods, while leaving others relatively unscathed. While there were few substantial differences between cities in the extent to which these crimes were of concern, differences between our study neighborhoods there were large and consistent in this regard. For Table 6.2 we have catalogued each of our neighborhoods in terms of the proportion of residents there who reported that crimes of various types were "big problems." The upper half of the matrix in this table presents correlations between these proportions. All were strong, indicating a tendency for crime problems to cluster in certain areas. Not unexpectedly, the weakest correlations are between burglary and personal crimes; burglary problems were common in our most middle-class community, where personal theft and assaults by strangers were much more rare. The strong, positive correlations in Table 6.2 are indicative of the substantial spatial clustering of the incidence of crime and crime problems, and suggest that the labels "bad places" and "good places" can fairly describe neighborhoods. Not unexpectedly, crime problems were reflected in our respondents' ratings of neighborhood conditions: the average correlation (gamma) between perceptions of crime problems and reports that the neighborhood was "getting worse" was .25.

The correlations to the left and below the diagonal in Table 6.2 are based upon responses by about 1200 individuals in our citywide surveys to the same set of questions. They parallel the citylevel findings, indicating a strong tendency for individuals who think that one type of crime is a serious problem (or not) in their area to report the same for the remainder. Those correlations averaged .35, which is quite substantial for such perceptual indicators. It indicates that there is a great deal of stability in ratings of local conditions across the domain of "crime." The reports of individuals analyzed at that level are less tightly interrelated than perceptions aggregated at the neighborhood level, precisely because crime and crime problems cluster tightly with other social and economic characteristics of small geographical areas. While citywide survey samples produce data from heterogeneous and broadly representative populations, neighborhood studies gather information from people who share a great deal in common across a broad range of personal, attitudinal, and experiential factors. As a result, when we aggregate their responses to questions about a related perceptual domain, they are much more likely to be homogeneous in their replies. At the city level we are aggregating the opinions of very diverse peoples, and thus should expect smaller differences and much less consistency in ratings.

The strong tendency even for individuals drawn from the general population to share consistent perceptions of conditions in their neighborhoods indicates that we can usefully combine those ratings into an omnibus scoring of the extent to which crime constitutes a problem in each of their immediate environments. A factor analysis of the four ratings of neighborhood conditions indicated that they were unidimensional, and when added together they formed a measure with a reliability (Cronbach's Alpha) of .67. The average score on that measure was 6, placing the average person exactly between "almost no problem" and "some problem" with respect to crime in his or her vicinity. The multivariate statistical analyses of the impact of these conditions presented in the following chapters will use this single rating score to represent all four types of crime problems.

While these ratings of community crime conditions are perceptual — they reflect our respondents' readings of the extent and personal significance of local crime — there is some evidence that we can use them as general indicators of the "objective" distribution of crime. As we noted in Chapter 1, we conducted a Chicago metropolitan area survey in mid 1979 which included many of the questions used in our three-city study, and which sampled residents using the same techniques. In that survey we were able to establish the place of residence of each respondent. For Chicago residents, we identified the community areas in which they lived. There are 76 such areas in the city, and each exhibits a great deal of social and economic homogeneity. We use those areas here as "neighborhoods," although of course they are larger in scope than is ordinarily implied by the term. For each area we secured official crime reports and up-to-date population estimates, and calculated the crime rate (per 100,000) for each respondent's locality. Although they certainly do not reflect the "true" rate of victimization in these neighborhoods, these figures give us an independent rating of the extent to which crime was a serious problem in each community, one which we can compare to our respondents' assessments.

That comparison is reported in Table 6.3. It indicates the average robbery, assault, and burglary rate for each respondent's area, in terms of whether they rated each crime as a "big problem," "some problem," or "almost no problem." Ratings of neighborhood conditions paralleled official crime counts for the area. Differences in average crime rates were largest for robbery; those who ranked predatory street crime a "big problem" lived in community areas where the official robbery rate was half again as that for the city as a whole, and almost twice as high as it was for those who rated robbery "almost no problem." The relation between assessments of assault problems and the official aggravated assault rate was almost as dra-

TABLE 6.3   Official Crime Rates and Ratings of Crime Problems in
             Chicago

Extent to Which Respondent Rates a Problem	Average Official Crime Rate per 100,000 Persons in the Respondent's Community Area		
	Robbery	Aggravated Assault	Burglary
Almost no problem	397 (405)	268 (498)	1058 (368)
Some problem	534 (235)	385 (160)	1123 (276)
Big problem	700 (112)	486 (89)	1197 (107)
Total	485 (753)	319 (747)	1101 (752)

NOTE: Differences in crime rates across ratings of problems all significant ($p < .01$). Number of cases is given in parentheses.

SOURCE: Crime counts from the Chicago Police Department (see Maxfield, 1979). Population figures for calculating rates from the Chicago Department of Planning. Computed from metropolitan area survey, central-city sample only.

matic. Differences in the official burglary rate were weakly but consistently related to ratings of burglary conditions.

There was some dispersion around these means. Correlations (Pearson's r) between crime assessments and crime rates were substantial and persistent, however. Among city residents, the correlation between their ratings of assault problems and the official assault rate for their community areas was $+.29$; for robbery the correlation was $+.21$, and for burglary $+.10$. These relationships were quite independent of whom our respondents were. Controlling for age, sex, race, and income affected those correlations hardly at all — they sank an average of only .04. While these indicators of vulnerability all were related to how much of a problem crime presented to our informants, the effects of vulnerability were independent of the connection between our survey measure and official crime rates.

All of this is evidence of the validity of this crime-problems measure as an indicator of actual neighborhood conditions. Like McPherson's (1978) survey of Minneapolis, these data indicate that citizens' assessments of conditions around them can be used as a useful "stand-in" measure of the incidence of crime, at least as recorded by the police. Robbery, assault, and burglary were ranked as a concern where independent measures of their incidence indicated they were more frequent. On the average, respondents in this parallel survey who indicated that a certain crime was a "big problem" lived in places where police came to the same conclusion.

The Distribution of the Burden of Crime

When we examine how individuals rate their immediate environments, the results resemble only in part the profile of social and
economic factors we drew to describe victimization. The poor are by
far more likely than those in middle- or upper-income categories to
report living in areas haunted by problems with robbery, purse snatching, and assaultive violence. While 31% of those in the lowest income
category reported that robbery was a big problem in their locales, and
16% reported that assault by strangers was of similar concern, for
those at the top of the financial ladder those proportions stood at 17%
and 6%, respectively. Only burglary reputedly was a problem in areas
in these three cities where upper-income people lived. The same
curve described the distribution of neighborhood problems with
burglary that we saw in relation to the distribution of victimization
itself: Those problems were least common for those in the $10,000 to
$20,000 income group, and peaked at virtually an identical level
among those at the top and bottom of the scale.

In sharp contrast to the higher levels of victimization and
neighborhood problems reported by the poor were the neighborhood
descriptions rendered by younger people; while they were more likely
than anyone to be victimized by every crime examined here, older
adults were the ones who were most likely to report that crime
constituted an important problem in their vicinities. In the case of
personal theft, concern about neighborhood conditions rose steadily
with age, peaking with almost 30% of those over 60 reporting that
robbery and purse snatching were big problems in their areas. The
same age gradient described how people perceived difficulties with
assaultive violence and sexual molestation, but not with burglary. In
general, the older the people, the more likely they were to express
concern about personal crime, ranking it a major problem in their
neighborhoods.

The relationship between race and the distribution of the burden
of crime rang a familiar note: Black residents of these cities were more
likely than whites to report that serious personal crimes plagued their
communities. Only 15% of whites, but 25% of Blacks, rated personal
theft a "big problem" in their areas. Blacks were more likely to
perceive rape problems nearby as well. On the other hand, Blacks
were only 3 percentage points more likely to report problems with
burglary — but this relationship became considerably stronger when
we controlled for the effects of differing income levels.

Finally, quite in opposition to their personal rates of victimization,
women were more likely than men to report that personal theft and

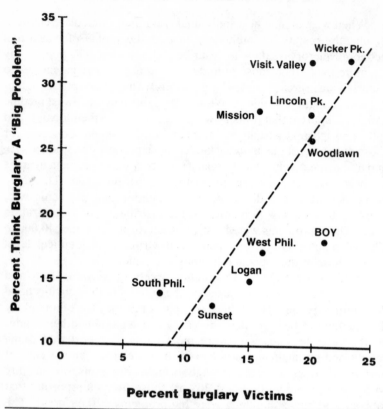

Figure 6.1 Neighborhood Victimization and Burglary as a Problem
SOURCE: Computed from ten neighborhood surveys.

assault were serious neighborhood problems. They also were more likely to share that perception of rape problems, although the difference between the sexes was not large in this regard — 2 percentage points.

All of this paints a picture which looks less like the distribution of victimization than that of fear. We indicated in Chapter 5 that fear levels do not accurately reflect who reports being a victim of what, and suggested that women and the elderly constituted two key components of this puzzle. Here we find that the distribution of perceived crime *problems,* which appear to reflect such factors as the potential consequences of victimization as well as the incidence of crime, does lie to the disadvantage of those groups. In Chapter 7 we shall see how neighborhood conditions independently affect how people assess their risks.

Finally, our data on victimization indicate that personal experience with neighborhood crime strongly affects how people rate general conditions in their neighborhoods. In our surveys we asked people, "Has anyone actually broken into your home in the past two years?" Overall, 15% indicated that someone had, and, among those who did, 41% indicated that burglary was a "big problem" nearby (the contrasting figure for nonvictims was 15%). When we classified our study neighborhoods by their burglary rates, based on this measure, the local incidence of burglary was very strongly related to estimates by people there of the magnitude of the problem. Figure 6.1 illustrates how the two covary. A high-burglary, big-problem area, Wicker Park in Chicago, anchors the top of the chart, while the low-rate low-concern neighborhoods of Sunset, in San Francisco, and South Philadelphia fell at the bottom. At both the individual and neighborhood levels our data point toward the incidence of the burden of crime itself (and the concomitant diffusion of that information among residents of the area) as an important force shaping perceptions of crime problems.

Signs of Disorder

In addition to asking about the incidence of problems with major crimes, we also inquired in our surveys about the extent to which selected facets of the local social order seemed to be in disarray. By "the social order" we mean people's expectations about fit and proper conditions and conduct, especially in public and semipublic places. Improper conduct includes boisterousness, drunkenness, and untidiness, as well as proneness to violent or acquisitive behavior. Where these standards seem to be in a decline, people feel thaty they are watching the disintegration of the rules that ought to govern public life. Within urban neighborhoods people are variously successful in negotiating with other users of their common space a working set of expectations about how they should behave (Hunter, 1978b). They may differ in the level at which those expectations are set and the degree to which diversity of behavior around these guidelines is tolerated, but everyone develops such norms and applies them as templates to gauge local conditions and events. In his study in Boston, Wilson (1968b) called these "standards of right and seemly conduct," and reported that distress about the failure of the community to control violations of those standards was widespread. He argued that this was a major contributor to the "sense of urban unease" which crept around us in the 1960s.

Based on our field investigations in three cities, we chose four particular signposts indicating the presumed health of the social order, in order to gauge how it affected residents' perceptions of crime. Over a decade ago Biderman et al. (1967: 16) argued that people's major impressions about crime derived from "the highly visible signs of what they regard as disorderly and disreputable behavior in their community." While few people witness crimes or personally experience them, they all associate danger from crime with selected aspects of the environment. They rely upon the presence or absence of those cues to warn them from dangerous locales; the environmental cues serve as what Stinchcombe et al. (1978) dubbed "the signs of crime."

Those signs of crime — in our terminology, potential "problems" — serve as early-warning signals of impending danger because people have learned to associate them with things they fear. For example, in our field investigations we learned that an abandoned building is a source of considerable distress to residents of a community. People believe that tramps will break into empty buildings to escape the cold and sleep; then "drug dealers" will ply their trade in them, marketing among youths in the area. Criminals of various sorts are thought to base their operations there, making it dangerous even to walk near an abandoned structure. At the very least vandals will deface an empty building, and perhaps loot it. Finally, abandoned buildings become targets for casual arson, and seem to have a high chance of being set afire. This threatens neighboring homes as well. It may not take much abandonment to constitute a community problem. A study by the Department of Housing and Urban Development (1973) indicated that building abandonment becomes a serious problem, with regard to future investment in a neighborhood, when between 3% and 6% of the buildings there fall empty. As a result, empty buildings often become a focus for neighborhood actiion. One Wicker Park woman was describing local events to a field interviewer:

> She then began to talk about buildings that had been abandoned. One was condemned, the other was standing empty but not boarded up. It scared the people in the neighborhood. The kids in the neighborhood were playing around it. It was really dangerous. They all got together and went to the precinct captain about the houses. One was torn down, and now they are trying to get them to tear the other one down [Wicker Park, July 1976].

Unsupervised teenagers also are seen as potential sources of disruption, harassment, and crime. Rifai (1976) reports that in Portland a large proportion of victimizations recalled by the elderly involved nonphysical, verbal harassment by teenagers. In a study of "dangerous place," Riger and Gordon (1979) asked respondents why they were so; the most frequent reason given for the most frequently nominated places (alleys and parks) was that "kids hang out there." Certainly they often seem to be "up to no good," and the police frequently are called to deal with bands of teenagers congregating on street corners, in alley ways, or in front of shops and arcades. Rubinstein (1973) reports that police likewise sense that trouble may be brewing in such groups, but that they are helpless to do more than encourage them to "move on."

A woman in South Philadelphia described problems with teenagers there:

> We had a meeting in the evening and my son was supposed to come in later and pick me up. I called him and told him not to go into the project. I asked him to pick me up around the corner. The kids harrassed people — they were throwing things out of windows. The shooting of the policeman made people fearful of being robbed, possibly being killed — the boys in Wilson Park carry knives and guns. The residents live in constant fear [South Philadelphis, October 26, 1976].

Three older Black men interviewed on the street in Chicago's Woodlawn expressed concern about the apparent irrationality of teenage violence.

> I then asked if they were afraid of young people. They answered not afraid exactly, but leery, extremely leery of young people, that you never know what's on a young person's mind. Then one of them said that a lot of young people he knows, some of the things they do are just to be mean, just to be ornery, it serves no purpose, it's really senseless [Woodlawn, August 1977].

Signs that drug use is frequent is a source of fear for neighbors because people believe that addicts are driven to crime to pay for drugs, and that they are crazed and irrational in their behavior when they are on the prowl. An informant in South Philadelphia talked about addicts this way:

> Well, people are really worried about all of them. The kids who take drugs commit crimes. It's mostly robbery. They rob to get money for the drugs. The girls, who don't participate in such activities, sell their body to get the money. The people around here got so scared of drug addicts they are afraid to leave the house. The junkies break in and take any small item they can carry — TVs, radios, jewelry, its unbelievable. Many houses belonging to local families were robbed by their own children [South Philadelphia, November 19, 1976]!

People also believe addicts are prone to killing or injuring people "when they don't have to." Thus, not only does drug use raise the crime rate, but the risks it generates are unpredictable, beyond understanding, and thus impossible to avoid. A woman in the Mission in San Francisco:

> When people are using heroin they are apt to use guns and knives and whatever. That's what I am most afraid of, and so are most of my neighbors; see, we don't care too much about losing our material things. It's coming in one time and finding somebody in your house. And say he has a gun or a knife. Well he may choose to kill you so that he will remain anonymous [Mission, December 1976].

Finally, graffiti and visible vandalism are physical signs of the breakdown of social control. The aerosol paint dispenser is simply the latest twist in the urban arms spiral, a counter to the adoption of Lexan plastic school windows which are virtually unbreakable. But in each case the damage is attributed to "kids" and not to predatory outsiders. Thus its appearance in a community signals a problem that is close to home: intergenerational conflict over appropriate behavior.

The Prevalence of Disorder

We probed our informants' perceptions of the local order following the same format we employed to measure the extent of crime problems: Respondents were asked "how much of a problem" the various conditions described above were in their neighborhoods. They were:

(1) Groups of teenagers hanging out on the streets;
(2) Buildings or storefronts sitting abandoned or burned out;
(3) People using illegal drugs;
(4) Vandalism — like kids breaking windows or writing on walls or things like that.

The most common of these problems proved to be drug use and teenage congregations, followed very closely by vandalism. All of these concerned about 20% of our respondents in a major way. Only abandoned or burned-out buildings posed a "big problem" for less than one in ten. The figures for each city are noted in Table 6.4. They indicate that residents of Chicago and Philadelphia held virtually identical perceptions of problems in the community, but that many

TABLE 6.4   Disorder Problems in the Neighborhood

| City | Percentage Responding "A Big Problem" | | | |
	Teenagers	Abandoned Buildings	Drug Use	Vandalism
Chicago	23	12	25	22
Philadelphia	22	14	23	21
San Francisco	12	3	14	10
(Significance of differences)	(.01+)	(.01+)	(.01+)	(.01+)
Average	19	9	20	17

SOURCE: Computed from citywide surveys.

fewer San Franciscans shared those concerns. The proportion of residents in the Bay City who saw them as "big problems" almost uniformly ran 10 percentage points less, and this difference accounted for the highly significant intercity differences recorded in Table 6.4.

The markedly lower rates of perceived social disorder registered by San Franciscans does not mean, of course, that conditions necessarily are better there. Rather, they may reflect the "labels" people there give them. As we noted at the outset, there doubtless is a great deal of variation from place to place in the extent to which people accommodate themselves to marginal behavior in public places. Becker (1971) and others have noted the high tolerance for diversity of behavior which characterizes San Franciscans. Becker argues that this tolerance is a stable and enduring feature of that city's life, one he dubbed "the culture of civility."

The figures in Table 6.4 also indicate that concern with social-order problems is fairly frequent, somewhat more common than concern about major crime problems and vastly more frequent than recent victimization. While in these cities perhaps 5% of the residents were robbed in the past year, three times that many were plagued by vandalism, bands of teenagers, and drug-related problems. This relatively high frequency of crime-*linked* problems led Hunter (1978b: 9) to conclude that

> Fear in the urban environment is above all a fear of social disorder that may come to threaten the individual. I suggest that this fear results more from experiencing incivility than from direct experience with crime itself. Within areas of a city incivility and crime may in fact be empirically correlated. As such, incivility would then be a

symbolic cue to the heightened possibility for more serious criminal victimization. Independent of this empirical question, incivility may still produce greater variation in fear than does crime because of its relative frequency in daily experience of urban dwellers.

High scores on these measures reflect truly troublesome neighborhood conditions. The most extremely disorganized community in our study, Wicker Park in Chicago, stood at the top of all four of them. Between 40% and 50% of residents there reported that teenagers, drug use, and vandalism were "big problems," and 30% gave a similar ranking to the presence of "buildings or storefronts sitting abandoned or burned out." Wicker Park is a severely deteriorated area. Boarded-up buildings, junk-filled vacant lots, and badly maintained apartment buildings can be seen everywhere. Bars in the area attract an unsavory clientele which spills out into the streets. It is the only one of our study sites where gangs are considered to be a major problem. Violence is frequent in the schools, and adults fear to be on the streets when school lets out in the afternoon. Suspected arson fires are frequent occurrences, and arson deaths in the area have led to significant political conflict between local groups and the city. Ethnic conflict in the area is endemic. The mostly elderly Polish population is particularly hostile to neighborhood Puerto Ricans, to whom they attribute their neighborhood's decay. Puerto Ricans feel that they are the most badly served group in the neighborhood, where minority programs seem to be geared to the needs of the Black population. As a result, residents of Wicker Park have great difficulty in dealing with the problems of teenagers, building deterioration and abandonment, and community decline.[1]

The Distribution of Disorder

An examination of responses to these questions about disorder indicates that demographic factors which geographically cluster most strongly also were most clearly related to readings of neighborhood conditions. Race and income were closely tied to these ratings, to the disadvantage of Blacks and the poor. For example, abandoned or burned-out buildings were a "big problem" in the neighborhoods of 17% of our Black respondents, but only for 5% of whites. The correlation between family income levels and our three-point "problem" measure for building abandonment was $-.28$; 13% of those at the bottom, but only 5% of those at the top of the income scale, were concerned about this problem. On the other hand, age and sex largely were unrelated to these ratings. Old people generally were *less* likely

TABLE 6.5   Disorder Measures at the Individual and Neighborhood
Levels

	Above Diagonal Neighborhood-Level Correlations			
Below Diagonal Individual-Level Correlations	*Teenagers*	*Abandoned Buildings*	*Drug Use*	*Vandalism*
Teenagers		.85	.85	.90
Abandoned Buildings	.35		.82	.76
Drug Use	.48	.43		.86
Vandalism	.44	.39	.49	

NOTE: Number of cases above diagonal was ten, the number of neighborhood surveys. Neighborhood scores were percentages indicating crime was a "big problem." Those scores were based upon responses by 200 to 450 residents in each area. Number of cases below diagonal was approximately 1200, the number of respondents to our citywide surveys. All correlations are Pearson's r.

to see these conditions as "big problems" in their vicinities, but differences between age groups were slight.

The clustering of these problems by income and race, but not by sex and age, suggests that responses to these questions reflect neighborhood conditions, and are less multifaceted judgments about events and their consequences. This is because households are spatially segregated most strongly on the basis of race and class. Two decades of research in the "social area analysis" tradition indicates that socioeconomic status and racial-ethnic heritage are two of the strongest social "factors" which describe the distribution of peoples within a metropolis. These two factors, but not sex and age splits, also are strong correlates (in a spatial sense) of the distribution of crime and delinquency.

All of this suggests that "the signs of crime" serve as environmental cues, stimulating the perception that crime is a major concern in the vicinity, while additional factors — including age and sex-linked vulnerabilities to crime — contribute to some individuals' assessments that it is a "big problem." Issues like these will be considered in the next chapter, where they will be tied to indicators of fear of crime.

Their close tie to environmental conditions also may be responsible for the very strong clustering of these indicators at the neighborhood and individual level. As Table 6.5 indicates, across our ten study neighborhoods reports about these problems "went together" in a very clear way. Overall, the average correlation between them was

.86, with building abandonment (doubtless because of its relatively low frequency as a "big problem") the least connected (but with an average correlation of .81) to the remaining conditions. At the individual level the average interproblem correlation was .43, with building abandonment again constituting the "outlier" because of its low frequency. As with problems with major crimes, people who felt they were affected by one concern also were likely to be plagued by another. The overlap among these problems was so substantial that only 33% of our respondents indicated that *any* of these four issues was a "big problem." The correlation between disorder and crime problems also was considerable, and 54% of all our respondents fell into the fortunate "no big crime problems/no big disorder problems" category.

As the high correlations between these indicators suggest, they usefully can be combined to form a single index of social disorganization. In the citywide surveys responses to the four items were single factored, and added together they formed a scale with a reliability (Cronbach's Alpha) of .76. The average score on this scale was 6.18, placing the average respondent almost exactly between "almost no problem" and "some problem" on this dimension.

Although problems with crime and disorder clearly are interrelated, these clusters of concerns were empirically as well as conceptually distinct. Entering responses to all eight of these questions into a single factor analysis revealed that each set of four formed a clear, separate factor. Thus we scaled them separately, although the correlation between the two resulting scores is a substantial +.45.

Neighborhood Integration

In the oldest traditions of urban sociology can be found most of the ways in which contemporary scholars characterize communities and the people who live in them. This is certainly true of the concept of "neighborhood integration," a key building block in theories of unbanization since the turn of the century (see Lewis, 1980). Integration is one of a small set of concepts which make up "social disorganization theory," one of the major intellectual tools which social scientists employ even today to understand social problems. There are at least two major classes of definitions of social integration, reflecting the social or psychological orientations of those researchers. Whatever their particular biases with regard to the operationalization of the concept, all see integration as an important causal antecedent of a variety of social pathologies, including crime.

In the "social" tradition, Keller (1968) has advanced a behavioral definition of integration, based on patterns of "neighboring" and other forms of spatially bounded activity. In this view, the very boundaries of a community can be delineated by the lines along which the frequency of such visiting drops off. Hunter (1974) emphasizes the psychological conponents of integration. He views it as a two-dimensional concept. One of those dimensions is cognitive, calling for indicators reflecting people's awareness of their communities and knowledge of their prominent features. The other dimension is sentimental. Following Wirth (1938), he stresses the importance of emotional attachment, identification, positive evaluations, and other affective components of people's assessments of their lifespace.

There are a variety of important theoretical reasons to dwell on the concept of integration. It has been hypothesized to be causally related to a variety of important crime-related factors, at both the individual and community levels. Among social disorganization theorists, integration measures the capacity of a community to exert social control over its members and even passers-by, thereby enforcing local versions of right and seemly conduct (Janowitz, 1978). Integration thus effects levels of crime and other untoward aspects of behavior, including "competition, aggrandizement, and mutual exploitation among residents" (Wirth, 1938).

Even where such pathologies are rampant, individuals who are more integrated into their communities may reap important benefits. They seem to know more intimately the groups, individuals, and dangerous situations to be avoided in their locales, and to have a clearer sense of the boundaries of secure areas. This knowledge of the rhythms of life around them enables them to more effectively manage the risks of that environment (Suttles, 1968). Because they have developed working social relations with their neighbors, those who are more integrated should find it easier to call upon community members for support in risky situations, and could depend upon them to intervene. This in turn reinforces their own willingness to act, and to join in concert with others in collective efforts to solve community problems (Taub and Taylor, 1979). This may be why Lewis et al. (1980) and Riger et al. (1978) both find that in more integrated communities residents seem less affected when they encounter what they call the "signs of crime."

Those who are more integrated into their communities' social systems may become more involved in collective efforts, because they are linked into communication networks which pass along information about local conditions and events, and because they know who to go to when they have a problem. This also may serve to reduce their sense of social isolation and vulnerability, which seems to be a powerful predictor of fear of crime. Finally, many definitions of integration stress factors (like home ownership) which are, in a direct sense, measures of people's investment in a community and their bets about its future. This hinges the concept of integration to economic interests, which usually are powerful predictors of a host of attitudes and behaviors.

In this analysis we will mean two things by integration, along dimensions which touch upon many of the conceptual issues reviewed above. We are concerned first with integration as it reflects residential commitment. People are more integrated into their communities when they have lived in an area for a long time, when they have a financial investment there, and when they plan to remain living there. We call our measure of this cluster "residential ties." We also were concerned with the social and identificational components of integration. People are more integrated when they know people in their neighborhoods, when they are able to differentiate between them and outsiders, and when they feel a sense of sentimental attachment to the area they live in. We call our measure of this cluster "social ties."

In order to assess these linkages and gauge their impact upon reactions to crime, we asked each of our respondents a number of questions about their connections with their neighborhoods. We found that these two distinct (but interrelated) factors effectively summarized them. The correlations between indicators of each of the dimensions are presented in Table 6.6. Those below the diagonal reflect the individual-level clustering of those measures, while those above the diagonal indicate the consistency with which our ten neighborhoods fell on these indicators.

The first indicators reflected our conceptualization of residential ties. We asked about length of residence, home ownership, and whether or not our respondents thought that they would be living in the same area in two years. Responses to these questions were positively related, with an average correlation (at the individual level) of +.32. (The gamma correlation was somewhat higher, but we will employ Pearson's r here to be consistent with the neighborhood-level data.) Added together in standardized form, they formed a simple additive scale with a reliability of .56.

The second set of indicators presented in Table 6.6 measures social ties. We asked each respondent about how easy it was to recognize strangers in their areas, how many of the children in the neighborhood they knew, and whether or not they "felt a part" of the

TABLE 6.6 Integration Measures at the Individual and Neighborhood
Levels

Below Diagonal *Individual-Level Correlations*	*Above Diagonal* *Neighborhood-Level Correlations*		
Residential Ties	Home ownership	Length of residence	Plan to stay
Home ownership		.48	.82
Length of residence	.38		.48
Plan to stay	.32	.26	
Social Ties	Feel a part of neighborhood	Easy to tell strangers	Know many children
Feel a part of neighborhood		.60	.72
Easy to tell strangers	.31		.86
Know many children	.28	.39	

NOTE: Number of cases above diagonals was ten, the number of neighborhood surveys.
Neighborhood scores are percentages in highest category named. These scores were based upon
responses by 200 to 450 residents in each area. Number of cases below diagonals was
approximately 1200, the number of respondents to our citywide surveys. All correlations are
Pearson's r.

neighborhood rather than thinking of it as "just a place to live." When
standardized, responses to these questions formed an additive scale
with a reliability of .58. A factor analysis of the six items indicated
that the set was indeed two-factored. These factors are not independent of one another, to be sure, and these additive scale scores are
correlated +.40.[2]

We also asked our respondents how often they had visited the
homes of their neighbors "in the last two weeks." This behavioral
report turned out to be independent of other measures of integration,
apparently because elderly persons (who generally are long-term,
home-owning, familiar members of the neighborhood) simply do not
go out very often.

The Distribution of Integration

Like concern about crime and the signs of disorder, the extent of
neighborhood integration varied from group to group and from place
to place. In comparison to crime and disorder, key population groups
did not differ dramatically or consistently with regard to how tightly

they were tied to their local communities. Neighborhood contrasts remained strong, however, and there were strong differences among our three cities with regard to the strength of social and residential ties there.

Residential ties were much stronger among older and more affluent city dwellers. The strongest relationship we observed was that between age and residential stability (gamma = .56). On every component of that measure the elderly were particularly likely to be among the highest scorers. On the other hand, the elderly were *not* among those with the strongest social ties. Those neighborhood linkages grew with age through the fifties, but then declined sharply. In particular, elderly residents of these cities did not report knowing youths in their neighborhoods, and they were modest about their capacities to recognize strangers in the area. Although their fates were linked to these urban neighborhoods through home ownership and anticipated residential stability, the elderly were somewhat estranged from the local social system.

Blacks and whites fell on opposite ends of the spectrum of these two measures as well, but ranked differently on each of them. There was a tendency for whites to report stronger residential ties, which was largely an income-and-ownership issue. Blacks were more likely to enjoy strong social ties with those in their communities, on the other hand, As this suggests, family income was positively related to residential ties, but was virtually uncorrelated with social linkages. There were no significant sex differences whatsoever. This is to be expected, for males and females are scattered in almost equal numbers across the remainder of these social dimensions. This also increases our confidence that these measures reflect economic and environmental conditions.

These characteristic social and residential ties also varied in strength across cities, and that variation was quite independent of each city's demographic composition. On every measure Philadelphians were substantially more integrated into their communities than were residents of Chicago, and those in San Francisco in turn scored much lower than the middle group. Of the respondents in Philadelphia, two-thirds reported that it was "easy to tell strangers" in their neighborhood, as contrasted to 55% in Chicago, and only 41% in San Francisco. These differences persisted when we controlled for the demographic characteristics of our respondents; these cities varied in the strength of residential and social ties there quite independently of the attributes of the individuals doing the reporting.

The consistent clustering of these measures across our ten study neighborhoods, documented by the above-diagonal correlations in

Table 6.6, suggests that they, too, can usefully be described by how they stand on these summary indicators of integration. At the neighborhood level our measures of residential and social ties were strongly related to each other ($r = +.79$), and each community ranked in approximately the same position on each dimension. The most integrated and the least integrated of these ten neighborhoods differed substantially on these factors. In the Mission in San Francisco only 37% of our respondents thought that it was "easy" to recognize strangers in their area, while in South Philadelphia 80% shared that assessment. Of those we interviewed in Chicago's Lincoln Park, 22% owned their homes; in West Philadelphia that figure was 60%. Consistent with the city differences we identified above, our three study neighborhoods in Philadelphia all stood near the top on our indicators of integration.

As these examples hint, our measures of neighborhood integration cut across many otherwise important differences between neighborhoods. In the most and least integrated categories were found some quite different communities. Of the four most highly integrated communities, two were predominately white neighborhoods (South Philadelphia and Back-of-the-Yards), and two were predominately Black (West Philadelphia and Logan). The least integrated of these areas, the Mission, was also among our most delapidated, but the very next neighborhood at the bottom of the list, Lincoln Park, was by far the most affluent place we investigated.

The Mission is a racially heterogeneous but predominantly Mexican-American community, located immediately to the south of San Francisco's downtown. Most people there are poor, and live in apartment buildings or in old Victorian houses which have been cut up into small flats. Many Blacks live in high-rise public housing projects in the area. Young, affluent whites also are busy renovating older houses in one end of the neighborhood. Nearby urban redevelopment and the construction of BART have disrupted parts of the area as well. In our survey, 48% of the population of the Mission had lived there two years or less.

In contrast, our next most un-integrated community was Lincoln Park. Of the population there, 33% had lived elsewhere three years before, but our survey indicates that residents of Lincoln Park are overwhelmingly white and affluent. They also usually live in rented apartments, but they often are single, rarely report having children, and mostly are college graduates. Given the many differences between these two communities, any experiences which their residents share because of their common status with regard to integration would be strong testimony to the power of the concept.

At the higher reaches of the integration scale are found communities where people recognize one another, feel at home, and intend to stay. At the top of the list stands South Philadelphia. The area is dominated by blue-collar Italians and other white ethnics, and the boundaries of some substantial Black enclaves which dot the community are patrolled by white youth gangs which maintain close watch over anyone crossing racial lines. Especially in light of its racial composition, the area is characterized by low levels of education and low family incomes. However, the streets are clean and well-maintained, and are lined with attractive single-family homes. Many have been remodeled. People stay in South Philadelphia; in our survey, 46% of those we interviewed had lived there 20 years or longer. The physical layout of the community encourages the development of social ties as well:

> South Philadelphia has few major thoroughfares, and a large number of narrow side streets and alleys. These may well have given rise to the typical "South Philly" street culture where all children have "their" corners and people meet on the street and sit on their front steps in the evening chatting with their neighbors [Lewis et al., 1980: 116].

Our next most integrated neighborhood was also in Philadelphia. West Philadelphia, however, is one of the oldest Black communities in the city. There is a high concentration of elderly residents there. Most of the housing in the area is in the form of single-family homes, either detached or row-style. Many sections of the community are well maintained, despite substantial levels of unemployment among residents of the area. Home ownership is quite common in West Philadelphia, almost 2.5 times more frequent than in very affluent Lincoln Park.

Neighborhood Integration and Crime

In the chapters which follow we will often employ these measures of crime problems, signs of disorder, and integration, to explain why individuals think and behave as they do, and why certain beliefs and activities cluster as they do within neighborhoods. It should be noted, however, that although we will treat them as independent variables in those analyses, they are intimately related to one another as well.

The obvious prediction of social disorganization theory, of course, is that both crime and disorder problems will be greatest in places where levels of integration are low. It is not clear which direction the causal paths implied by this prediction take. There are reasons to suspect that low levels of integration spawn crime and related problems, and that these in turn undermine the social cohesion and economic viability of the community. What is clear in our data is that the two are strongly, negatively related.

The causal path leading from integration to crime and disorder reflects the efficacy of informal social control. In integrated areas adults keep an eye on children, and the whole community eyes strangers carefully. Adults who do not comply with local standards regarding home maintenance and household lifestyle are spoken to. People with a stake in the community and its future "police" events there with vigor.

The reciprocal process reflects the corrosive consequences of crime and fear, which reputedly cause people to restrict their social activity, forego opportunities to use community facilities, and avoid contact with strangers on the street. Crime and disorder may lead people to be less sociable, more suspicious, and less trustful even of their neighbors. As Wilson (1975: 21) argues:

> Predatory crime does not merely victimize individuals, it impedes and, in the extreme case, prevents the formation and maintenance of community. By disrupting the delicate nexus of ties, formal and informal, by which we are linked with our neighbors, crime atomizes society and makes of its members mere individual calculators estimating their own advantage.

Whatever the direction of these causal processes, the resulting distribution of crime and integration in our data indicates that they are quite powerful. Close-knit, stable neighborhoods are characteristically places where crime problems tend to be less severe. To illustrate this point, Figure 6.2 presents a comparision of the ten neighborhoods on their aggregate scores for residential ties and the extent to which these four types of crime were thought to be a problem in the area. When divided at the mean on each of those measures, nine of the ten areas fall clearly at opposite poles — either they were highly integrated and did not have severe difficulties with crime (five areas) or they were relatively disorganized and had serious crime problems (four areas). Only Visitacion Valley in San Francisco does not fit the pattern; it is a relatively high-income, homeowning, yet ethnically heterogeneous area, characterized by a high crime rate and high levels of organizational activity around crime. Many of the crime problems of the area reportedly stem from a public housing complex which lies nearby, but outside of the locally defined boundaries of the neighbor-

MAJOR CRIME PROBLEMS

	LOW	HIGH
LOW		Mission Lincoln Park Woodlawn Wicker Park
HIGH	Back-of-the-Yards Logan Sunset West Philadelphia South Philadelphia	Visitacion Valley

(left vertical axis label: NEIGHBORHOOD INTEGRATION)

Figure 6.2   Neighborhood Levels of Integration and Crime Problems
NOTE: Neighborhoods classified by dividing each measure at its mean. Integration is represented here by scores on the residential ties measure.
SOURCE: Computed from ten neighborhood surveys, averaging scale scores of residents of each area.

hood. In isolation, Visitacion Valley probably would fall neatly in the high-integration, low-problems category. Including all ten neighborhoods, the aggregate-level correlation between our residential-ties measure and crime-problems scale score was $-.48$; excluding Visitacion Valley it was $-.71$. The correlation between measures of the extent of crime problems and the strength of social ties was $-.56$.

Summary

In this chapter we described two related dimensions along which neighborhood crime and disorder can be assessed. The first reflects the extent to which an area's residents believe that serious crimes are a concern in their community. In our city and neighborhood surveys we assayed the extent to which burglary, street robbery, stranger assault, and rape constituted problems in our respondents' neighborhoods. We also inquired about a related set of neighborhood conditions, including building abandonment, drug use, vandalism, and teenage troublemaking. These may serve as the "signs" of crime, pointing to serious trouble because they indicate major rents in the local social fabric.

In general these data suggest that assessments that crime is a problem do not vary much from city to city, but that within cities they vary considerably from neighborhood to neighborhood. Both crime and disorder problems cluster together very tightly, and it is possible to fairly describe neighborhoods as troubled or not troubled, and people as in trouble or not. Blacks and the poor bore the brunt of both sets of problems. Women and the elderly also were more likely to perceive that crime constituted an important concern in their communities. All of this paints a picture which resembles closely the distribution of fear, and places scoring near the top on these measures are fearsome places indeed.

We also examined the strength of the ties which bind individuals to these neighborhoods. One of these ties involves residential commitment, and the other integration into the local social system. Like concern about crime and disorder, neighborhoods varied considerably in the degree to which residents evidenced those forms of involvement in local affairs. Our measures of integration were less strongly linked to the personal characteristics of our respondents than were those describing crime and disorder, and they drew similar profiles of some surprisingly dissimilar neighborhoods. However, integration was strongly, negatively related to the incidence of crime-related conditions in our ten study neighborhoods, and there are strong theoretical reasons to suspect that they will be linked to fear and behavior as well.

NOTES

1. This discussion is drawn from Lewis et al., 1980.
2. Because we saw these measures as all reflecting integration, we allowed for the factors to be correlated by confirming their separate status using oblique factor analysis.
3. These neighborhood descriptions are drawn from Lewis et al., 1980.

Chapter 7

NEIGHBORHOOD CONDITIONS AND FEAR

Introduction

In principle, people's assessments of local crime conditions and their integration into neighborhood affairs should play an important role in shaping their perceptions of the risks they face there and the dangers they are exposed to when they brave the streets after dark. The crimes we have focused on are serious ones, and areas where they seem to be common should be fearsome places indeed. Where the "signs of crime" abound, people should be more circumspect about their activity as well. Our surveys in three cities indicated that these effects were quite strong. Numerically, we found that perhaps the most unsettling characteristic of a community was the direction in which the forces of change seemed to be taking it. A substantial number of city residents thought that things were getting worse rather than better in their neighborhoods, a trend which did not augur well for their perceptions of community security. As Furstenberg (1971: 607) put it, "people take their cues from the neighborhood about how afraid to be."

There has been considerable speculation that some people may take these cues more to heart than do others. We have seen in Part I that people vary in the extent to which they are vulnerable to crime, and that this is reflected in their fear of its occurrence. Some argue that certain vulnerable groups — notably, women and the elderly — may be more affected by the events and conditions which surround them. However, in this chapter we report that within major population groups, neighborhood conditions seem to have about the same fear-provoking consequences. We did not find that women, the elderly, Blacks, or the poor, were more sensitive than others to untoward environmental conditions around them. But because the groups are more likely than whites or the well-to-do to live in areas plagued by these problems, more of them suffer the consequences.

On the other hand, there is some evidence that community integration can have positive benefits with respect to fear of crime. For example, a research project conducted for the National Council of Senior Citizens found that, among the urban elderly, those who were more integrated into their communities (using measures of the strength of social ties) were less likely than others to report being fearful (Jaycox, 1978). Perhaps this is because they were more likely to feel that adults in the area (whom they know) would intervene if they found themselves in risky situations. Baumer and Hunter (1979) found that, in Hartford, citizens of all ages who were attached to the community more frequently relied on their neighbors for mutual support and believed that such efforts would actually reduce crime. Or, those who are more closely attuned to the local scene may be able to avoid dangerous situations in the first place. Their "mental maps" of dangerous places in the area may be more accurate.

Integration into the community may also yield indirect benefits with respect to fear, through its impact upon the relationship between neighborhood problems and fear. Like the selected "invulnerabilities" we described, extensive community knowledge and experience may weaken the effect of crime or disorder on levels of fear. The National Council of Senior Citizens found that neighborhood victimization rates were positively correlated with fear among older persons who were not closely attached to their communities, but among those who were most integrated into local affairs there was virtually no relationship between crime rates and fear.

Crime, Signs of Disorder, and Fear

Our measures of neighborhood conditions included questions about "how much of a problem" was presented by some of the most prominent crimes which strike individuals and households: robbery, burglary, assault, and rape. These crimes are of the type that Conklin (1975), the Crime Commission (President's Commission on Law Enforcement and Administration of Justice, 1967), and others speculate are the major causes of fear. All involve direct or potential personal confrontations with offenders, and thus may possibly lead to injury or death. They generally involve strangers, and they often are attributed to "outsiders" to the community (Garofalo and Laub, 1978); thus their incidence (from the point of view of the victim) is quite unpredictable, and they may seem impossible to completely avoid. The neighborhoods where these crimes are viewed as constituting a big problem are frightening places. Surprisingly few residents of our three cities reported that this was the case, but among those who did, levels of fear were substantial.

The clear differentiation between neighborhoods reporting higher and lower crime problems is illustrated in Figure 7.1, which relates levels of fear in each of our study neighborhoods to the average "crime problems index" reported by those living there. Places where such problems were reported to be less serious, including Logan, West Philadelphia, South Philadelphia, and Sunset, all were characterized by relatively low levels of fear among their residents. On the other hand, communities in which crime constituted a serious problem were very high on fear — in three neighborhoods more than 50% of our respondents reported being afraid, and these were our most crime-ridden study areas. The most notable "outlier" of this otherwise strong relationship was the Lincoln Park neighborhood in Chicago. In that community, which is made up of younger, middle-class, often single whites, burglary was rated a very serious problem; in every other way, however, it "belongs" where it lies on our aggregated measure of fear.

In addition to asking questions about the nature of crime problems, these surveys inquired about the extent to which the local social order seemed to be in disarray. Respondents were asked about "how much of a problem" teenagers, vandalism, building abandonment, and drug use seemed to be in their neighborhoods. As we argued in the previous chapter, people rely upon the incidence of problems like these to warn them of dangerous locales.

Stinchcombe et al. (1978) argue that the most debilitating fears are associated with such conditions. Because they reflect perceptions of local conditions, the anxiety they generate is enduring. Unlike the adrenalin shock sparked by a specific encounter or incident, the assessment that one's neighborhood is unsafe is a constant phychological irritant. Unlike with many accident situations, we can recognize from conditions around us that we are in a high risk environment, so "we can be afraid in advance, not just when danger suddenly appears. . . . Perception of risk depends both on the concentration of risk in time and space and on the presence of early signs of impending danger" (Stinchcombe et al., 1978: 2-4). At the neighborhood level the correlation between our measures of local disorder and fear was +.66.

Finally, we included in the analysis a measure of the direction in which these communities seem to be evolving, a question asking if the neighborhood was getting "better or worse." Lemert (1951) and

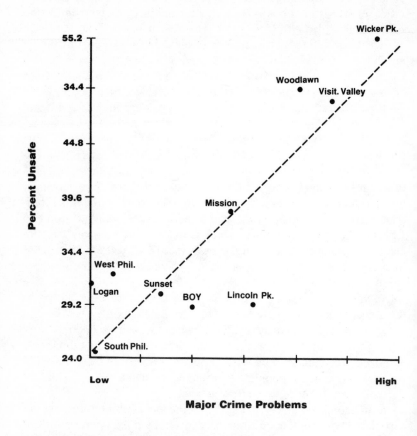

Figure 7.1 Neighborhood Rating of Crime Problems and Fear
SOURCE: Computed from ten neighborhood surveys.

others have suggested that changes in conditions, rather than the current level of neighborhood problems, are the most significant bellwether of fear. People develop routines for coping with the physical and psychological risks presented by most environments. They are at least familiar with their surroundings, regardless of the level of threat they present. As a result, even those living in higher crime areas may not be incapacitated by fear. LEAA's city surveys inquired whether respondents thought their neighborhoods were above or below average with respect to crime, and very few chose the more pessimistic rating. But while residents of a neighborhood may become accustomed to conditions prevailing there, shifts in their envi-

TABLE 7.1   Neighborhood Conditions and Fear

Measure of Neighborhood Conditions	Correlation With Fear Measure	Percentage Responding "A Big Problem"	(N)
Major Crime Problems			
Burglary	.32	18.7	(1261)
Robbery/purse snatching	.46	18.2	(1248)
Stranger assault	.45	7.9	(1248)
Rape	.39	5.9	(1186)
Scale score	.43	—	(1325)
Local Social Order Problems			
Teens hanging out	.29	18.8	(1309)
Abandoned buildings	.31	9.2	(1314)
Use of drugs	.30	20.4	(1065)
Vandalism	.26	17.4	(1316)
Scale score	.26	—	(1330)
Neighborhood Conditions			
Getting worse	.28	26.5	(1185)

NOTE: For neighborhood trends, percentage is those who think things are "worse" rather than "better" or "about the same."

SOURCE: Computed from combined citywide surveys. All correlations (gamma) are significant (p < .01).

ronment may disrupt their accommodation to its risks and rewards. That familiarity may be lost. Instability in the neighborhood and new unpredictability in relationships in nearby public places may generate anxiety and spread alarm, and hold out little hope for the future. At the neighborhood level, the correlation between fear and belief that things have been "getting worse" was +.56.

Table 7.1 presents the correlation (gamma) between each of these indicators and our measure of fear. In addition, it reports the association between fear and the multi-item scales which summarize the extent of crime and community order problems. The strongest linkages are to be found with assessments of personal crime problems, and the summary measure of major crime problems is correlated +.43 with fear of walking the neighborhood at night.

Indicators of the condition of the local social order all were related to fear as well. Perception of the seriousness of a vandalism problem seemed to be the least important determinant of fear, but there was little item-by-item variation in this regard. Finally, reports of general neighborhood trends were correlated with fear at about the same level as the remaining "signs of crime." Together, the trend measure and our two "problem" indices were related to fear in simple additive

TABLE 7.2   Net Effects of Neighborhood Conditions on Fear

Neighborhood Conditions	Net Effect: Percentage Responding "A Big Problem" Who Also Feel Unsafe
Neighborhood getting worse	13.4
Robbery and purse snatching	11.3
Use of drugs	10.1
Burglary	9.4
Teenagers hanging out	9.4
Vandalism	8.7
Stranger assault	5.4
Abandoned buildings	4.5
Rape	3.3

NOTE: For neighborhood trends, percentage is those who think things are "worse" and feel unsafe. Number of cases is approximately 1320.

SOURCE: Computed from combined citywide surveys.

fashion (there was no statistical interaction between them), and explained slightly over 20% of the variance (R = .45) in our measure of fear.

In addition to the correlation, or measure of statistical impact of a particular problem upon fear, Table 7.1 also reports the proportion of our respondents who perceived that each of them indeed constituted a "big problem" in their communities. The proportion varied considerably, and played a major role in determining the overall net effect of each of them. For example, while the impacts of perceptions of rape and burglary problems upon fear were quite similar in magnitude (the correlations were +.39 and +.32, respectively), more than three times as many people were concerned about burglary in these cities as reported that rape was a big problem. Examining those relationships in detail, we find that 9% of our respondents thought that burglary was a big problem in their neighborhoods *and* reported that they felt unsafe at night, while only 3% of the total were in the comparable "fear of rape" category. Because the frequency with which various problems were rated as serious varied greatly, we calculated such "net effect" measures for each of them; they are presented in Table 7.2.

By this accounting, the most important facet of their evaluations of their communities were respondents' estimates of the directions in which they had been changing. Table 7.2 indicates that about 13% of residents of these cities felt that their neighborhoods were getting worse and they felt unsafe at night. This high ranking stems from the large proportion (26%) of our respondents who felt that things were getting worse; it was by a substantial margin the most frequent pessimistic assessment of their neighborhoods that they had to offer.

TABLE 7.3   Official Crime Rates and Fear of Crime in Chicago

| Fear of Crime: Respondents Who Feel- | Type of Crime Average Official Crime Rate per 100,000 Residents | | | |
	Robbery	Aggravated Assault	Burglary	(N)
Very safe	358	233	922	(201)
Somewhat safe	462	300	1065	(310)
Somewhat unsafe	539	358	1232	(140)
Very unsafe	740	464	1353	(126)
Total	494	320	1105	(777)

NOTE: Differences in crime rates across ratings of safety are all significant (p < .01).

SOURCE: Crime counts from the Chicago Police Department (see Maxfield, 1979). Population figures for calculating rates from the Chicago Department of Planning. Computed from metropolitan area survey, central-city sample only.

Following neighborhood trends came two other high-correlation and high-frequency problems, the perceived seriousness of drug use, and street muggings in our respondents' neighborhoods, while at the bottom of the list fell the least frequently mentioned problems, abandoned buildings and rape.

The same relationship between crime and fear can be found by substituting police reports of the extent of crime for our respondents' assessments of neighborhood conditions. The higher the official rate of crime in their areas, the more likely our city respondents were to indicate fear. Again, these data were drawn from a parallel survey conducted in Chicago two years after our original city studies. The results are presented in Table 7.3.

Reported crime was higher in neighborhoods where respondents who felt "somewhat unsafe" or "very unsafe" lived. Those averages differ most sharply for robbery. Robbery rates were more than twice as high for those who indicated they were very unsafe than they were for those who felt very safe. Differences in rates for aggravated assault from category to category were almost as sharp, and burglary rates were consistently related to fear.

As before, the importance of these findings lies in the totally independent fashion in which the crime data were collected. They are official police accounts of neighborhood crime. They point to the same substantial relationship between neighborhood conditions and fear found in the survey data. The correlation (Pearson's r) between community robbery rates and fear was +.22, while the comparable figure for assault was +.27, and for burglary, +.23. Those correlations remain virtually unaffected when they are controlled for age, sex, race, and income.

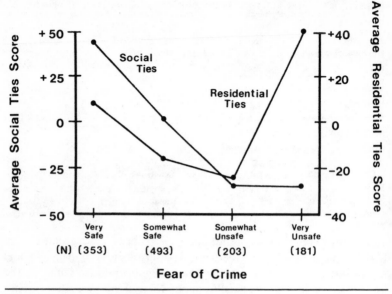

Figure 7.2 Integration and Fear
SOURCE: Computed from combined citywide surveys.

Integration and Fear

Relationships between social and residential integration and fear of crime were somewhat more complex than those above. Suttles' (1968) notion of the "segmented community" implies that residents of an area who are knowledgeable of the comings and goings of local toughs, who know clearly the boundaries they dare not cross, and who have become acclimated to prevailing levels of crime and incivility, should be less fearful than those for whom the night holds great mysteries. The most direct measure of this form of integration, that tapping the strength of social ties, was linked to fear of crime in the expected fashion. However, residential ties, which generally are positively correlated with knowing local youths, recognizing strangers, and feeling a part of the community, were related to fear of crime in sharply curvilinear fashion. The shape of those relationships is depicted in Figure 7.2, which plots average residential and social ties scores for those reporting various levels of fear.

The most striking feature of Figure 7.2 is the sharp upturn it describes in levels of residential integration among those in the most fearful category. While the residential ties measure generally descends with increasing levels of fear (the gamma correlation between the two is a very moderate −.16), the relation between residential integration and fear is far from linear (and the gamma correlation between them is a neat .00).

This apparent mystery is easily solved, however, by examining these interrelations among key population groups. The guilty group turns out to be the elderly. Those over sixty years of age report high levels of fear, and they were much more likely than anyone else to be long-time residents of their neighborhoods, home owners, and to plan to stay where they are. In multivariate analyses which take age into account, the correlation between residential ties and fear becomes mildly negative, as it should.

Neither of these effects is particularly strong, however, and it should not be surprising that the neighborhood-level correlations between integration and fear were weak, both standing at about $-.40$ (not significant with an N of only 10). In a Canadian study, Hartnagel (1979) also found no strong connection between neighborhood integration and fear. He speculated that this might have been due to the restricted range in which integration may vary in modern urban communities. In cities, even the "most integrated" areas may not be very integrated in absolute terms, at least not enough to affect such a powerful concern as fear of crime. The connections between integration and fear also were confounded by other important correlates of fear, including race and class. Remember that two Black neighborhoods were among our most integrated communities, and that the most affluent area stood near the bottom of the list on both integration measures. Two of the least fearful neighborhoods that were surveyed were the middle-class areas of Lincoln Park and Sunset, both places where residents reported weak social ties.

Factors Moderating the Impact of Neighborhood

While the association between assessments of neighborhood crime conditions and fear of crime is a substantial one, there is reason to suspect that the "overall" effects reported above mask some significant differences among population groups. While people generally are responsive to the opportunities and risks presented by the context within which they are operating, some may be more attuned than others to receiving and acting upon messages from their environments. Analytically, this is a hypothesis concerning statistical interaction, for it posits that the relationship between perceptions of environmental conditions and fear of crime varies in some systematic way, depending upon who people are.

One key difference among population groups is their vulnerability to crime. Stinchcombe et al. (1978: 2-24) argue that vulnerable groups are "more sensitive to cues that precede danger, to their own defenselessness." Because they are prone to suffer more heavily if victimized, it may be that vulnerable persons are more attentive to aspects of their environment which signal danger, that they "read" their surroundings on a more frequent basis to establish the existence of potential threats, and that they react more quickly when danger looms on the horizon.

The concept of vulnerability is, of course, not confined to the physical and social attributes analyzed in detail in this section. Other research on fear of crime has indicated that alternative measures of vulnerability exhibit some of the features anticipated here. For example, Cook et al. (forthcoming) argue that living alone enhances vulnerability both to victimization and to the consequences of crime, and find that being without the social support of living with others is most directly linked to fear of crime among the elderly. They also find a higher correlation between city size and fear among the elderly; presumably the former represents variations in the probability of victimization by personal crime, and hence "objective threat." Doob and MacDonald (1979) found that television viewing affected fear only in high-risk neighborhoods. Stinchcombe et al. (1978) report that race and neighborhood racial composition interact to produce higher levels of fear among whites in heterogeneous areas. Conklin (1976) concludes that perceptions of crime and fear of crime are positively related only in communities where crime rates are high enough to surpass some "threshold" marking the point at which the threat of victimization is a real one.

In each case the general lesson is that among persons sharing some form of vulnerability risks or threats in the environment may be more directly related to fear. Those persons are more affected by (or responsive to) events and conditions which surround them, and (by inference) they are more influenced by changes in their environments as well. If this is the case, we should find that including in our statistical analyses a separate interaction term, indicating those respondents who are more vulnerable and who live in higher-risk environments, should grant us predictive power above that contributed by measures of their vulnerability and their perceptions of environmental conditions alone.

Figure 7.3 examines in detail the relationship between environmental conditions (here represented by perceptions of the seriousness of major crime problems) and fear of crime, for males and females and for those under and over fifty years of age. If women (for example) are, as hypothesized, more responsive to variations in environmental

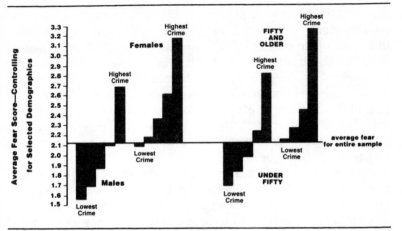

Figure 7.3 Neighborhood Crime Problems and Fear, by Sex and Age, Controlling for Remaining Personal Attributes

SOURCE: Computed from combined citywide surveys. Values estimated using multiple regression. All controlled for race and income, plus sex or age.

conditions, we should find that differences between those who live in higher-risk areas and their counterparts in safer places are greater than differences among men across places presenting varying levels of threat. Figure 7.3 indicates that this is not the case. It is clear that the "main effects" discussed above, those of physical vulnerability and neighborhood conditions, are at work here: Women were more fearful than men, and where neighborhood conditions seemed worse so did their assessments of the situation. However, the steady "stepladder" effect of worsening conditions did not appear to vary much between the sexes. The most substantial differences attributable to neighborhood conditions were those in the very worst places (making up about 12% of the total). However, that jump also characterized the fears of males in the highest risk locations, putting them above all but the most threatened females.

The same even-handed effect of neighborhood conditions seems to characterize the fears of older persons as well. Those in the worst locations and those fifty years of age and older fell much above the overall population mean illustrated in Figure 7.3, but the effects of perceived neighborhood conditions did not vary by age. In neither case is there much evidence here that the attitudes of those in the most vulnerable groups are more affected by their assessments of their environments. Neither do the data support Conklin's (1976: 105) hypothesis that there is a "critical threshold" of risk below which variations in perceptions of crime do not affect fear. He found that in areas little bothered by crime (measured by official statistics), fear did not vary much with perceptions of crime; on the other hand, in these three cities fear mounts steadily even at lower levels of crime and disorder. The data linking local official crime rates and fear point to the same conclusion. The figure presented in Table 7.3 indicate that the relationship between crime and fear is quite linear. Only in the case of the indicator of neighborhood trends are these relationships not generally linear; in that case, there was no difference in fear between those who thought things were "better" or those who thought they were "the same."

The visual interpretation debunking the "attentiveness" hypothesis is confirmed by a more rigorous statistical analysis, the results of which are presented in Table 7.4. Each indicator of physical and social vulnerability was analyzed in conjunction with the major crime problems scale to establish the importance of their joint, as opposed to separate and cumulative, effect. Table 7.4 indicates that in no case were these interaction terms significantly related to fear of crime, and in no case did they account for more than 1 or 2% of the variance which was explained by all of them in conjunction. The effect of local crime conditions remained steady at about 40-45% of the total explained variance. Indicators of physical vulnerability were much more important in explaining fear than were those reflecting social vulnerability. Both personal vulnerability and neighborhood conditions were independently related to fear, in simple and additive fashion. (The same could be said using official community crime rates to measure those conditions.) There seems to be little utility to complicating our understanding of fear with allusions to a greater attentiveness to crime problems by those in more vulnerable categories.

These data also provide no evidence that integration into community affairs paid any significant indirect benefits with regard to fear. City residents who perceived high levels of crime and disorder were more fearful, but the hypothesis that those among them who were socially or residentially integrated would be able to better handle those problems was not supported. The relationship between crime conditions and fear was virtually the same for those reporting quite different degrees of community attachment.

Figure 7.4 summarizes the linkages between crime problems, social ties, and fear for residents of the three cities. It depicts the relationship between crime problems and fear for people in each of four categories of integration. In general, those reporting the weakest social ties described themselves as the most fearful, and those with the strongest ties were the least fearful. While levels of fear varied

TABLE 7.4 Interaction Between Vulnerability and Crime Conditions and Fear

Measures of Vulnerability and Neighborhood Conditions	Percentage of Explained Variance	Significance
Physical Vulnerability		
Sex (female)	19	.01+
Crime problems	41	.01+
Interaction — sex and problems	1	.20 (n.s.)
Remaining personal attributes	39	.01+
Old age	16	.01+
Crime problems	45	.01+
Interaction — age and problems	2	.13 (n.s.)
Remaining personal attributes	37	.01+
Social Vulnerability		
Race (Black)	4	.01+
Crime problems	44	.01+
Interaction — race and problems	1	.26 (n.s.)
Remaining personal attributes	51	.01+
Low income	2	.01+
Crime problems	42	.02+
Interaction — income and problems	—	.65 (n.s.)
Remaining personal attributes	55	.01+

NOTE: Calculated using multiple regression estimates. "Remaining personal attributes" includes other appropriate age, sex, race, and income measures.

SOURCE: Computed from combined citywide surveys.

with the degree of integration, the shape of the upwardly curving lines illustrating how crime problems were related to fear did not vary significantly from group to group. Crime affected fear in the same fashion among those who were more and less integrated into their communities. There was no significant decrement in fear among those in the high crime (or disorder) but high attachment category.

Summary

This section examined community contexts which seem to engender problems with victimization and fear. Fear of crime is higher in places where neighborhood trends point in the wrong direction; people who perceived that their communities were in decline also were more fearful. In places where robberies, assaults, and other major crimes constituted a serious problem, people also were concerned about exposing themselves to risk. They also were negatively effected by more subtle signs that the social order was in disarray.

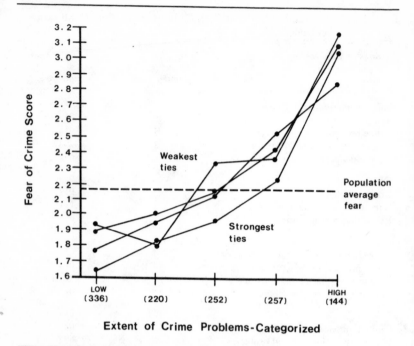

Figure 7.4 Relationship Between Crime Problems and Fear, for Varying Levels of
           Social Ties

SOURCE: Computed from combined citywide surveys.

There were significant (but weaker) positive contributions to the
fear problem attributable to community integration. There was a
weak-to-moderate tendency for people enjoying stronger social and
residential ties to their neighborhoods to report being less afraid.

All of these neighborhood factors and linkages were related to one
another, however, and many were strongly linked to personal attributes of the respondents which signal their social and physical vulnerability to crime. In their study of public housing developments,
Newman and Franck (1979) found that variations in crime rates within
buildings did not effect the level of fear among residents, nor their
desire to move out. The simple correlations between these factors
were strong, but disappeared when they controlled for confounding
variables. This was a very surprising discovery. Thus it is necessary
to sort out the relative contribution of each of these factors while
taking the effect of the others into account. This task is simplified by
the fact that there was no evidence that any population groups were
more responsive than any others to these conditions. Rather, people

TABLE 7.5   Analysis of Neighborhood Conditions and Fear

Summary Concept Index	Simple Correlation	Standardized Regression Coefficient	(Significance)
Personal vulnerability	.37	.33	(.01+)
Crime and disorder problems	.43	.38	(.01+)
Social and residential integration	−.06	−.09	(.01+)
R^2 = .29			
N = 1011			

NOTE: Summary indices are summed standard scores of sets of individual measures.

SOURCE: Computed from combined citywide surveys.

of all kinds were more wary when the vital signs of their localities were poor. This allows us to concentrate on the simple linear effects of community problems and linkages on fear.

To make the results of this analysis more interpretable, many of the measures employed here were combined into summary indices. This makes statistical analysis more interpretable, at a cost of only a slight decline in the predictive power of those measures. To summarize personal vulnerability, we standardized,[1] then summed scores representing the age, sex, and race of each of our respondents. The resulting measure increased in value with vulnerability. The same procedure was followed with the two measures of integration and with the three measures of community problems. These three independent variables were then employed in a regression analysis of reports of fear. The results of this analysis are summarized in Table 7.5.

Table 7.5 indicated that problems with neighborhood crime and disorder remain the most important predictors of fear, even when community integration and personal vulnerability are taken into account. Next in importance ranks vulnerability, followed by integration. The effect of the latter remains significant, but relatively weak.

The causal ordering of these indicators remains, of course, judgmental. We assumed that in the short run, and among individuals, factors like vulnerability and community conditions engender fear. On the other hand, Conklin (1971, 1975) and others argue that, over time, fear in turn generates neighborhood crime and disorder, reduces levels of integration, and reshapes a community's demography. When people are fearful their solidarity with those around them and their trust in others declines, their attachment to the community weakens, and their satisfaction with the neighborhood as a place to live disappears. Those who can afford to may leave, while those who cannot huddle behind closed doors. Part IV examines the behavioral consequences of the factors detailed here, and while that analysis provides some evidence supporting this "feedback" model, a study of the over-time reciprocal relationship between community and fear requires data far beyond the cross-sectional surveys that we have at our disposal.

NOTE

1. These are the "Z-scores," which standardize the means and variances of measures. This gives them equal value in an index when they are added together.

PART III

LEARNING ABOUT CRIME

In this section we examine in detail two of the ways in which people may gain impressions of the daily risks of urban life: through the media and by talking to others. In Chapter 8 we examine the crime content of newspapers and television in our cities, and we document patterns of media attentiveness there. In Chapter 9 we explore the diffusion of information about local victims and events through neighborhood social networks. In the final chapter in this section we probe the impact of these factors on people's assessments of neighborhood safety.

Chapter 8

CRIME IN THE MEDIA

Introduction

To understand how people cope with crime it is important to clarify how they acquire information about the problem. These impressions should play a major role in shaping how people assess the potential risks which surround them and how they adapt to the situation by altering their day-to-day behavior.

People acquire information about crime from several sources: by observation, from reports by those around them, from the media, and through direct personal experience. They come across this information casually, in the course of their daily routines. During one field interview in San Francisco an informant mentioned such an incident.

> The stove man who was here the other day fixing the stove was saying to me that he thought that this area is the third highest crime area in the city. In fact, he used to be assigned to the Towers (a nearby housing project), but he asked to be transferred to another area because it was getting so dangerous. He was in the hospital three times from stuff that happened to him while he was working in the Towers [Visitacion Valley, August 1976].

Chapter 2 indicated that recent and direct victimization experience is not the primary source of impressions about crime for most people. Few residents of these cities were victimized recently by serious crime, and few of them had actually observed any crimes taking place. Crime is furtive activity, and criminals try to avoid being identified by an eyewitness or bothered by an intrusive bystander. However, as we discussed in Chapter 6, people do pick up visual cues from their environments which they interpret as signs that their communities are troubled. These include such neighborhood conditions as vandalism, residential abandonment, and youth activity.

Because of the limited role that recent personal experience and direct observation play in obtaining information about crime, people generally must rely upon the media and personal conversations with others to learn about the nature of the crime problem. In this survey respondents were asked about their "best source of information" about neighborhood crime; with the exception of radio (6%) and miscellaneous sources (8%), the newspapers, television, and personal conversation accounted for all of them.

Media coverage of crime seems ubiquitous. Graber's (1977) content analysis of network and local Chicago television news broadcasts revealed that almost 20% of all stories on local news shows and 10% of those carried over the networks concerned crime and criminal justice. A content analysis of eight metropolitan newspapers in these three cities (described below) found that every day each paper reported at least one story about a violent crime in a prominent position. It revealed between 4.4 and 6.8 stories about violent crime per paper, per day. Not surprisingly, this survey found that more than three-quarters of the residents of these cities reported hearing about a crime story on television or reading about one in the newspapers on the previous day.

Other research and our own surveys indicate that people think of crime largely in terms of homicide, robbery, and assaultive violence. The overrepresentation of violence in people's recollections of criminal events parallels findings from detailed studies of the content of mass communications. Hurley and Antunes (1977), Graber (1977), Gordon et al. (1979), and others have documented this emphasis on violence in the media and the generally inverse relationship between newspaper coverage of crime and the actual frequency of events in a community. The similarity of the profile of events in the media to popular images of crime was one reason why the Crime Commission pointed an accusatory finger at newspapers and television in their report to the president (President's Commission on Law Enforcement and Administration of Justice, 1967). The commission charged that the media were exaggerating the dimensions of the crime problem and that their emphasis on violent crime encouraged unrealistic levels of fear.

By their very frequency, personal conversation and media accounts of crime must be suspect as sources of fear. In the fourth chapter we pointed out the discrepancy between the magnitude of fear and actual levels of victimization. Unlike victimization, the reiteration of stories about crime is not a "rare event." Crime stories make up an important component of the crime environments which surround the residents of our three cities, one which is brought to their attention almost on a daily basis. In fact, in a study in Portland, Yaden et al. (1973) found that many thought there was more talk about crime than the problem warranted, and 40% felt (like the Crime Commission) that such talk was stirring up excessive concern about crime.

In order to gauge the frequency with which people encounter media messages concerning crime, we asked our respondents if "yesterday" they had watched any television news shows or "shows involving police or crime," and if "yesterday" they had read any stories about crime in a newspaper. They were asked only about their media contact on the previous day in order to measure as accurately as possible the impact of the newspapers and television, specifically. The longer the reference period for these questions, the more likely it was that our respondents' replies would be colored by the welter of crime information bombarding them on a daily basis, and by the tendency of people to forget about trivial occurrences very rapidly (Sudman and Bradburn, 1974).

The results indicate that people are very attentive to crime news. Based on this measure, 45% of respondents very recently had read about crime. Of that group, about three in five regularly read both metropolitan and local community newspapers, about one-third read only the citywide dailies, and about 1% only read their local papers.

For many respondents newspapers were the major source of crime news. In another question they were asked:

Considering all the sources you use to get information, what's your best source of information about crime in your neighborhood?

Of those who were questioned, 31% indicated that a major daily newspaper (20%) or the local community paper (11%) was their most important source of local crime news.

The other major media source of information about crime is television. Among those questioned, 17% indicated that it was their most important source of crime data. They were also asked whether or not they had watched local and national television news programs on the previous night. While we did not ask them specifically if they had seen a story about crime that evening, content analysis of television news indicates that crime news is a staple on those programs. Graber (1977) reports that in Chicago 19% of all the stories and 22% of all the topics covered on local television news programs concern crime (there could be more than one story on a topic), about twice the national figure for the three major networks. Thus we can safely assume that people who watch (especially local) news programs are exposed to stories about crime. In this survey 3% of the respondents watched only national news, while 14% watched local news programs and 26% tuned in to both. We also inquired about exposure to fictional accounts of crime on television. People were asked, regarding the previous evening, "Did you watch any shows involving police or crime? (Like Kojack, Charlie's Angels, Hawaii Five-O, Adam-12, or Baretta?)" About 36% indicated that they had seen such programs.

There were no differences of any import in these figures from city to city. Not only newspaper and television news generally reach about equal proportions of the population, there were no significant differences among residents of different cities in how often they were exposed to stories about crime in the media. As we shall see, there are great variations in the receptivity of various audiences to secondhand crime news, but those differences can be attributed to individual factors, and not to city of residence. Whatever the content of media stories about crime, the stories reach about equal proportions of the population in each of these communities.

In the remainder of this chapter we explore the issues of media coverage of crime and the consumption of crime news. We examine in detail what can be seen about crime in the newspapers and on television, including both the frequency and the substantive content of that coverage. We then turn to the question of who actually picked up those messages. The answer, it appears, is that — in one way or another — virtually everyone does.

Media Coverage of Crime

Most research on crime in the media has examined the correspondence between media images and other indicators of the distribution of crime, usually official statistics. It is apparent that a selection process generally restricts media coverage of crime to only a subset of potential stories. Since the media are restricted to covering crimes which are known to the police, these two versions of reality could be similar, but because of this selection process (in which police and reporters each play a role) the picture of crime portrayed in the press and on television differs from aggregate police statistics on crime. Davis (1951) compared changes in official crime reports to changes in coverage of crime stories by four Colorado newspapers from 1948 to 1950. He found that changes in newspaper coverage were not related to changes in police records of the extent of serious crime. Reported crime and the frequency of newspaper stories about crime were also the foci of Jones's (1976) analysis in St. Louis. He found that newspaper representations of crime were highly distorted, both with respect to the relative frequency of different types of offenses and the locations of those crimes. One of the city's two major papers concentrated on crime in white areas of the city, while the other reported more crime in Black neighborhoods. Jones concluded that reliance on St. Louis newspapers for information about crime in that city would cause readers to make erroneous judgments about the level and distribution of different types of crime. Graber (1977) and Hurley and Antunes (1977) examined crime news in Chicago and Houston newspapers, respectively. They both found that the papers disproportionately reported violent personal crimes. Murder and rape constituted less than 1% of all index crime reports in Chicago, while stories about those offenses made up almost 30% of crime stories in the Chicago *Tribune* (Graber, 1977). Murder and rape made up about 0.8% of the total index crimes in Houston for the period studied by Antunes and Hurley, but one paper there devoted 45% and the other 56% of their crime space to these offenses. An analysis of crime news in British newspapers by Roshier (1973) turned up similar findings: The papers concentrated on the most serious offenses, so that their coverage disproportionately portrayed serious crime relative to its incidence according to official statistics.

The consistency of these findings reflects the fact that a commitment to "newsworthiness," or to report unusual or unique stories, affects the decisions of newspaper editors regarding which crime stories to print. The generality of this decision rule is indicated by the similarity of news decisions in newspapers and on television. Graber compared coverage of three common types of crime by Chicago newspapers and television stations. There was no relationship between the types of crimes protrayed in newspapers or on television news and those in police reports, but the images of crime presented to the public were similar across news organizations. This suggests that there is a general standard by which journalists evaluate whether or not to publish or broadcast crime stories. Roshier (1973) discusses characteristics of crime stories which meet this standard. Serious crimes are more often covered than minor offenses, as are crimes involving whimsical or dramatic circumstances and those in which a famous or high-status person is the victim or offender. Newspapers are more likely to print stories when the offenders are captured, for reporters can write about the characteristics and motivations of the perpetrators only when they are known to police and in custody.

The use of themes to organize accounts of events also affects the content of crime stories. By suggesting associations between particular instances of a type of crime, reporters imply that they are part of a pattern. While crime waves may be created simply by focusing media attention on certain offenses, readers may gain the impression that the actual incidence of crime is increasing.

> In place of any theoretical understanding of the phenomena they report, (television) newsworkers make incidents meaningful only as *instances of themes* — themes which are generated within the news production process. Thus something becomes a "serious type of crime" on the basis of what is going on inside newsrooms, not outside them [Fishman, 1978: 536; italics in original].

The need for a common thread to tie news stories together creates an image of a crime wave, and a journalistic paradigm contributes to the content of news about crime stories.

There has been a great deal of research investigating the content of television entertainment programs concerning crime. The study of dramatic programs was sparked by the speculation that television violence may stimulate violent behavior on the part of viewers. One study by Dominick (1973) analyzed the characteristics of crimes, victims, and offenders presented on dramatic television shows and compared them to the attributes of crime, victims, and offenders in official statistics. His findings are similar to studies of newspaper and television crime news, for dramatic crime programs also overrepresented violent personal crime, and offenders were more often caught in fiction than in real life. In addition, Dominick found the following:

— Criminals on television are more often white and middle-class, and older than actual criminals;

— Whites are overrepresented as murder victims;

— Intrafamily violence is underrepresented on television;

— Television overrepresents premeditated crimes.

Graber also found that crime reports in Chicago's newspapers and television news shows tend to overrepresent criminals and victims as white and middle-class.

Newspapers serving our three cities also emphasized violent crime. In order to assess what our survey respondents were reading, we systematically coded samples of newspapers serving those cities during the period in which the interviews were conducted. Those data thus depict part of the immediate "media environment" which surrounded our respondents while they were being interviewed.[1] We examined in detail reports of violent crime in the papers, and can employ these data to characterize the print media in each of the cities.

TABLE 8.1   Newspaper Coverage of Violent Crime

Type of Crime	Average Number of Stories per Issue			
	Total[a]	Philadelphia[b]	Chicago[b]	San Francisco[b]
Murder and attempts	3.2	2.8	2.9	3.8
Rape and sexual assault	0.2	0.2	0.2	0.4
Assault and robbery	1.3	1.4	1.3	1.3
Child abuse	0.2	0.1	0.2	0.1
Kidnapping and hijacking	0.4	0.2	0.4	0.6
Other[c]	0.6	0.8	0.5	0.6
Total	6.0	5.4	5.6	7.0
Total number of issues coded	402	113	171	118

a. Stories summed across eight citywide daily newspapers, divided by number of issues coded.

b. Stories summed across citywide newspapers within each city, divided by number of issues coded.

c. The "other" category includes stories about arson, the criminal justice system's dealings with violent crimes, and so on.

SOURCE: Calculated from content analysis data for October-November 1977.

Table 8.1 reports the average number of stories about violent crime which appeared in the citywide daily newspapers in each community. The newspapers included the *Chronicle* and *Examiner* in San Francisco, the *Tribune, Daily News,* and *Sun Times* in Chicago, and the *Bulletin, Inquirer,* and *Daily News* in Philadelphia. In each of these eight papers readers could find an average of almost six stories about violent crime each day, a figure that was lowest in Philadelphia and highest in San Francisco. The most common category of violent crime reported was homicide; as a proportion of all crime stories, accounts of murders and attempted murders constituted 50% of the total. On an average day, there was at least one story about a robbery or assault, while kidnapping and hijacking tended to receive coverage every other day. There were fewer stories about rape and sexual assaults, and reports of child abuse were even less frequent.

As Table 8.1 indicates, there was a discernible tendency for residents of San Francisco to wake up more often to stories about homicides, rapes, and terrorism. Newspapers in Philadelphia and Chicago painted less strident and relatively similar portraits of crime for their readers. While there are both newspaper and city differences in crime coverage at work here, the higher coverage of violent crime in San Francisco was a city phenomenon. Both San Francisco papers gave murders, sex cases, and terrorism more coverage than any of our other six daily newspapers, and their levels of coverage were more like one another than like the coverage patterns within either of the remaining cities. While the dailies in Chicago covered an average of 2.9 homicide stories per day, and in Philadelphia 2.8, the *Chronicle* in San Francisco reported 3.7 per day, and the *Examiner* 4.0.

On the other hand, when viewed from the perspective of the number of crimes which could have been covered each day, these figures display remarkable consistency. For example, residents of the Chicago metropolitan area reported 1.5 times as many rapes and nearly 3 times as many homicides as those in the San Francisco-Oakland SMSA in 1977 (Federal Bureau of Investigation, 1978), a difference not reflected in newspaper crime coverage. Chicagoans reported about 1.5 times as many murders and rapes as residents of the Philadelphia metropolitan area, yet the coverage of those crimes in the newspapers of the two communities was virtually identical. This remarkable consistency suggests that there is a relatively constant amount of space, or "newshole," devoted to stories on violent crime in these cities. The newshole varies somewhat by community (it seems larger in San Francisco), and newspapers serving the same market resemble one another in their coverage. The magnitude of crime coverage does not seem to reflect differences in potential "inputs" to the news-gathering system — the pool of reported crime in each area — but it may be driven by journalistic decision rules about the size of the newshole appropriate for crime each day and by city-specific marketing decisions reflecting businesslike estimates of the local demand for crime coverage. The coverage of crime also may be as consistent as it is because such stories are reliable "filler" material. Because the supply of crime stories available from the wire services and the local police is quite predictable and plentiful, it always can be tapped to space out the newspapers (Gordon et al., 1979). As a result, in the newspapers these cities look more like one another than they do in victimization surveys or in the *Uniform Crime Report*.

Interestingly, one distinctive feature of crime stories carried by the San Francisco newspapers is that they report upon events that occur outside the city. It generally is easier to "cover" such stories because they can be rewritten from wire service reports, and do not even require a trip to police headquarters (Gordon et al., 1979). There seems to be more variation across cities and papers in the tendency of newspapers to emphasize this form of coverage than there is in their coverage of local crime news. Newspapers within cities look more like one another in their coverage of local events than they do in their overall attention to crime. San Francisco newspapers contained the smallest proportion of stories about crimes which actually took place in the central city, as well as the fewest stories about crime in the immediate suburbs. Rather, the *Examiner* and the *Chronicle* more frequently reported crimes which occurred in other cities. In examining this we focused upon reports of three crimes included in Table 8.1; murder, rape, and the robbery-assault category. These types of incidents are most feared by urban residents, and were the most likely to be associated with levels of fear among the respondents in our surveys (Skogan, 1977b). For these crimes, about three in five newspaper stories (60% in the *Chronicle* and 63% in the *Examiner*) were about incidents outside of metropolitan San Francisco, as compared to an average of 41% in Philadelphia and 34% in Chicago.

In all the papers, when suburban crimes are reported they are almost universally homicides. Murders also are the primary grist for out-of-town-crime coverage, but almost one-quarter of those stories are concerned with robberies and assaults, and rape stories from other places occasionally appear. Assaults and robberies make up one-third of all stories originating within these three cities.

Because they describe violent events it is possible that *any* stories about crime may provoke fear or concern, and in this light the disproportionate coverage of violent events by the San Francisco papers may be significant. On the other hand, media consumers may be selective in their attention to stimuli, and perhaps only accounts of local events have much of an effect upon their perceptions. However, even from this perspective, crime is disproportionately reported in the San Francisco newspapers. Based upon the ratio of stories about local murders, rapes, robberies, and assaults to police reports of the numbers of those crimes which occurred there, we still find that San Francisco newspapers report more "stories per thousand crimes" than those in either of the remaining cities. Even with their extensive coverage of violence in other places, the papers in the Bay City still magnified the apparent frequency of local violent crime more extensively than newspapers in other places.

In addition to asking about newspapers as sources of information about crime, our surveys inquired whether or not the respondents

TABLE 8.2   Crime News on Chicago Television

| | Percentage Distribution of Crime Stories | | | | |
| | Chicago Programs | | Network News Programs | | |
	CBS Local	NBC Local	ABC National	CBS National	NBC National
Street crimes	49.9	46.8	46.8	43.0	47.0
Terrorism	12.5	24.2	22.8	23.0	16.6
Corruption	21.7	13.2	20.5	22.3	24.0
Drug offenses	4.5	4.7	3.3	3.8	3.7
Business crimes	11.2	10.8	6.3	7.6	8.5
(Number of crime stories)	(815)	(1501)	(568)	(599)	(587)
Number of broadcasts April-December 1976	197	197	197	197	197
Mean total crime stories per broadcast	4.1	7.6	2.9	3.0	3.0
Mean street-crime stories per broadcast	2.1	3.6	1.3	1.3	1.4

SOURCE: Graber (1977).

recently had watched network and local television news broadcasts. We were not able to examine directly the presentation of crime news on television stations in our three cities. We can, however, make some rough estimates of the crime content of national news programs, and of local television news in Chicago, using data gathered by other researchers.

As we noted earlier, Graber and her associates coded all crime stories broadcast on the three networks' evening news programs and on Chicago's CBS and NBC local news programs from April through December in 1976. The top of Table 8.2 presents the distribution of crime stories for different types of crime from that analysis. The "street crimes" category includes murder, rape, robbery, and assault, the incidents which we have been discussing with respect to newspaper content. It is thus possible to compare the relative emphasis given to different types of crime stories in the two media.

Street-crime stories are the largest single group of crime stories which were described on all news programs, as shown in Table 8.2.

There were few differences among the three networks, or between network and local news programs, in the proportion of crime stories which dealt with street crime. Of the stories dealing with crime, 43% of those on the CBS evening news described street crime, while 50% of local news crime stories concerned those offenses. The other local Chicago station and the remaining networks fell between these extremes with respect to the relative frequency of street-crime stories. There were greater differences between them in other crime categories, but the various television news organizations broadcast about the same proportion of street-crime stories.

The two local news programs presented considerably more crime news than the national networks. The average number of crime stories per broadcast on local news programs was 4.1 for the Chicago CBS outlet, and 7.6 for the NBC station. The number of crime stories on network telecasts was both smaller than the number on local TV and very similar across networks. The average number of crime stories per program on the network news shows was 3.0 for CBS and NBC, and 2.9 for the ABC national evening news.

We are not able to separate stories about local crime from stories about crimes which occurred elsewhere using these data, but we can compare the usual number of street-crime stories from television news shows to the average number of street-crime stories per issue of the newspapers in our three cities. There were an average of 2.1 such stories per broadcast on the Chicago CBS station, and an average of 3.6 on the local NBC station. A typical national television news program described 1.3 stories about street crime on ABC and CBS, and 1.4 stories on NBC. In Table 8.1 we saw that the average number of comparable stories per daily issue of newspapers in Chicago was 4.4. Compared to the number of crime stories in newspapers there were slightly fewer stories about crime per broadcast on local television news programs. Viewers of local news shows in Chicago were exposed to about one-half as many stories about street crime as readers in Chicago newspapers.

There are, of course, many fewer stories of any kind on a television news broadcast than are found in a daily newspaper. In a study of political news coverage during the 1972 election period, Hofstetter (1976) found that there were an average of 15 "hard" news stories on each ABC news broadcast, 18 on CBS, and 16 on NBC. Thus, the proportion of the newshole devoted to crime on television is much larger than comparable figures for newspaper coverage. Using those figures, crime stories constituted between 16.6% and 19.3% of all stories broadcast by network news shows, and street crimes consumed from 7.3% to 9% of broadcast "space." Using as a comparable newshole estimate the total square inches devoted to news in each of our newspapers, crime coverage in our three newspapers consumed from 1% to 2.6% of the space available for news, and street crimes substantially less. Daily newspapers in these cities set aside an average of 1.8% of their news space for crime.

While the television programs analyzed here appeared some 12 to 20 months before our surveys, we feel confident about making these very general comparisons. Graber's data show remarkable consistency in the relative coverage of different types of crime stories across national and local news programs for a nine-month period. Like the similarity of crime coverage across newspapers described above, this suggests that media messages about crime depend not so much on the volume of crimes as they do upon the application of a consistent set of criteria regarding what constitutes an acceptable news product. The pool of crimes described in newspapers or on television may vary, but the proportion of news content set aside for crime stories remains constant.

If there are few differences in the proportions of different types of crime shown on television news, there will be some variation in the actual events which are covered. There will be times when the media focus on a single newsworthy event, and periods when crime news concerns "garden variety" rapes, robberies, and assaults. The content of television news stories about crime will vary, but these data, together with the findings of Fishman (1978) and Epstein (1973) suggest that the volume of crime news relative to the volume of other news stories on television programs will remain relatively stable, subject to sharp variation only in the case of rare and spectacular crime stories.

In summary, we have suggested in this section that the media give a great deal of attention to personal and violent crime, especially in relation to its relative frequency and vis-à-vis other newsworthy events. Both television and newspaper stories about crime emphasize violent crimes at the expense of other, more frequent kinds of predation. Television in particular devotes a large proportion of its newshole to crime.

One of the most striking aspects of this coverage is its consistency. There are relatively few differences among newspapers in their attention to violent events, especially within a given city. There was never a single issue of any of our newspapers which failed to report at least one major violent crime, and the average number of violent crime stories per issue varied only slightly from paper to paper. Television news coverage of crime was quite uniform, especially that by the networks. This uniformity was even higher when we examined "street crimes" in detail, for they constituted nearly a constant proportion of all crime stories reported and a fairly even proportion of all news stories broadcast.

There were some city-by-city differences in patterns of newspaper coverage. Both absolutely (crime stories per issue) and relative to the pool of reportable events (crime stories per thousand crimes), San Francisco's newspapers devoted disproportionate attention to violence. They also reported out-of-town events in great profusion, which increased the total volume of stories about violence. We have no evidence about differences in the coverage of crime news by local television stations in these cities, but the Chicago data suggest that local broadcasts report upon crime more often than the networks.

These data indicate that readers of the newspapers and viewers of television news programs in our three cities are exposed to stories about violent crime on a daily basis. This large volume of crime information may significantly affect the perceptions and beliefs of those exposed to it, and may increase levels of fear about crime. There are, however, reasons to suspect that this might not be the case. Only about one-half of the stories about violent crimes reported in Chicago and Philadelphia papers took place in the city, and in San Francisco this figure was even smaller. This means that although readers of those newspapers were exposed each day to accounts of fearsome events, few of those accounts described crimes which could have been viewed as posing a direct threat to the reader. The same is certainly more true of events depicted on network television news.

If people use information they acquire from these sources as guides to behavior, it is likely that they will pick up little that is directly useful. We are particularly unlikely to detect its consequences in our survey data, for we focused throughout on neighborhood conditions and events, and upon the neighborhood as a context for individual and collective action in response to crime.

We also are unlikly to detect much of an impact because of the consistency with which most crime news is disseminated. If reading about crime or watching crime news on television affects fear, there should be few differences among readers of different papers, or the watchers of various television news shows, because the message everywhere is largely the same. Further, because of the nationalization of the news-gathering process and the substantial attention given to events in other places by all our media, the very events being depicted may be the same from city to city. Since we have only very tenuous evidence concerning the content of local television news programs, and that for only one city, we are unable to make many claims about the effects of differential television coverage on viewers, except to note that the distribution of crime stories across different categories is relatively invariant for news shows by the two Chicago stations.

All of this suggests that the effects of the media are not to be found among the consumers of different media, but rather between consumers and abstainers. The crucial issue in understanding how people learn about crime may be that of media attentiveness rather than variations in specific media content. One of our most important findings in this regard is that three-quarters of the residents of these three cities were exposed to crime information in one way or another.

Attentiveness to Crime News

Based on our surveys, most residents of American cities are hooked on the media. Of our informants, 85% indicated that they had read daily newspapers during the past week, and almost two-thirds had watched television on the previous night. Only 6% escaped either dose of popular culture. There was a discernible fall-off in the proportion who were exposed to media reports about crime, however. Virtually identical proportions of adults reported reading a crime story the previous evening (45%) and watching television news (44%). Despite their similar numbers these were not the same people. Patterns of readership and viewership, as well as attentiveness to the crime-related content of the media, varied considerably across the two forms of mass communication. Different people "got the message" in different ways, and as a result that message was widely disseminated.

Despite the high level of newspaper readership in our three cities there was some variation in news consumption among different population groups. In our target neighborhoods newspaper readership was highest in the two most middle-class areas, Lincoln Park and Sunset. In general, males, high-income persons, whites, and those with more education were more likely to report regularly reading a newspaper. These figures are shown in Table 8.3. Many fewer people — often one-half as many — remembered reading a crime story on the previous day, however. Again, males, whites, and the more highly educated were more likely to recall this. Age was related to general and crime news consumption in curvilinear fashion: Those in younger age categories were by far the least likely to read anything in a paper, while people in their late thirties and forties were the most likely, and

TABLE 8.3 Correlates of Media Attentiveness

Personal Attributes		Watched Television	Watched Television News	Read a Newspaper	Read a Crime Story	(N)
		Percentage Recalling Media Contact				
Sex	Males	(63)	(43)	90	48	(653)
	Females			86	40	(716)
Age	Under fifty	59	39	(88)	(44)	(922)
	Fifty and older	73	56			(350)
Race	Whites and others	(63)	(43)	91	47	(873)
	Blacks			85	41	(377)
Education	No College	68	47	84	42	(647)
	College	56	39	93	47	(672)

NOTE: When differences between subgroups are not significant (p > .05) average values for both groups are given in parentheses. All other differences are significant (p. < .05).

SOURCE: Computed from combined citywide surveys.

the elderly fell somewhere in between. The fall-off in attentiveness specifically to crime news (reading newspapers regularly but not remembering a crime story) also was greatest among the kinds of people who generally were less likely to read a newspaper at all, magnifying demographic differences between those who did and did not see such stories.

Within each city it was clear that newspapers serve particular markets which vary in demographic profile. Across the board, Philadelphians were more likely than those elsewhere to read a major daily newspaper. In Philadelphia, Blacks read the *Daily News* while whites and older readers stick to the *Inquirer* and the *Bulletin*. In San Francisco, young readers, whites, and the more educated choose the *Chronicle* over the *Examiner*. In Chicago, young readers, Blacks, and less educated respondents report reading the *Sun Times,* while *Tribune* readers are older, white, and more highly educated. Few of our respondents read the *Chicago Daily News,* perhaps explaining why it went out of business shortly thereafter. Despite clear differences in patterns of readership we are uncertain of their significance. Because newspapers serving a single city tend to resemble one another in the volume and content of their crime news, differences in which newspaper our respondents read should be less important than differences between readers and nonreaders in general.

Television viewing patterns are a mirror image of those describing news readership. Our respondents reported watching an average of 1.7 hours of prime-time television the previous evening. In general, television viewing was much more frequent among older and less educated persons, and (although the difference was not significant) women. Television viewing was heaviest in our poorer and white ethnic neighborhoods. There was a slight tendency for television viewing to be more frequent among our youngest respondents than for those in their mid twenties, but consumption then rose steadily with age for the remainder of the population. At least some of these differences may reflect variations in lifestyle, for television viewing was highest for retired and disabled persons, the unemployed, and home managers, and it was lowest for those who were working or in school. The most intensive viewing in all groups is found among those with less than a high school education. Of that group, 25% reported watching 4 hours of television or more the night before we called, more than 2.5 times the comparable figure for high school graduates. Exposure to television news simply was an extension of these differences between general viewers and nonviewers.

All of this indicates that different people are exposed to crime information in these two media sources. Less educated and older viewers more often tune in television news, and they are (but only slightly) more likely than nonviewers to be Black and poor. Reading about crime in the newspapers, on the other hand, is more often reported by males and more highly educated persons, who also are more likely to be white and affluent. As a result, although virtually identical proportions of our respondents reported watching television news (44%) and reading about crime (45%), only 24% were exposed to crime information in both ways.

Potential Consequences

The media are a source of vicarious information about crime. In addition to their other experiences, information gleaned from newspapers and television may cause people to form impressions about the nature and magnitude of the crime problem. However, most research on the effects of media have focused only on television, and those studies have emphasized its criminogenic appeal rather than its possible corrosive effects on citizen morale.

We have seen in this chapter a number of reasons why the media might be accused of engendering fear. Media coverage of crime emphasizes violence. Its coverage of violence, and in particular homicide, is frequent and consistent. No matter where we turn, things look bad, for both newspapers and television news present essentially the same images of crime. Television in particular devotes a substantial proportion of its total news coverage to crime, while the newspapers report a number of stories of violent crime in every issue.

From a consumer perspective, these messages are widely diffused. Viewing television news or reading about crime in the newspapers is very frequent, even when we ask only about "yesterday." Different people get the message in different ways, due to sex, age, and educational differences in media consumption. As a result, "everyone" (in categorical terms) is exposed to media messages concerning crime, in one way or another. Crime information is spread widely, and does not parallel the distribution of actual victimization. Further, other studies (including our own, to be reported in Chapter 10) indicate that violence is what people remember when we ask them about crime. Thus both the frequency of exposure to crime news and the content of the message matches the frequency and content of popular fears about crime. While the frequency of actual victimization and the relative proportions of violent and property crime do not match people's concerns, the media are more suspect. When we chart its impact, media coverage of crime may be an important source of "vicarious victimization."

On the other hand, there are a number of reasons to believe that the attitudinal and behavioral impact of media messages about crime may not be that significant. The media are sources of impressions about crime which are remote from actual events. Being at best secondhand accounts of crime, stories of specific incidents which are channeled to the citizenry in this way may be stripped of most of their emotional content. The personal impact of vicariously experienced victimization may be far from that of the real thing. Also, as sources of information on crime, the media are most likely to concern themselves with distant events. Rarely will they focus upon a victim that the average viewer knows, or even on a crime in the viewer's neighborhood. In fact, most media stories about crime contain little useful information for readers which would enable them to assess their own risks. The location of crime is often not specified, and there is seldom sufficient information about victims and offenders for readers to estimate the risks to people like themselves. Research we reviewed above indicates that crimes involving run-of-the-mill victims (that is, most people) are unlikely to be reported. In addition, many media accounts concern crimes that take place in other cities or nations, or involve very unlikely (and thus "newsworthy") circumstances. Presumably, these stories are neutral with respect to cues about risks facing the common person, or what he or she should do about crime. Television drama is not even concerned with real events, and tends to be an unreliable guide to real-world risks.

Despite their frequency, media stories about specific crimes also may often not specify enough detail about those events to provide a consumer with meaningful cues for action or raw material for reevaluating their personal assessments of risk. In their content analysis of newspapers in these cities, Gordon et al. (1979) noted the presence or absence of pertinent facts about violent crimes and their victims. They found that the age of victims was noted in these stories less than one-half of the time, that the victim's race rarely was specified, and that the neighborhood where the crime occurred could not be discerned in about 15% of stories. The time of day in which the incident took place was not noted 75% of the time, and there was no speculation about the relationship between the parties in the case in 60% of stories. The secondhand version of reality that these narrations may create in the minds of readers is likely to be vague on many key points.

Finally, we may not be able to discern much of an effect of the media because it does not vary much. There is little variation from place to place in terms of media coverage. Newspapers within a city greatly resemble one another in coverage, and both television and the newspapers dispense largely the same message. In one way or another, the bulk of the population is exposed to these messages. When almost everyone receives virtually the same message, studies of individual differences in media consumption and fear cannot reveal its consequences.

NOTE

1. The newspaper content analysis project covered papers issued until April 1978. For a detailed discussion of the entire content analysis and the coding procedures employed, see Gordon et al., 1979.

Chapter 9

CRIME AND NEIGHBORHOOD NETWORKS

Introduction

In addition to reports in the media, there is a large store of second-hand accounts of crime which can be tapped by talking to other people. Because most of us have little personal experience with crime, these vicarious sources of experience should play a great role in shaping our impressions of the crime problem. Further, unlike those in the media, stories about crime that we hear from friends and neighbors should be rich in information about local events and victims. Personal conversations about crime should be a key source of knowledge about neighborhood conditions. This suggests that it is important to understand the operation of neighborhood communication networks and the way in which crime news flows through those linkages.

There is a great deal of talk about crime. Interviews with victims of street robbery suggest that they recount their experiences to others with great frequency, thus spreading the word widely (Lejeune and Alex, 1973). As a result, Lawton et al. (1976) found that one-half of the elderly residents in a low-income housing project could describe crimes against their fellow tenants.

One of our field observers visited such a project, a senior citizen center in the Wicker Park area of Chicago. He noted:

The room was filled with about 50-60 old white men and women. . . . Most were in their 60s or 70s and had lived in the area for a long time. They all said they were very afraid. . . . A woman in her early 60s said you have to take chances. She shops at the Jewel and . . . she got in a struggle with a Black kid for her purse at 2:00 in the afternoon. An old woman in her 70s told a few stories I couldn't understand because of her thick, possibly Polish accent. . . . Another guy in his 70s, unshaven, wore an old gray suitcoat and a bandage above his left eye. He had gotten hit recently according to the others. He wore glasses. V said they generally come up behind you and sock you in the eye before you have a chance to react. They they steal your purse or whatever while you're thinking about your eye. . . .

One of the employees was a woman in her 60s who was very authoritative. She yelled at everyone that the meal would not begin until everyone quieted down [Wicker Park, April 1976].

In our city surveys we gathered reports of the frequency with which people were exposed to different sources of information about crime, including face-to-face conversations with others. Local informants were most often mentioned as a source of neighborhood crime information. We asked our respondents about the "best source of information about crime in your neighborhood." Almost 40% indicated that "friends," "relatives," or "neighbors" fell into this category. When we asked if, "in the past week or two," they actually had talked with anyone about crime, 43% answered in the affirmative. However, much of that conversation was not centered in their neighborhoods. The most frequent category of persons with whom they had recently talked were friends or persons at work or school; these groups constituted almost 60% of all conversational partners. Of our respondents, 20% indicated they had talked to members of their families and 17% said they had talked to their neighbors. When we take into account people who did not talk to anyone at all, only 16% of our respondents conversed about crime with neighbors or family members, those from whom they would be most likely to pick up new information about local crime activity.

In this chapter we first consider the issues of who talks about crime, and with whom they talk. Because of the importance of neighborhood communication networks for the flow of local information, we will explore in detail patterns of personal conversation about crime. It appears that the extent to which people in a neighborhood talk about crime is a consequence of two independent social processes; different factors motivate people to (a) talk about crime in the first place, and (b) talk to their neighbors rather than to others. The density of communication in a neighborhood lies in the intersection of these processes.

We then trace people's knowledge of local victims and the impressions they have gained about patterns of victimization in their communities. Being linked into a neighborhood communication network increases the chances that one will know local victims. People know a surprising number of victims, and the relative frequency of serious violent crime seems to be magnified by the way in which their stories get around. Impressions about what kinds of people in the neighborhood are being victimized also are at odds with the true distribution of crime in ways that may enhance both individual and collective levels of fear.

Models of Networking

We consider here competing explanations for the operation of personal communication networks with regard to crime: a Crime Problems model and a Neighborhood Integration model. Both models emphasize the role of environmental rather than personal factors in stimulating discussion about crime and shaping choices of conversational partners. The Crime Problems model proposes that conversation about an issue is encouraged by its frequency or seriousness in the immediate environment. In this case we employ two measures of neighborhood crime conditions which reflect the frequency and seriousness of crime: our index of the extent to which four types of serious crime constituted a problem in the area, and our respondents' estimates of the number of burglaries which occurred in their neighborhoods during the previous year.

The Crime Problems model postulates that reports of untoward neighborhood conditions enhanced the likelihood that our respondents talked to others about crime. The experience of "B," a young Polish woman employed as a church receptionist in the Wicker Park area of Chicago, illustrates this explanation:

> Last summer, every few days someone would be hit (burglarized). The neighborhood got together. . . . We have no formal neighborhood organization. We just visit back and forth and sit out in front and talk about what is going on. We compare notes on what happened to who. . . . Maybe at that time (last summer) ten on one block had been robbed [Wicker Park, July 1976].

There has been little previous research on this hypothesis. In Conklin's (1975) study of two cities, concern about crime was highest in the high crime community, but in Furstenberg's (1971) study in Baltimore those who lived in low-risk neighborhoods were more likely than those who lived in high crime areas to indicate concern about crime. Neither study provides evidence about the relationship between concern about crime and talking to one's neighbors about the topic.

There is, on the other hand, some evidence supporting a Neighborhood Integration explanation of crime communication. This model postulates that the discussion of neighborhood problems is facilitated by linkages to the community. In a major study of Philadelphia neighborhoods, Yancey and Ericksen (1979) found a strong relationship between residential stability and the development of close interpersonal networks in the area. The longer people lived in one place, the more closed their circles of friends and relatives became, and the more they centered on the neighborhood. Gubrium (1974) observed in his studies of the elderly that high levels of social interaction between them often led to widespread sharing of information about crime, which in turn enhanced their concern about the issue. We reported above upon the widespread diffusion of individual crime stories among the elderly residents of a public housing project, which is the sort of age-homogeneous environment which facilitates extensive friendship networks (Sundeen and Mathieu, 1976b; Gubrium, 1974).

Following Hunter's (1974) typology, we employ here two measures of neighborhood integration based on reports of residential commitment and social ties with neighbors.

Again, there are two dependent variables of interest: whether or not an individual recently had talked to another about crime, and — among those who had done so — with whom they had conversed. Because we are interested in intraneighborhood networks, responses concerning the latter are divided into those indicating nonlocal and local conversational partners.

Figures 9.1 and 9.2 detail the differential impact of the extent of crime problems and neighborhood integration. Measures of these competing factors are presented in relation to patterns of personal communication about crime.

We see in Figure 9.1 that while assessments of crime problems distinguished those who talked about the problem from those who did not, the Crime Problems model does not explain with whom they talked. The largest difference on the left side is reserved for ratings of sexual assault as a neighborhood problem. Where rape was a concern 54% talked about crime; where it was not, only 38% did so. On the other hand, the proportions who talked to neighbors rather than to outsiders about crime (on the right side of Figure 9.1) generally were less affected by the magnitude of crime problems.

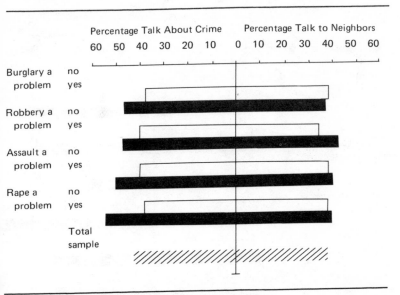

Figure 9.1 Crime Problems and Conversation About Crime

NOTE: "Percentage who talk to neighbors" is of those who talked about crime.
SOURCE: Computed from citywide surveys.

More dramatic is the differential relationship between our measures of neighborhood integration and patterns of conversation about crime, presented in Figure 9.2. Very little variation is reported in the tendency of persons to talk about crime (on the lefthand side of Figure 9.2). However, there were considerable differences in choices of conversational partners between those who were more tied and those who were less tied to their neighborhoods.

The largest differences in the tendency to talk to neighbors were to be found between those who found it easy to recognize strangers in their area and those who did not (63% to 37%), and between owners (52%) and renters (29%). The first three indicators in Figure 9.2 constituted our scale of residential ties, while the last three formed the social ties measure. Figure 9.2 shows that all of these measures, except length of residence, were individually related to patterns of crime communication in the expected fashion.

This suggests that each of our explanations for the extent and locus of personal conversation about crime was partially correct. Talk about crime is stimulated by crime conditions. Among those who do talk about crime, whether or not they talk with neighbors is dependent upon integration into the neighborhood.

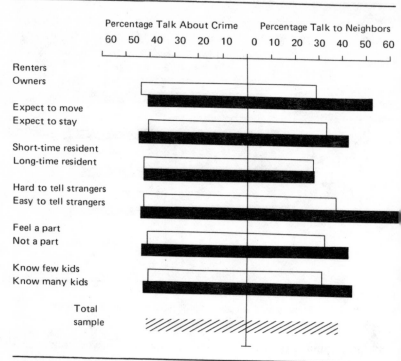

Figure 9.2 Neighborhood Integration and Conversation About Crime
NOTE: "Percentage who talk to neighbors" is of those who talked about crime.
SOURCE: Computed from citywide surveys.

A more stringent test of the contrasting explanatory powers of the Crime Problem and Neighborhood Integration models involves entering the major indicators of each into the same regression equation and testing the significance of the resulting coefficients. The results of this test are presented in Table 9.1, which matches the four indicators against one another in competitive fashion. Table 9.1 also presents the simple bivariate correlation between each indicator and our measures of crime communication.

As the figures in Table 9.1 indicate, the data are quite consistent with the existence of two processes shaping crime communication. Both measures of crime problems were significant predictors of talking about crime, while neither measure of neighborhood integration affected it significantly. On the other hand, both crime measures paled in significance when compared to the importance of integration in explaining neighborhood talk about crime. People talked to their neighbors about crime when neighborhood ties were strong. The

TABLE 9.1 Test of Contrasting Models of Crime Communication

Indicators	Talk About Crime At All			Talk to Neighbors Rather than Others About Crime		
	Simple	Multivariate		Simple	Multivariate	
	r	Beta	(Significance)	r	Beta	(Significance)
Residential ties	−.01	−.02	(.62)	.25	.23	(.01+)
Social ties	−.04	.04	(.33)	.16	.12	(.04)
Major crime problems	.17	.13	(.01+)	.04	.07	(.24)
Burglary frequency	.14	.10	(.02)	.05	.07	(.22)
Multiple R		.19	(.01+)		.29	(.01+)
(N)		(1142)			(468)	

NOTE: There is no significant statistical interaction effect among the independent variables. Main effects are significant as shown.

SOURCE: Computed from combined citywide surveys.

same pattern can be observed in the bivariate correlations, attesting to the independence of the two social processes that underlie patterns of personal communication about crime.

The strong neighborhood basis of personal communication is further attested to by the absence of any substantial personal correlates of talk about crime. In a regression analysis (not shown) we examined the relationship between six key demographic attributes of our respondents and the frequency and locus of their conversations about crime problems. Only one of the twelve correlations was significant; older people were more likely than others to talk to their neighbors. This relationship disappeared, however, when we controlled for our measures of neighborhood integration. Conditions, events, and community linkages seem to play the predominant role here. Finally, when we controlled for assessments of neighborhood conditions and integration, all significant differences between cities in crime communication patterns disappeared.

In summary, this analysis suggests that two steps underlie the word-of-mouth diffusion of crime news through a community. First, discussion is sparked by the belief that there are serious crime problems in the area. Discussion about crime was not related in any significant way to the personal characteristics of our respondents, but rather to their assessments of conditions in their immediate environments. Because most of the residents of these three cities did not perceive conditions in their vicinities to be extreme (70% reported no "big problems" in this regard), well over half of them did not become involved in conversations about the issue. However, once people began to talk about crime, variations in the seriousness of crime problems in their area did not affect with whom they talked. Rather, those who reported strong residential and social ties with their neighborhoods — and this was most common among our older respondents — spoke more frequently with residents of their own areas. However many were talking about crime, the locus of their conversation was shaped by the strength of their linkages to the community.

Networks in Neighborhoods

One important consequence of this complex communication process is that there is relatively little variation from place to place in the amount of talk about crime which goes on there. Many people in our special target neighborhoods had conversations about crime: that proportion ranged from 37% in South Philadelphia to 52% in the San Francisco community of Sunset. There also was some variation in with whom people conversed. The proportion of all adults who reported conversing with their neighbors about anything ranged from 34% in San Francisco's Visitacion Valley to 49% in Chicago's Back-of-the-Yards. However, the amount of talk which goes on in a neighborhood lies in the conjunction of these figures, and in the main the two did not go together. Across our ten selected big-city neighborhoods an average of about 17% of all adults recently had engaged in conversation with people from their neighborhoods about crime. Conversation about crime is sparked by the existence of serious neighborhood crime problems, but, as we saw in Chapter 6, close-knit neighborhood networks are much more characteristic of places where crime problems tend to be less severe. Crime problems and neighborhood integration do not go together.

As a result of the existence of two mutually conflicting processes there is very little neighborhood-by-neighborhood variation in the amount of crime talk going on there. That figure ranges from 13% of all adults in South Philadelphia (a low crime area with the least talk about crime at all) to 20% in San Francisco's Sunset. Because the survey samples for our study areas often are as small as 200 respondents, we cannot confidently say more about these proportions than that they are "very similar." However, the relatively similar levels of crime-related conversation taking place in these diverse neighborhoods means that some people are talking about crime everywhere, although the reasons for this vary considerably from place to place. Thus talk about crime may seem ubiquitous, to be heard no matter where we go, but at the same time it clearly is not a reliable guide to how much crime actually plagues a community.

The similar effects of these two different contextual factors also may explain why talk about crime was most frequent in Chicago and least frequent in San Francisco. Chicagoans were more likely than others to indicate that major crimes constituted a "big problem" in their neighborhoods; concomitantly, they also were the most likely to report talking to someone about the crime problem. Philadelphians stood between the others in terms of crime conversation, and scored at the top on both of our measures of neighborhood integration. Residents of San Francisco were the least likely to report talking with their neighbors about crime (26% did); and they were, in general, the least tied to their places of residence and the least likely to express concern about crime problems.

Learning About Local Crime

In light of what we have found about patterns of conversation about crime — that it is shaped by crime problems and linkages to the community — it is not surprising that contact with neighbors brings with it more information about crimes and victims in the neighborhood. Kleinman and David (1973) found that Black residents of the Bedford-Stuyvesant area of New York City who reported more social contacts in their community were more likely to perceive high rates of crime there. Further, the more crime there is in the area, the more local stories there are to tell. People who live in an area with serious crime problems have more things to learn about, and gossip with neighbors is an important means of spreading that information through the community.

Under those conditions, being linked to local communication networks is another source of what we have called "vicarious victimization." There are more people who know of crime than there are victimizations; in the case of burglary the "vicarious victimization rate" for local crime is perhaps four times the direct victimization rate. As a result, talk about crime may have greater consequences — in the aggregate — than the direct action of criminals. Some of those consequences are psychological, for vicarious victimization is linked to fear of crime. Others are behavioral, for (as we shall see in Part IV) those who are linked to communication networks and who are "victimized" in this way also are more likely to report doing things about crime to protect both their persons and their households.

In order to assess the spread of accounts of local crime through the community, each of our respondents was asked if he or she knew anyone who had experienced each of four types of crime: burglary, personal theft, assault by a stranger, and rape. In the case of burglary, the interviewer inquired:

> Do you personally know of anyone, other than yourself, whose home or apartment has been broken into in the past couple of years or so?

They also were quizzed about their knowledge of persons who had "been robbed or had their purse or wallet taken," who were "a victim of an attack by strangers," or who were "sexually assaulted." We followed positive responses to find out if those crimes took place in the respondent's neighborhood or not. We also probed the content of those accounts by asking our respondents to describe who they had heard about being victimized in their neighborhoods.

The data can be used to categorize our informants in terms of their contact with victims. Overall, 57% of city residents reported knowing a victim of a burglary, while 48% knew a victim of personal theft, 32% a stranger assault victim, and 22% someone who had been sexually assaulted. Of course, knowledge of victims was far from uniformly distributed in the population, and contacts with victims of different kinds of crime overlapped somewhat. In all, 66% of our respondents reported knowing at least one victim of any of these crimes. City-by-city breakdowns in the distribution of contact with crime victims are presented in Table 9.2.

It should be apparent at first glance that "personally knowing" crime victims is very common everywhere. While very few residents of these three cities were robbed in a recent year (in the victimization surveys the figure was 5.5%), almost one-half of them knew someone who was. Rape rates are relatively low, and that crime presumably is less widely discussed by its victims, but one in five of our respondents knew someone who had been sexually molested. While many crimes, and especially serious personal ones, are relatively infrequent from an individual perspective, contacts with victims of crime are very widespread.

The manner in which this indirect victimization was distributed generally parallels other indicators of harm. Compared with official figures, the ranking of our three cities in terms of the frequency with which people knew crime victims duplicated police crime counts: San Francisco stands at the top, while Philadelphia is at the bottom of the list. Although differences between the cities are not as striking as

TABLE 9.2   Knowledge of Crime Victims

City of Residence	Percentage Who Knew a Victim of:				
	Burglary	Personal Theft	Stranger Assault	Rape	(N)
Chicago	54	51	31	23	(428)
Philadelphia	57	42	29	20	(453)
San Francisco	61	51	37	28	(483)
Average	57	48	32	22	

NOTE: Number of cases varies slightly from crime to crime; averages are given here.
SOURCE: Computed from citywide surveys.

crime rates would lead us to expect (and differences between them with respect to burglary were not significant), the distribution of this form of "vicarious victimization" parallels reported crime levels for these communities.

Reports of victim contact also are in rough accord with the frequency with which these crimes occur as measured in the victimization surveys. In terms of volume, burglary was the most common of these crimes, followed by personal theft, stranger assault, and rape. This is exactly the order in which residents of the cities reported knowing victims. It is important to note, however, that the magnitude of the differences among these figures on victim contact is somewhat askew. Burglary is far more common than each of the personal crimes; it is more frequent than robbery by a factor of seven in official statistics and by a factor of four in the victim surveys. However, contact with burglary victims is only slightly more common than contact with victims of personal theft. At the other end of the scale, rape registers at a very low rate on all measures of victimization, far lower than our one-in-five finding reflects. Like media coverage of crime, the processes which lead victims' stories of their experiences to "get around" seem to accentuate the apparent volume of personal as opposed to property crime. Because personal and indirect experiences with violent crime have substantial consequences for what people think and do, this magnification of their apparent frequency has important implication for collective levels of fear.

Not surprisingly, contact with victims of crime is distributed in the population much like victimization itself. Violent crime in particular is not widely dispersed geographically; rather, it clusters in particular locales. People also are clustered in characteristic ways according to race, class, and lifestyle. The two often go together. Further, most

TABLE 9.3   Conversation About Crime and Knowledge of Victims

| Conversation Locus | Percentage Who Knew Local Victim of: | | | | |
	Burglary	Personal Theft	Stranger Assault	Rape	(N)
No talk about crime	40.0	18.7	12.2	4.5	(779)
Talk to nonlocals	49.7	24.0	18.7	7.6	(329)
Talk to neighbors	56.7	35.7	29.4	8.3	(206)
Gamma	+.23	+.27	+.35	+.25	
(Significance)	(.01+)	(.01+)	(.01+)	(.01+)	

NOTE: Number of cases varied slightly from crime to crime. Averages are given here.
Correlation is between conversation locus and knowledge of a local crime victim, for each type of offense.
SOURCE: Computed from citywide surveys.

criminals (being young and opportunistic) tend to do their work close to home, and generally victimize people like themselves. Finally, people mostly know people like themselves, victims and nonvictims alike, and thus contacts with victims tend to follow patterns of predation. As a result, in our data 80% of those who reported knowing a burglary victim indicated that the crime took place in the respondents' immediate neighborhood.

In general, personal contact with victims increased in frequency toward the bottom of the income ladder and among Blacks. For assault and personal theft the poor were most heavily victimized, and their acquaintances were the ones who heard the stories. The only exception to this rule was burglary. As we have seen, burglary strikes widely; in many places people at the top of the economic heap are victimized more frequently than those at the bottom. Because victim contact generally follows the social distribution of offenses, we found positive correlations between family income levels and contact with burglary victims in each of our cities. While the concentration of personal contact with crime victims in various social strata was less clear-cut than the distribution of crime, its burden fell generally on the same social groups.

It is apparent that being linked to local communication channels led people to know of more *local* crime. Among those who had not recently engaged in discussion about crime, about 50% reported knowing a victim of a crime in their neighborhoods, while among those who had discussed crime with their neighbors, fully 72% knew at least one victim of a local crime. The proportion who knew of a crime in their neighborhoods varied by type of crime, with burglary

TABLE 9.4 Conversation About Crime and Knowledge of Victims, by Seriousness of Neighborhood Crime Problem

| Conversation Locus | Percentage Who Knew a Local Crime Victim, by Degree Crime a Problem | | | |
	No Problem	Some Problem	Big Problem	(N)
No talk about crime	27	57	67	(779)
Talk to nonlocals	25	63	74	(335)
Talk to neighbors	38	73	87	(206)
(N)	(371)	(471)	(469)	
Gamma	+.08	+.21	+.33	
(Significance)	(.16)	(.01)	(.01+)	

NOTE: Crime problem categories created by trichotomizing the crime problems scale. Correlation is between conversation locus and knowledge of a victim, within each of the three levels of crime problems.

SOURCE: Computed from combined citywide surveys.

being the most prominent. Table 9.3 presents a breakdown of knowledge of local crime by patterns of conversation. Burglary victims were most widely known, but in terms of proportional differences, personal conversations magnified the frequency of predatory and assaultive violence more dramatically. People who talked to their neighbors were almost twice as likely as those who did not to know victims of rape and personal theft, and two and one-half times as likely to know victims of stranger assault. This dovetails with Tyler's (1978) findings in a Los Angeles survey. When he asked people specifically about what crimes they had discussed with others they were by far most likely to report talking about serious violent crimes and those involving atypical victims. These data suggest that interpersonal neighborhood communication networks substantially magnify the apparent volume of local violence.

There is doubtless a reciprocal relationship between the knowledge about crime thus gained and assessments of neighborhood conditions. If crime is a serious local problem, being linked into neighborhood networks will more often lead one to learn about events there. On the other hand, hearing of serious crime surely rebounds to shape assessments of conditions.

The data can only demonstrate the simple relationship between these factors. People who report that crime is a big problem in their neighborhoods more often report knowing victims. However, the causal linkage in that direction is through neighborhood communications networks that spread the stories of individual events. We find that personal communication spreads the stories more strikingly in areas plagued by crime problems. The data are presented in Table 9.4. In communities where residents did not think that crime was a problem, relatively few reported knowing a local victim, and the relation between neighborhood communication patterns and knowing a victim was relatively slight (a gamma of only +.08). However, in more troubled areas, being linked to local communication nets had a substantial impact upon knowledge of local events, and almost 9 out of 10 of those reporting the most troubled conditions *and* talking with neighbors about crime thought that one of the serious crimes discussed here had hit close to home. In areas where residents perceived crime to be a major problem, conversation about the problem magnified the apparent frequency of victimization even more greatly.

Profiles of Local Victims

In addition to asking about the incidence of various crimes in the community, we quizzed our respondents about stories that circulate concerning local victims. We were not at all sure that the popular image of crime victims would actually match the profile of victims as revealed by either official statistics or victimization surveys. We have seen above that only about one-quarter of our respondents knew a victim of a personal crime, and that many more garnered what they knew of such things through secondhand (or more removed) media sources. We have also seen that stories about crime did not spread in consistent fashion. Attention either to the media or to interpersonal channels of communication was far from random, and doubtless would play a role in determining who heard what, as well as from whom. While youths and males make up the bulk of crime victims, both the "sending" and "receiving" components of these channels may garble the message considerably. We have already seen that media messages convey distorted pictures of crime, and cannot assume that people heard about crime stories which predominantly concerned youths and males.

We hypothesized that people would be more fearful when they thought that people like themselves were being victimized in their neighborhoods, and to test this we needed to know who they thought the victims were. In order to gauge the content of stories circulating about crime, we asked:

What kinds of people do you hear about being attacked, beaten up, or robbed in your neighborhood?

TABLE 9.5   Perceptions of Neighborhood Victims

Profile of "People Heard About Being Attacked . . ."	Percentage of Total
Females	44
Males	18
Both sexes	25
No specifics	13
	100
Older people	56
Younger people	15
Children	2
Multiple ages	11
No specifics	16
	100

NOTE: Total is 1082 for sex and 1143 for age profiles. This excludes those who volunteered "no crime here," or replied "don't know," and so on.

SOURCE: Computed from combined citywide surveys.

Respondents were asked first, "Are the victims mostly older people, younger people, or children?" and then, "Are the victims generally male or female?"

A few respondents (6%) were unwilling or unable to hazard a response to this question, and 10% insisted that there was no crime in their neighborhoods, on which to report. Among the remainder opinions were mixed, but in general people's perceptions of victims did not seem to match the "true" distribution of crime. As Table 9.5 reports, the bulk of our respondents reported hearing about women and older people as victims. Almost 70% said that "females" or "both sexes" were victims of personal crime in their vicinities and 67% indicated that "older persons" or combinations of our age categories were involved. Only 18% indicated that they heard about "males" being attacked or robbed, and 15% chose the "younger people" category with respect to age.

While the age categories presented to our respondents were broad, it does not appear that their profile of victims very closely matches other descriptions of the victim population. For example, in the San Francisco victim survey of 1974, about 47% of all assaults struck people between 12 and 24 years of age, and only 12% involved those 50 years old and older. This age skew was less marked for robbery, 34% and 26% for the younger and older groups, respectively, but it clearly pointed in the same direction. The mismatch between popular and survey-based profiles of victims is even more extreme when we contrast victimization rates across the sexes. In San Francisco about 62%

of all robberies and 57% of all assaults involved male victims, and the differences were even greater for the other two cities (U.S. Department of Justice, 1975: Table 3). Yet only a small proportion in each city reported hearing that men were the "kind of people" victimized in their areas.

Based on age and sex profiles of victims, we thus find that public perceptions of who is victimized are skewed in the direction of more vulnerable groups, those who also may be perceived as being less culpable in their predicament. Those who are less able physically to resist attack, who seem to have the most to lose from personal victimization, and who generally take the most precautions against crime, are reported to be "the kind of people" who are victimized in a large majority of neighborhoods.

The causes of this distribution of victims in the public's mind are of considerable interest. At a minimum, it suggests that the social processes behind conversation about crime encourage the dissemination of atypical stories, or that only atypical stories are remembered. It may be that only stories which do not fit the norm are "newsworthy," even within the community. This is not unlike the pattern by which editors pick crime stories worthy of publication in daily newspapers or broadcast on television. Alternately, people may tend to talk about people like themselves who are victimized, or be more attentive to those messages when they come by. This profile of victims might match that of people who talk about crime. However, we found no important age or sex correlates of conversations about crime. We also find it interesting that popular images of victims more closely match those broadcast by the media than those uncovered in the victimization surveys. Dominick (1973), Graber (1977), and others have documented how television and the newspapers exaggerate the extent to which women, middle-class people, the elderly, and innocent bystanders become involved in crime as victims. Fishman (1978) has described how the newsgathering process behind this operates, examining in detail media coverage of crimes against the elderly in New York City.

Potential Consequences

Unlike images of crime transmitted by the media, which are likely to concern remote events and atypical persons and circumstances, the web of interpersonal relationships ties together many community members and is likely to facilitate the spread of crime stories which concern local residents and events close to home. That knowledge should play an important role in shaping how people assess the risks of their environments and the measures they take to prevent becoming victims.

Unlike victimization, which from the point of view of most persons is a "rare event," knowing crime victims is very common. We found that two-thirds of our respondents knew a victim of a serious crime. Further, in terms of the relative frequency of events, they were disproportionately acquainted with victims of violent crimes. In light of the infrequency of crimes like rape, the extent to which knowledge of victims of those crimes had spread through these communities was quite surprising. As we shall see, these crimes are the most likely to engender fear among those whose acquaintances have fallen victim. Thus, the apparent magnification of the relative frequency of personal crime by the mechanisms through which this knowledge spreads becomes quite significant.

Not surprisingly, contact with crime victims was distributed in much the same fashion as victimization itself. Blacks and the poor were more likely to know victims of personal crimes, while people of all races and classes were likely to have had contact with burglary victims. Perhaps significantly, this knowledge of victims of personal crime was distributed in the population in much the same fashion as fear. But, unlike victimization, it also was frequent enough potentially to serve as an explanation for much of that fear.

Most of the victims that people knew were close to home. This was encouraged by the consistent impact of participation in neighborhood communication networks on the diffusion of crime stories. Those who were linked to those networks knew more local victims. Further, it seems that those networks serve to magnify the relative frequency of local violence. Participation seemed to have a greater effect on spreading the word concerning stranger assault and rape than it did on knowledge of local household burglary.

Because our respondents disproportionately nominated women and the elderly as victims of violent crime in their localities, the consequences of this view of events may be considerable. It may raise our collective level of fear. Crime as a social phenomenon might be interpreted quite differently if victims were seen primarily to be young toughs, people who drink too much and get involved in disputes, roughhousing boys, gang members, and others who largely bring their fates upon themselves. However, the imagery attached to victims who are old and female is quite different. As we suggested, they may seem less likely to be culpable, more likely to be victims of calculated predatory abuse, and more likely to suffer horribly at the hands of their attackers. For law-abiding citizens the message may be, "You could be next."

At the individual level the message may ring loudest among women and the elderly. We have seen from victimization surveys that they are less likely than most to be involved in the majority of serious crimes. But crime is an atomistic force, striking individually, here and there. It is not known collectively except through social mechanisms which distribute the reports of victims. People know what they hear and read, and in this case that presents quite a different picture than the statistical record. It seems that by word-of-mouth sources, women and the elderly could gain a greatly exaggerated picture of the risks they face. While popular images of victims may raise our collective level of fear, they should impact more heavily upon those two vulnerable groups.

The social processes which underlie the spread of crime stories through a community also may account for the relatively widespread distribution of fear of crime. For different reasons, crime news spreads by word of mouth in communities of all kinds. Discussion of crime is common even in places where crime does not constitute much of a problem. As a result, while there is a tendency for word of crime to follow its distribution in the social structure, there are also forces which potentially foster fear among those who are not often victimized, and who live in places where victimization is rare.

Chapter 10

THE IMPACT OF MEDIA AND NEIGHBORHOOD NETWORKS ON FEAR

Introduction

The victimization surveys conducted by the Census Bureau for LEAA provide a wealth of data on the frequency of crime and fear. However, Chapter 2 noted that the frequency of recent personal victimization as documented by those surveys simply is too low to provide an explanation for the relatively high level of fear reported by urban dwellers. Thus in gathering our own data we cast our net more widely in order to examine the consequences of other significant events and conditions. This chapter assesses the impact of two vicarious sources of information about crime — the media and personal conversation — on fear of crime in the three cities. Respondents in this survey report that watching television news, reading about crime in the newspapers, and talking to neighbors about local events are, unlike victimization, quite common features of daily life. If these experiences affect their assessments of their personal safety, they may account for the high level of fear among urban residents. Because personal conversation about crime and media contact do not always parallel the distribution of victimization but often seem to parallel that fear, they also may account for the high incidence of fear among subgroups in the population that are not usually victimized.

Some fear may arise when individuals come into contact with victims or learn that people they know have been victimized. People may be more fearful when they learn of crimes which struck friends and neighbors, with whom they often share some bond or sense of common fate. Not only are people sorrowful when the consequences of those crimes are tragic, but they are reminded of their own vulnerability. The impact of these events doubtless is greatest when the bond is close. The impact of crime also may be greater when it occurs nearby, serving as a direct reminder that no locale is free from threat. Finally, people should feel more threatened when victims (especially those nearby) resemble themselves; when "people like me" are being attacked, the perceived threat of crime should soar. Fear also may follow from learning of crime via more impersonal sources. From the media people may come to believe that violence is casually inflicted and ubiquitous, and that it strikes "innocent bystanders" like themselves with great frequency. From the sheer volume of violence featured on television and in the newspapers they may gain an exaggerated view of the actual frequency of such crimes.

Our research indicates that violent crime is what people recall when asked about crime. We inquired of each respondent:

> Thinking of all the crime stories you've read, seen, or heard about in the last couple of weeks, is there a particular one that you remember, or that sticks out in your mind?

One-half (52%) did recall such a story and were able to describe it in sufficient detail that it could be placed in one of several categories.

The most striking, if not unexpected, feature of those stories was the frequency with which they depicted dramatic and violent confrontations. Almost 50% of the stories involved a murder or attempted murder, another fifth a kidnapping or hijacking, and 13% a rape or other sexual assault. The other large classes of stories included assaults and robberies (8%) and cases of child abuse (5%). Lost in the "other" (5%) category were reports of burglaries and thefts, the most common crimes, and a host of other offenses.

This profile of "memorable" crimes greatly overrepresents the frequency of violent incidents. By using official "crimes known" statistics for Part I offenses and arrest totals for Part II crime (Federal Bureau of Investigation, 1978), it is possible to compare the distribution of memorable events to the official picture of crime in America. Based on police records, homicides make up 0.1% of all known offenses, while violent sex offenses constitute 0.3%, assaults and robberies 5%, and child abuse cases less than 0.3% of the total. By official count the "other" category of memorable crimes in our survey includes 95% of all incidents.

Our research question is the extent to which vicarious knowledge of crime may constitute a form of indirect victimization. Although it takes the form of information, communicated either in person or through the media, vicarious victimization affects fear through imagined participation in the depicted violent event. Thus an important dimension upon which such experiences vary is the extent to which they strike close to their "victims" either in social or geographical distance.

Research in other psychological domains indicates that vicariously experienced events can affect people's judgments, and that their content is generalized to provide cues for behavior (Hansen and Donoghue, 1977). This is especially true in the absence of any direct experience. This is reflected in the findings of Gerbner and Gross (1976), who argue that heavy viewers of television tend to generalize the information acquired there. They find that high consumers are more likely than others to perceive a high risk of becoming involved in violence, to be more apprehensive about crime, and to feel less safe. Tyler (1978), on the other hand, finds that indirect experiences with crime affect only a selected subset of our perceptions of the problem. He finds that judgments of the amount of crime in an area or of the general crime rate are affected by exposure to media accounts of crime and personal conversations on the topic. Estimates of one's own risk of victimization are unaffected by such experiences. Doob and MacDonald (1979) found a strong correlation between television viewing and only the most general perceptions of crime, and then only in higher crime neighborhoods. The media and other sources of vicarious experience are major determinants of guesses about the amount of crime, but those assessments are not related to the social backgrounds or attitudes of individuals, nor do they seem to affect their behavior. Estimates of risk are a function of things which affect us directly. Thus, Tyler's research suggests that vicarious victimization does not play an important role in generating widespread fear of crime.

In this chapter we examine first the impact of knowing local crime victims upon fear of crime. Chapter 9 reported that knowing of victims from the vicinity was a function of participation in personal communication networks, especially when there was a significant crime problem in the area to discuss. The popular image of victims also overemphasized the risks facing women and the elderly. This chapter traces the consequences of that knowledge. It examines whether or not knowing about various kinds of neighborhood victimizations affects fear. We find that predatory personal crimes had the greatest impact upon those who heard about them. However, far more respondents knew local victims of burglary, and calculating the "net effect" of knowing victims, based upon both the frequency and apparent consequences of such contact, lends great importance to the role of burglary in stimulating aggregate levels of fear. We then test the importance of the content of the stories which circulate concerning crime and find that hearing of local victims "like you" has consistently adverse consequences for assessments of personal safety.

This chapter then turns to the impact of the media upon fear. Television viewing and fear of crime are similarly distributed in the population; both are higher among the old and the less educated and among women and Blacks (although not significantly so in the case of television viewing) than among their counterparts. Thus it is necessary to determine whether or not the relationship between television viewing and fear is spurious, in fact reflecting patterns of victimization, vulnerability, neighborhood conditions, and contact with victims. A correlational analysis indicates that the relationship between television viewing and fear of crime is indeed an artifact of "who watches television," particularly the elderly. Newspaper readers tend to resemble those who are less victimized, but again we find no independent effects of this form of media involvement.

Neighborhood Events and Fear

Learning about crime in their communities is related to people's assessments of their personal safety. As hypothesized, geographical proximity plays an important role in determining the consequences of such information. Hearing about crime in one's neighborhood is related to fear of walking the streets there, while knowledge of events elsewhere has much less impact. Some kinds of crime seem to have more of an effect than others in shaping people's assessments of their personal safety. However, the seriousness of crimes must be balanced against their frequency in making this assessment. The multiplier effect of indirect victimization is considerable, for knowledge of local crimes is much more common than personal victimization. Further, there are differences in this multiplier effect among various kinds of crime, increasing the apparent importance of burglary in generating fear at all levels of the social ladder. Finally, hearing about a lot of crime is worse than hearing about a little; although relatively few people hear about more than a few local incidents, there is a cumulative effect of such information.

There is some research that indicates that knowing crime victims contributes to fear. Skogan (1977b) has reported a relationship between living in a household in which someone else was victimized and being fearful. Klecka and Bishop (1978) found that knowing about the victimization of a friend had a significant effect upon fear of crime among the elderly. They constructed an index measuring the number of friends and acquaintances of their respondents who had been robbed or burglarized "in the past few years." This had a greater impact on perceptions of neighborhood conditions than did demographic attributes, measures of neighborhood integration, reports of neighborhood conditions, or anything else. Both of these cases involve only one component of what we have dubbed indirect victimization, personal contact with the victim. This suggests either that the various modes by which information about crime spreads may have different effects, or that a prior relationship with the offended party is crucial.

The work of Klecka and Bishop also documents the extent to which vicarious victimization, by "multiplying" the apparent frequency with which criminal events take place, may increase the overall level of fear. They examined the impact of victimization by personal crimes in high and low crime neighborhoods (Flatbush, in New York City, and Sherman Park, in Milwaukee, respectively). When they compared victimization rates per 1.000 elderly residents of these areas, they found that indirect victimization was as much as *14* times as frequent as that experienced directly. In Sherman Park those rates were 39 and 520 per thousand, respectively. Thus even if their effects on fear were relatively weak, vicarious experiences could have wide-ranging effects on the community due to their great frequency. Further, they found that indirect victimization experiences of this sort were only slightly less common in low crime areas than in higher crime areas. While direct victimization of the elderly was over four times as frequent in Flatbush as in Sherman Park, rates of indirect victimization were only 20% higher. Clearly, crime stories were "getting around" with vigor even where personal experiences with crime were relatively rare.

There is also experimental evidence that the geographical proximity of those victims has consequences for fear as well. Shotland et al. (1979) gave contrived newspaper stories depicting crimes to samples of women. They found that reports of events which were described as occurring in the vicinity led to more fearful evaluations of the stories than did reports of crimes which occurred elsewhere.

Having heard about crime in their neighborhoods affected our respondents' assessments of their personal safety. For each of the major crimes examined here — burglary, robbery, stranger assault, and rape — we determined if our informants "personally knew" victims of such predations which had taken place "in the past couple of years." If they had, we asked where those crimes took place. Table 10.1 reports the proportion who felt "very unsafe" after dark in each of three categories: those who had heard of no specific crimes, those who had only heard of attacks which occurred elsewhere, and those

TABLE 10.1   Proximity of Crime Victims and Fear

Type of Crime	Percentage Feeling "Very Unsafe"		
	Knew No Victim	Knew Victim Out of Area	Knew Local Victim
Burglary	13	7	18
Robbery	11	10	28
Stranger assault	12	11	28
Rape	15	10	26

NOTE: All differences significant at $p > .01$ level. Number of cases for each type of crime approximately 1320.

SOURCE: Computed from combined citywide surveys.

who indicated that they knew victims of events that had taken place in their own neighborhoods (some of whom also knew victims from elsewhere). It is apparent that knowing any type of crime victim was related to higher levels of fear, but only if that incident had occurred in the immediate vicinity. Of those who recalled knowing a victim of a local robbery or stranger assault, 28% also reported feeling "very unsafe," a figure that was virtually the same for those who knew rape victims (26%), but that dropped to 18% for those who knew local victims of burglary. For all but burglary these respondents were twice as likely to report being afraid than were those who did not know a victim.

On the other hand, people who only recalled knowing victims of crimes which took place somewhere else (including "out of town," "other place in city," and so on), seemed *less* afraid of personal crime than those who knew no victims at all. While on first blush this might suggest that people take delight in the plight of others, in fact it reflects who they are and whom they know. In general those who reported knowing victims in other communities were younger and more educated than most residents of our three cities, and presumably more cosmopolitan in their social contacts. This was suggested by their proclivity toward talking to persons outside their neighborhoods when they discussed crime problems. Probably as a result, they recalled knowing more distant victims, while at the same time enjoying age and educational levels generally associated with lower fear. People also might not know local victims because there is no significant local crime. Knowledge of victims and assessments of neighborhood crime problems were positively related, as we have seen. Once the age, sex, race, and education of respondents are accounted for, the relationship between knowing a crime victim and fear of crime becomes straightforward: Those who knew only more distant victims were slightly more fearful than those who knew none at all, while those who knew victims from the immediate vicinity were considerably more fearful.

The previous chapter indicated that much of this knowledge concerning victims was due to integration into local communication networks. People who were hooked into neighborhood networks were more likely to know of local victims, while those who conversed with people at work or elsewhere knew more victims from outside their neighborhoods. A simple test of this talk-knowledge-fear model is to examine the relationship between talking about crime and fear of crime — which is positive and significant — after controlling for the intermediate link in the model, knowing victims. When this is done in a regression analysis, the relation between crime conversation and fear disappears. It is apparent that learning about victimization is the key consequence of personal conversation for this model and is instrumental in increasing fear.

The individual-level relationship between knowledge of crime victims and fear has a parallel at the neighborhood level. In areas where many people knew local victims of personal predatory crime many more of them reported being fearful of crime. Figure 10.1 depicts the extent to which the two measures covaried across our ten target neighborhoods.

Figure 10.1 is dominated by three neighborhoods in which large numbers of adults knew robbery victims from the vicinity: Woodlawn, Wicker Park, and Visitacion Valley. They contribute disproportionately to the correlation between knowledge of robbery victims and fear of crime at the neighborhood level, which was $+.78$. All were communities with high crime rates in all categories. At the other end of the scale lay our more placid neighborhoods, where knowledge of robbery victims was less widespread and where levels of fear generally were low.

In addition, knowledge of local victims seemed to have a cumulative effect on fear. Summing across all four categories of victimization, the *number* of local victims our respondents reported knowing was positively related (gamma = $+.26$) to fear. Successively greater and more diverse information about local crime was associated with higher levels of fear in our cities.

As Table 10.1 showed, knowledge of different types of victimization had different effects upon our respondents' assessments of their personal safety. Differences in fear levels between those who knew no

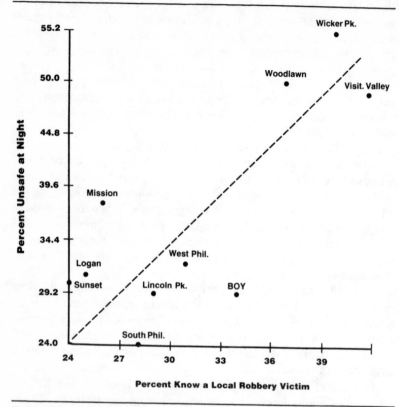

Figure 10.1 Neighborhood Knowledge of Robbery Victims and Fear
SOURCE: Computed from ten neighborhood surveys.

victims and those who knew one in the vicinity were greater for
personal crimes than for burglary; the greatest disparity was for
robbery. Table 10.2 presents the correlation between knowing a local
victim or not (here a dichotomy) and our measure of fear, for each type
of crime.

Table 10.2 suggests that knowing that robbers were active in the
vicinity had the greatest impact upon assessments of safety, followed
by knowledge about stranger assaults, rape, and burglary. As described above, however, the number of people who know about these
crimes shapes the overall impact of the flow of crime information
upon levels of fear. Table 10.2 also indicates that the percentage of
people who knew local victims varied considerably by type of crime.
While 23% of our informants knew local robbery victims and 17%

TABLE 10.2   Net Effect of Knowledge of Victims

Type of Crime Respondent Knew Local Victim of	Correlation With Fear	Percentage Who Knew Local Victim	Net Effect – Percentage Knew Local Victim and Felt Unsafe
Robbery	+.40	23	11.5
Stranger assault	+.32	17	7.6
Burglary	+.16	45	16.4
Rape	+.28	6	2.7

NOTE: Correlation is gamma. "Knowing a local victim" is a dichotomy which combines those who only knew victims outside the neighborhood with those who knew none at all.

SOURCE: Computed from combined citywide surveys.

knew local victims of assaults by strangers, 45% knew about burglaries in the vicinity. Thus, although the difference in fear between the informed and the uninformed in this regard was the greatest for personal crimes, more people could be found in the "knew of burglary/felt afraid" category because of the significantly greater number of burglary stories to tell. The net effect of particular kinds of information about crime is reported in Table 10.2 for each type of victimization. Burglary was closely followed in net effect by robbery. This is because its lesser frequency was balanced by the greater impact that knowledge of local robberies had upon assessments of personal safety. At the bottom of the list fell the distribution of information about sexual assaults, the net effect of which was very small because so few of our respondents knew of any such crimes in their neighborhoods.

All of this places in a different light the consequences of the dissemination of various types of crime information in a community. Personal violence and predatory attacks indeed have greater effect upon those who "get the message," and they become more pessimistic about conditions in their communities as a result. Because personal and impersonal communication channels seem to deliver messages about this kind of crime disproportionately, they help spread knowledge of victims — and thus fear — more widely than the frequency of violent personal crimes would suggest. As we saw above, 48% of respondents knew a victim of a robbery or purse snatching, while 57% knew a burglary victim. More people know victims of burglaries because of its sheer frequency and wide distribution, and the overall impact of the dissemination of stories about burglary probably is greater as a result. In these three cities about 9% of the respondents to the victimization surveys sponsored by LEAA reported being victimized by robbery or purse snatching, and 23% lived in burglarized households. Thus local indirect victimization by burglary took place at more than twice the rate of direct victimization. Remember that burglary also is a crime which strikes a broad cross section of people in American society. Assaultive violence, on the other hand, is much more class-linked, and the bulk of offenses of that type strike those at the bottom of the social ladder. As we saw in the previous chapter, news of local crimes of assaultive violence are more concentrated among the less well-to-do and in poorer neighborhoods, while "vicarious victimization" by burglary is widely distributed in the community.

Figure 10.2 illustrates the differential distribution of knowledge of nearby burglary and stranger assault in these three cities. Among our respondents those in the lowest income group were more likely to know about local assaultive violence, while knowledge of burglary in the neighborhood generally rose with income. Both of these relationships are quite consistent with the distribution of victimization for these crimes (compare them to the slopes in Figure 2.1 and 2.9). They also parallel the way in which these crimes are rated as problems in the neighborhood. Family income is negatively related to reported problems with assaultive violence, while it is positively related to burglary problems. As a result of these differences in the distribution of direct and vicarious victimization, fear of crime is stimulated to at least some degree at every level of the income ladder.

Victim Proximity and Fear

While hearing about crime in the neighborhood may stimulate concern and fear, many of these stories may not seem "close to home" except in geographic proximity. Chapter 2 documented that many kinds of serious crime — and especially violent personal victimizations — do not strike everyone with the same frequency. Rather, they tend to be concentrated among young males, who often put themselves in risky situations and generally take fewer precautions than most people against crime. Blacks and the poor, people living in high-rises, and renters also are more likely than others to be victimized (U.S. Department of Justice, 1977b). If the crime stories which circulate through a neighborhood tend to follow patterns of victimization, many may continue to feel relatively immune from

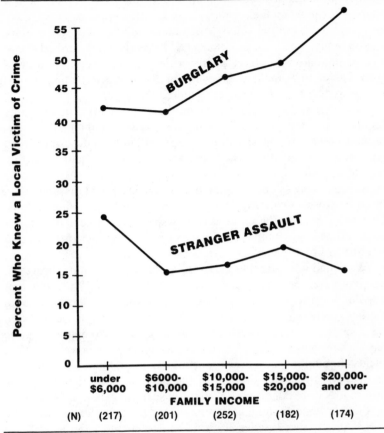

Figure 10.2 Knowledge of Local Victims of Assault and Burglary, by Income
SOURCE: Computed from combined citywide surveys.

predation. Rates of victimization for most kinds of crime usually are lower for women and older people, and those who can take precautions to protect themselves may feel relatively invulnerable regardless of local events.

This suggests that all crime stories may not be of equal import when one looks at why people assess the risks of their immediate environments in the ways they do. Knowledge that people like *themselves* were being victimized should prove most distressing to our big-city dwellers. Conklin (1975) argued that the more people "identify" with victims of highly threatening crimes the more they will do to avoid victimization. These surveys do not have measures of such identification, but hearing about crimes that happen to "other kinds of people," even when their geographical location is close, should have less impact on people than stories about victims who share their station in life. The Shotland et al. (1979) experiment described above also manipulated the descriptions of the victims in contrived news stories given to women, and they found that stories depicting victims who were like their subjects engendered more fear.

As noted in the previous chapter, there was a dramatic tendency for our respondents to recall hearing about elderly and female victims in their community. The patterns of predation they described were quite at odds with either official or survey data on the actual distribution of victimization. At the least this suggests that there is some systematic process encouraging the more widespread dissemination of crime stories involving "atypical" or sympathy-arousing victims. Other research on the content of newspaper and television stories about crime suggests that this image of victims is in accord with that put forward by the media.

We found considerable variation in these perceptions, however, and that variation was systematically related to fear. While all major population groups seem to share these erroneous opinions about victims, there was a tendency for people to hear about victims who were similar to themselves. Thus, in these data, women were more likely than men to recall hearing about women being victimized in their communities, and the proportion reporting that "older people" are victims rose with the age of the person telling the story. The differences were not dramatic. In the case of sex, about 21% of males and 15% of females thought that victims of their neighborhoods were men. Among those under 30 years of age, about 48% thought that older people were victims, while that figure rose to 55% for those in the 30-49 category and to 66% among those 50 years of age and older. The tendency of people to hear of victims who are like themselves clearly is working at the margins of whatever social processes are shewing those profiles in the direction of women and older persons, but the probability of "likes hearing about likes" persists.

The central concern for this chapter is, " Does this make people more fearful?" At the aggregate level it may be that the widespread diffusion of stories involving women and older persons as victims raises the collective level of fear, but remaining individual differences in the effect of "profile matches" should persist as well. That is, while most men think that women are the victims in their neighborhoods, those who think that the victims are males should be more fearful than others as a result. This hypothesis implies that there is a "social

TABLE 10.3   Social Proximity and Fear

Perceived Victim Profile Match With Respondent	Fear of Crime Measure– Percentage Who Feel:				
	Very Safe	Somewhat Safe	Somewhat Unsafe	Very Unsafe	(N)
None	35	41	15	9	(763)
Sex or age	20	42	18	20	(411)
Sex and age	16	34	21	28	(162)
Gamma = .32					

SOURCE: Computed from combined three-city surveys.

proximity" as well as a "geographical proximity" dimension to crime stories which affects their impact on recipients of the message.

In order to examine this social proximity hypothesis we matched each respondent against his or her description of victims in their neighborhood. In the case of age, persons were scored in the "younger" category if they were under 30, and in the "older" group if they were 50 or older. Then, it was determined whether or not the respondents' descriptions of local victims matched their personal age and sex proviles. People only were matched when they chose an unequivocal victim profile (not "both sexes," or "combinations of ages," or "children"); otherwise they remained in the "not matched" pool. As a result, each respondent could resemble victims as they saw them in their vicinities in age *and* sex, they could match them on one of the two attributes, or they could resemble them in neither way. Across the three cities, 57% of our respondents did not at all resemble their images of victims, while 12% did so on both dimensions.

Table 10.3 reports upon the relationship between demographic similarity to victims and fear of crime. The two are moderately related, with the proportion in the "very unsafe" category rising by a factor of three across the three categories. As people more closely resemble their images of local victims, they are more fearful of crime.

One important characteristic of this social proximity effect is that it is extremely robust. It persists among males and females; an age match alone has the hypothesized effect. It persists as well when we control for age. In addition, in multivariate analyses it remains significant even when other important predictors of fear are taken into account. When entered in a multiple regression analysis with other demographic factors, it proved more important than either income or race in predicting fear. It also was independent of how many local victims people knew, and of what kind of crimes. The extent to which "people like me" are victimized in the vicinity seems to be an important component in the dynamics of fear.

Media Exposure and Fear

As we noted at the outset, there is relatively little research on the relationship between media exposure and fear. The bulk of media-related studies have dwelled upon the effect of television on predispositions toward committing crime. Chapter 8 reported that the media tend to exaggerate the relative frequency of violent crime. Surveys in 26 cities in fact suggest that many people (about 40%) tend to think that "crime is *more* serious than newspapers and TV say," and few (less than 10%) think that it is less serious (Garofalo, 1977a). Surveys by Conklin (1971) found no relationship between television or newspaper attentiveness and either perceptions of crime rates or fear of crime. On the other hand, Gerbner and Gross (1976) found that heavy viewers of television (those who watched four hours a day or more) were more likely than light viewers (two hours or less) to think they would become involved in violence. The most recent study of the problem (Doob and MacDonald, 1979) reports mixed results, but concludes that among people living in high crime areas of Toronto (where the threat of victimization presumably is real) television viewing is substantially correlated with levels of fear. If such effects were more general, indirect victimization via the media might explain the high levels of fear in many segments of the population not particularly plagued by crime. As we also saw above, fictional and even news accounts of violent crime tend to picture it striking people at the middle and top of the economic and social ladder more frequently than it actually does. Thus the bulk of the population (which is white and middle income) might be more likely to gain the impression that "people like them" are victimized through media sources than through either direct or indirect personal experiences. If the media have any effect, then the fears of the general population should be more closely related to the media's mapping of crime than to the actual distribution of ebents. Further, Tyler (1978) reports that crime stories in the media that people remember (presumably those that affect them the most) are more serious than those they directly experience, perhaps further enhancing their effect.

Turning first to the influence of television, there is a moderate relationship between exposure to television news (on the previous night) and reports of fear. The correlation (gamma) between these two

TABLE 10.4   Analysis of Media Impact on Fear

| Personal Attributes and Media Measure | Relation to Fear of Crime Measure | | | |
| | Viewing News on Television | | Reading of Crime in Newspaper | |
	Beta	(Significance)	Beta	(Significance)
Media contact	.03	(.23-ns)	.02	(.55-ns)
Sex (female)	.27	(.01+)	.27	(.01+)
Age	.23	(.01+)	.23	(.01+)
Race (Black)	.10	(.01+)	.10	(.01+)
Education	−.07	(.02)	−.07	(.01)
$R^2 = .18$				
$N = 1151$				

NOTE: Direction of coding independent variables given in parentheses. Analysis of variance indicates there is no significant statistical interaction among these independent variables affecting the dependent variable, fear.

SOURCE: Computed from combined citywide surveys.

measures was +.14, with about 6 percentqge points differentiating viewers and nonviewers in both the "very unsafe" and "very safe" categories. However, television viewing is also related to several measures of personal and social vulnerability to crime, principally age and education, and more weakly to sex and race. The elderly in particular report substantial levels of television viewing and high levels of fear; more educated persons, on the other hand, watch less television and recall fewer victimizations from robbery, rape, and purse snatching. This raises the question of whether or not the observed relationship between television viewing and fear is a spurious one. The kinds of people who watch television may also be more fearful, but for other reasons. Thus we attempt to ferret out the incremental effect of television news, taking those known correlates of the two into account.

With these data this can only be done using statistical techniques. The most credible examination of the problem would employ an experimental design, randomizing people into viewing and nonviewing groups in order to control for the possible "self-selection" of more fearful persons into the high viewing category. Here we can only control for our measures of personal and social vulnerability and observe whether or not recent exposure to television news and reading about crime is independently related to our measure of fear. The results of this analysis are presented in Table 10.4.

Table 10.4 indicates that recent exposure to television news was unrelated to fear when other factors are taken into account. Its relative impact on fear was very small (reflected in the beta weight, or standardized regression coefficient) and was statistically insignificant. A parallel analysis (not shown) of the relationship between viewing dramatic television productions and fear revealed the same findings. There was no independent effect of recently tuning in "cops and robbers" shows on expressions of fear of crime. A close examination of the data indicated that the effect of controlling for age was especially important in this analysis. Age is the strongest correlate of television viewing, and it consistently is the second strongest correlate (after gender) of fear. Among the elderly, 73% reported watching television the previous evening, and 59% said they watched television news. The comparable figures for all others were 59% and 39%, respectively. However, within each of seven standard age categories television viewing was unrelated to fear — except among those over 60. People in this group accounted for most of the correlation between television news consumption and fear. Among the elderly watching television was positively and significantly related (gamma = +.24) to fear. There was no evidence of statistical interaction between age and exposure to television, but this doubtless is worth pursuing in the future. Otherwise, we can discern no independent effect of television viewing on fear.

Table 10.4 also reports the results of a regression analysis of the relationship between attentiveness to crime in the newspapers and fear. A simple cross tabulation of these variables does not reveal even a slim connection between the two. In the "very unsafe" category readers and nonreaders differed by only one percentage point, and those who recalled reading about a crime in the newspapers actually were more likely than others to think they were "very unsafe."

This lack of a relationship also may be spurious. In this case, factors which are positively related to newspaper exposure generally are negatively related to fear. Males, whites, more educated respondents, and those in higher income categories were more likely to report reading a crime story the previous day, and they are, as a group, less fearful than most. However, controlling for indicators of personal and social vulnerability did not strengthen this association. It can be observed in Table 10.4 that newspaper attentiveness and fear are virtually unrelated when we controlled for those factors, and an examination of the relation between this form of media exposure and fear in many demographic subgroups did not reveal any significant linkages between the two. The situation is not improved by taking television and newspaper exposure into account together, nor by examining their cumulative interactive effect. The results of the two regression analyses presented in Table 10.4 are virtually identical, for both measures of media involvement have about the same mean and standard deviation. They also point toward the same substantive conclusion: There is no evidence here of any relation between media attentiveness and fear of crime.

Vulnerability and the Impact of Indirect Victimization

While the relation between vulnerability and fear of crime appears to be straightforward, there still is the possibility that differences in the potential impact of crime or in the threat of crime in their environments might heighten certain people's sensitivity to stories about crimes and victims. Those who are more vulnerable to crime may be more sensitive to messages which are discounted by people who are (or feel) more insulated from crime and its consequences. Residents of these cities who are socially more vulnerable suffer higher rates of victimization, and presumably stories about crimes or contact with victims will have concrete implications for their possible fates. Doob and MacDonald (1979) found that television viewing was related positively to fear only in higher crime areas of Toronto. They argued that media messages had an impact in these areas because the risk of actual victimization was high. By extension, it is quite possible that women and the elderly, who are extremely vulnerable to the potential consequences of victimization and who generally have more difficulty warding off attack when it occurs, would be more responsive to personal or media messages about crime. When they "get the word" they should feel more unsafe than their counterparts.

The city survey data can be employed to test the hypothesis that among people who are more vulnerable reports of indirect victimization will be related to an additional increment of fear. Statistically it is a statement about interaction between measures of vulnerability and victim or media contact as they affect fear. An examination of the data for residents of these three cities failed to find any support for this notion. Recalling a crime story was positively related to fear, but that relation was constant among more vulnerable and less vulnerable groups. Neither were there significant interactions between knowledge of a local crime victim, viewing television news, or reading of crime in the paper and the vulnerability of our respondents. Two interactions were noticeably stronger than others observed in this analysis. There was a tendency for older people and Blacks who knew victims to be more fearful than they "should have been" based upon those factors taken separately. These are indicators of different dimensions of vulnerability, and although their impact was not very strong (all of the interactions together added only 0.3% to the explained variance), they probably are worthy of further investigation.

A direct replication of Doob and MacDonald's (1979) Toronto study also failed to reveal any impact of neighborhood crime conditions on the relationship between media consumption and fear of crime. In these cities there was no significant statistical interaction between television viewing or reading of crime in the newspaper and the scale measuring assessments of local crime conditions. This was true controlling for the age, sex, race, and educational covariates of fear and television or newspaper attentiveness, and it was also the case when we examined media influences and crime conditions in isolation. There was no strong tendency for people in more problem-prone areas to be more affected by media messages concerning crime.

Summary of Part III

In this section we have demonstrated that some forms of vicarious experience with crime have a significant impact upon the distribution of fear in great cities. Unlike direct victimization, indirect exposure to crime is frequent and relatively widespread. We have examined two very different sources of information about crime: the mass media and personal communications among neighbors and others. Although the sources are different, the content of these communications is similar. The message is one of violence directed at atypical victims, whether people learn about crime from the media or from each other. These images of crime and the means by which they are disseminated are important because of their content, their frequency, and their impact on urban residents.

Our examination of newspaper stories about crime in three cities echoes the findings of others with respect to the nature of the message. Media images of crime focus on the most violent events, particularly those directed at what we have identified as vulnerable groups in the population. Furthermore, the message does not vary much in newspapers within a city, or between the three cities, for that matter. People who read newspapers are exposed to very similar doses of information about violent crime. Some respondents also depend upon television to learn about crime. Once again, the image of violence is broadcast, and although fewer stories about crime are presented in a typical newscast, crime represents a larger proportion of the total news product. TV viewers and newspaper readers are different people, but because the message carried by each medium is similar, consumers of these different media learn essentially the same stories.

Urban residents also learn about crime from each other, and again the stories which are told concentrate on crimes of violence. However, personal communication about crime differs from mass media images in one important respect: Talking to others is a source of information about crime in one's own neighborhood. The message here is also widely spread, but people in different areas hear about crime stories for different reasons. Talk about crime is found in high and low crime neighborhoods alike, but as a result of different social and communication processes.

Knowing crime victims is related to higher levels of fear, particularly when those events occur close to home. People who had contact with victims of personal predatory crime were most affected. On the other hand, knowledge of burglary victims was more common than knowledge of the less frequent personal crime. As a result the telling of tales about burglary appears to have had the greatest effect on fear in these three cities. In addition, burglary strikes both at the top and the bottom of the social hierarchy, and as a result produces a more egalitarian distribution of fear in American society. Social as well as geographic proximity plays an important role in shaping reactions to crime. When the respondents thought that victims of crime in their area were people like themselves they were more frightened.

We found no systematic evidence of the effects of more impersonal sources of crime information. Like Tyler (1978), Hansen and Donoghue (1977), and others, we find that media exposure had little effect on assessments of personal safety.

This may contravene a great deal of common wisdom on the role of the media in provoking fear of crime, but a careful reading of the research literature on the subject does not reveal convincing evidence of any stronger linkage between media exposure and fear. In fact, many pronouncements on the subject have been based upon the inability of researchers to find other explanations for widely dispersed levels of fear in American cities. Because the distribution of fear more closely resembles the distribution of attentiveness to television than it does actual victimization, there is a tendency to infer an association between TV viewing and fear of crime.

However, the weak effects of television reported in the few empirical studies of the impact of the media have led others to reconceptualize the issue. Gerbner and Gross (1975) argue that television may

have so radically affected our culture that everyone is different because of it, and that this "washes out" differences at the margin
between individuals. Because the cultural symbols communicated by
television are so widely shared, there is little variance in the population on these matters, and as a result the effects of television are both
ubiquitous and untestable. While this is an ingenious effort to salvage
something from a collection of weak research findings, we prefer the
explanation that people look to sources of information which are more
personal and close to home for guidance in making judgements about
how crime affects their lives. This is certainly in accord with our
findings. When people hear about nearby events, and when they think
the victims are "people like them," they are afraid. For everyone who
is affected by images of crime disseminated by the media we suspect
that there are many others who believe, like the young robbery victim
who told Charles Silberman (1978: 12) of her experience, "this kind of
thing happens on television, but not in real life."

PART IV

THE NEIGHBORHOOD AS A LOCUS FOR ACTION

This section focuses in turn on four reactions to crime. Chapter 11 examines the tactics that individuals employ in their own neighborhoods to protect themselves from personal harm. The next explores the way in which city dwellers fortify their homes against intruders, mobilize their neighbors to deter suspicious persons, and insure themselves against loss. Chapter 13 details patterns of participation in organizations which are attempting to do something about neighborhood crime. The final chapter profiles those who have taken the option of moving to the suburbs, and examines the role of central-city crime in precipitating that flight.

Chapter 11

PERSONAL PRECAUTION

Introduction

Preceding chapters examined how city residents learn about crime, how they assess their neighborhood conditions, and how these factors — along with their victimization experiences and vulnerability — are translated into fear of crime. Now we turn our attention to what people do about the problem. Part IV is concerned with the range of strategies they adopt to limit their chances of becoming crime victims, to minimize their losses if they are victimized, and to reduce crime in their communities. This chapter examines the particular kinds of precautions that people take in the face of personal crime: to limit their exposure to risk and to adopt tactics to reduce the level of these risks when they are exposed to threat.

The changing of one's activities to deal with personal threats is perhaps the most thoroughly researched behavior concerning crime. In Biderman's report to the Crime Commission he and his associates examined behavioral changes in response to crime, including staying off of city streets entirely (Biderman et al., 1967). In his inventory of responses to crime, Conklin (1975) includes reducing contact with other people, especially strangers. Studies of the elderly indicate that "not going out" is a very common description of their behavior. Rifai (1976) and Lawton et al. (1976) report that between 69% and 89% of those over 65 years of age say they never go out at night. Gordon et al. (1980) asked a sample of women about how often they found themselves in 12 common situations (for example, "home alone after dark") and how worried they were in these situations. The two sets of responses were strongly negatively correlated. On the other hand, Hindelang et al. (1978) concluded that most people do not alter their behavior drastically in response to crime; rather, they subtly change the way in which they do things, the manner in which they conduct themselves in public places, and the time of day when they go out, in order to reduce their frequency of exposure to what they perceive to be the threat of crime. In LEAA's victimization surveys in these cities, 48% of respondents reported limiting their activity due to crime, and 68% thought that their neighbors had done so.

We are interested in how crime and people's perceptions of crime affect the way in which individuals structure their lives. Interestingly, in these cities doing something about crime was much more frequent than reports of fear or pessimistic assessments of the magnitude of the crime problem. People in 96% of the households we interviewed reported taking at least one action against burglars, yet only 19% reported that burglary was a "big problem" in their neighborhoods. Almost 60% of those who were questioned indicated that they had adopted at least one tactic to reduce their chances of victimization from personal attack in their neighborhoods, although only one-third of them reported feeling at all unsafe there, even after dark. More than one-quarter reported severely limiting their exposure to risk, staying indoors after dark every night. When questioned about their participation in community life, over one-third of our respondents indicated that they had gotten together with neighbors about local problems, and 20% had been involved in a neighborhood organization. Somewhat fewer (13%) were active in a group that did something about crime, and 10% were themselves involved in those efforts.

Those who are fearful presumably will be most inclined to take extra steps to protect themselves. It is widely believed that fear of crime has enormous consequences for the way we live (Rosenthal, 1969). Urban dwellers are reported to be "prisoners of fear," barricaded behind doors and unwilling to risk any but the most necessary excursions. On the other hand, DuBow's (1979) review of studies of the problem reports mixed findings with respect to the influence of perceptions of crime on behavior.

People most frequently report staying away from dangerous areas. When pressed on that category they nominate parks (Kleinman and David, 1973; Malt Associates, 1971), subways (Savitz et al., 1977), underground parking areas, and downtown (Zion, 1978; Institute for Social Research, 1975). Among the least frequent strategies for dealing with personal crime seems to be that of carrying a weapon. In a study of high crime areas in Hartford, Mangione and Noble (1975) found that less than 10% of respondents recalled "taking something with them for protection" when they went out. Kleinman and David (1973) report that 14% of Bedford-Stuyvesant area residents in New York City said they carried a gun when they went out. In this survey a substantial proportion (about 60%) of our respondents reported taking simple precautionary measures against personal victimization, and more did single things to protect themselves from burglary. They did not seem to be completely immobilized in the face of crime, nor did crime cause them to fortify their homes at great cost in terms of dollars and opportunities foregone.

There is no consistent evidence that concern about crime is directly taking its toll by excessively restricting the behavior of large numbers of residents even in high crime areas. In a report to the President's Commission on Law Enforcement and Administration of Justice, Ennis (1967) concluded that people were more likely to take security measures when they perceived high levels of risk of robbery and burglary, and when they specifically expressed fear. Ennis's index of security precautions was based on a number of different types of protective behavior, including locking doors at night, having a watchdog, keeping firearms for protection, staying off the streets, and insuring one's life and property. Reiss's (1967) analysis of two neighborhoods in Boston and Chicago indicated that similar kinds of protective behaviors were common in neighborhoods with high levels of fear. However, Biderman's analysis of crime and its effects in the District of Columbia did not find the same relationships between fear, concern, and security measures that were uncovered in the national survey conducted by Ennis (Biderman et al., 1967). Ennis found some relationship between fear and property protection, while Biderman concluded that fear of crime only affected the steps individuals take to reduce their chances of personal attack. Corrado et al. (1980) find that levels of fear of crime are almost as high in metropolitan Vancouver as they are in American cities, despite the fact that victimization rates there are generally much lower than comparable figures from below the border.

It is also apparent that human activity is not always based upon simple calculations of the costs and benefits of actions aimed at a particular problem. Opportunities and constraints unrelated to the problem at hand shape how people react to crime. These forces derive from the social and economic structure. People do some things, and do not do others, almost regardless of their desires and often in the face of their fears, when those constraints are strong. Some must go out at dangerous times or to dangerous places because of work or social demands, while others may never be exposed to risk because they are physically incapacitated. The National Council on Aging (1978) reports that nearly one-half of those over 65 years of age suffer some limitation of activity due to chronic health conditions; of that group, 40% are at least partially immobilized. Some who would prefer not to use public transportation because of concern about crime may not have that choice. Not everyone has equal access to an automobile, a problem shared by the elderly and younger persons. The expectations of others based upon social role, the strictures of race and class, the discipline of the time clock, the demands of family life, and neighborhood customs and physical design all shape what we can and cannot do about crime. A model of crime-related behavior faithful to life must take these exogenous factors into account.

Personal Caution and Exposure to Risk

One striking finding of this research is the large proportion of city residents who habitually do simple, routine things that may have the effect of reducing their chances of being assaulted or robbed. These things fall into two categories: actions people take to limit their exposure to risk in the first place, and tactics they adopt when they are exposed to threat which may reduce their chances of being attacked. Suttles (1972) has pointed out that these both are characteristic ways in which urban swellers find security. He found that in a high crime neighborhood residents tended to segregate their activities in time and space to avoid particularly risky circumstances. They developed "street sense" about when to go out, where they could go, and appropriate precautions to take in dangerous situations. As a result, residents of the area could coexist with crime and contending social groups, creating order and reducing their chances of victimization in a potentially threatening environment.

One reaction to crime, and to other real or imagined threats, is to stay home. Generally people feel safest at home, the place to which they can withdraw in time of stress.

> Housing as an element of material culture has as its prime purpose
> . . . protection from potentially damaging or unpleasant trauma.
> . . . The most primitive evaluation of housing, therefore, has to do
> with the question of how adequately it shelters the individuals who
> abide in it from threats in their environment [Rainwater, 1966: 23].

Many fewer threatening things occur at home. There people are safe from chills, automobile accidents, and attacks by strangers. Data from the victimization surveys suggest the significance of that protection: Nationally, only about 8% of all robberies and 5% of all assaults by strangers were described by victims as taking place "at home" (U.S. Department of Justice, 1977b).

Many people are concerned primarily about limiting their exposure to risk after dark, although differences in crime rates between day and night are less substantial than locational differences. About 63% of all rapes and 54% of all robberies and assaults by strangers took place at night, according to their victims. Most common at night are robberies resulting in serious physical injuries, and robberies and assaults involving the use of guns (U.S. Department of Justice, 1977b). Police reports indicate even a greater concentration of violent crime during the after-dark hours (Hindelang et al., 1978).

The day-night distinction is in accord with people's expressed fears. Popular attention is fixed upon after-dark dangers. In the Census Bureau's surveys in the nation's five largest cities, for example, only 11% indicated that they felt any degree of danger in their neighborhoods during the day, as contrasted to 48% after dark.

At one extreme, limiting one's exposure to risk may entail almost complete withdrawal from public life. For example, in the literature on crime among the elderly this is known as the "prisoners of fear" phenomenon. Many argue that few seniors are victimized by personal crime because they do not often expose themselves to attack; rather, they remain at home, behind locked doors, in fear for their lives (see Antunes et al., forthcoming).

In an interview with a police captain in Philadelphia we heard a most extreme example of this:

> As far as victimization, I got a call today. There's a mother and daughter in Wynnefield living in a 15-room house. They're barricaded in the bedroom and claimed they had 5 locks on the door. We found only 3 locks. They want a full time policeman out there. They offered to pay us to provide a full time policeman [West Philadelphia, July 13, 1977].

In addition to limiting their exposure to risk by staying home (or enjoying the same effect when immobilized for other reasons), people can deal with the threat of personal attack by acting judiciously when they are exposed to potential danger. A survey in Baltimore found that 40% of those interviewed had taken taxicabs or driven in their own cars somewhere because they were afraid to walk there (DuBow, 1979). Most people may adapt to prevailing levels of danger by adjusting their daily routines to bring their risk of victimization within acceptable bounds. They instinctively avoid places or persons they think are dangerous, walk in groups, and avoid using public transportation. In any case, they proceed about their business and carry on with their lives.

Avoiding dangerous places was a strategy which was mentioned frequently in field interviews. A woman in Wicker Park described her accommodation to crime:

> I have lived here all of my life. It is really dangerous around Pulaski Park. There are a lot of gangs and gang fights. I don't go into that neighborhood now. I used to walk there all the time. . . . I don't know it anymore. I feel uncomfortable and afraid. My neighborhood now is from Milwaukee to Armitage. I walk there all the time. I guess someone coming in might feel strange here. I feel strange in other neighborhoods [Wicker Park, July 1976].

Most surveys indicate that taking precautions against victimization is very common. In the 26 cities surveyed for LEAA by the Census Bureau almost 50% of those questioned indicated that they had changed or limited their activities because of crime. In surveys of high crime areas in three cities, Reiss (1967) found that 60% reported such behavior changes. On the other hand, in a study in Portland only 20% reported changing their behavior due to crime (DuBow, 1979).

It seems that people adopt these strategies in part because they are easier and cheaper than doing more fundamental things about crime. When asked about the causes of crime, people rate programs and activities aimed at reducing crime through attacking its causes as ultimately having more impact than simply doing things to protect themselves. At the same time, they think that taking steps to reduce their own victimization is practical and simple. Although they believe thtat crime is caused by broken families, poverty, and drug dependence, what they do about it is to stay indoors. And the less control they think they have over the incidence of crime, the more they adopt a personal crime-avoidance stance toward it (Cohn, 1978).

One of the goals of our three-city survey was to assess the frequency with which people take precautions to avoid personal victimization. Our respondents were quizzed about four particular tactics: going out by car rather than walking, going out with someone else, avoiding "certain places" in the neighborhood, and "taking something with you . . . like a dog, whistle, knife, or gun." They were asked if they did these things "most of the time," "sometimes," or "almost never." Because other surveys found that few people take substantial precautions against crime during the daylight hours we added the phrase "at night" to each item. The question also indicated that we were interested in these things if they were done "because of crime." This recognizes that, for example, people may drive because there is nothing nearby to walk to, and couples may habitually go out

TABLE 11.1   Precautionary Behavior and Exposure to Risk

| City | *Percentage Who Do It "Most of Time" After Dark* | | | | | |
	Drive Not Walk	*Take An Escort*	*Avoid Places*	*Take Something*	*Percentage Who Did Not Go Out At All*	*(N)*
Chicago	52	28	31	22	28	(408)
Philadelphia	50	30	25	23	27	(444)
San Francisco	44	26	23	14	23	(481)
(Significance of Differences)	(.02)	(.15)	(.01+)	(.01+)	(.17)	
Average	48	28	26	19	26	(1333)

NOTE: Number of cases varies somewhat from behavior to behavior; averages are given here.
SOURCE: Computed from citywide surveys.

together. It should be noted that these strategies all would serve to reduce victimization in nearby public places. Thus they specifically relate to reducing the risk of personal and potentially violent confrontations with non-family members, presumably strangers, but close to home.

Table 11.1 presents city-by-city accounts of the proportion of our informants who indicated that they did each of these things "most of the time." By far the most common risk-reduction strategy adopted by residents of these cities was to go out by car rather than walk at night. Almost 50% of those questioned indicated that they did this "most of the time." About one in four indicated that they frequently went out with other people and avoided certain places in their neighborhoods because of crime, and one in five usually "took something" (a euphemism we employed to grant anonymity to gun users) when they went out at night. There was considerable overlap in these efforts to avoid victimization. In all, 33% of our respondents reported doing two or more of these things most of the time, 27% one of them, and 40% none of them.

In order to judge their exposure to risk we asked our respondents:

> During the past week, about how many times did you leave your home and go outside after dark?

About 40% of the respondents recalled going out four or more times during that period, indicating considerable nocturnal mobility. On the other hand, one-quarter of them indicated that they did not go out at all. This proportion is given for each city in Table 11.1. In every case exposure to risk was highest and precautionary behavior was least frequent among San Franciscans, but these city differences were not significant.

There were generally few differences in the precautionary activities of residents of Philadelphia and Chicago; the bulk of the intercity differences recorded in Table 11.1 stem from the less cautious stance of San Franciscans vis-à-vis the world. They were significantly less likely to report driving, avoiding areas in their vicinities, and carrying something with them because of crime. When asked how often they had gone out after dark during the previous week, San Franciscans also reported doing so more frequently. Interestingly, rates of violent and predatory crime were higher there than in the other two cities. If the opposite side of precaution is the creation of opportunities for criminals, San Franciscans were consistent in their position on both measures. While victims in LEAA's surveys were more likely than nonvictims to report changing their behavior because of crime, in the place where people were least cautious they also reported the highest rate of crime.

Most of the differences between San Francisco and our other two cities can be attributed to its racial composition. The correlation between race and these measures of precautionary behavior was substantial; only 21% of whites, but 32% of Blacks, reported that they did not go out at all after dark in their neighborhoods during the week before our interviews. When we control for the demographic makeup of our three city samples, city differences in precautionary behavior virtually disappear. The only visible "effect" of city which remains affects the elderly. Controlling for all other factors, there was a significant (and strong — more substantial than the main effect of income) tendency for older respondents in San Francisco to report taking more precautions. For this group, which in Chapter 2 we also identified as being particularly victimized by street crime only a few years before, levels of caution were high.

Among individuals, exposure to risk was low and avoidance measures generally were adopted more frequently by the same groups who indicated that violent and predatory crime was a big problem: women, Blacks, and the poor. Senior citizens who indicated that they went out at night during the previous week were not particularly likely to report adopting any of these strategies, but almost two-thirds of them indicated that they did not go out at all during that period. In the study neighborhoods, the areas in which the largest proportion of residents indicated that they restricted their activity also were those that reported the worst problems with personal crimes: Woodlawn and Wicker Park in Chicago, and Visitacion Valley in San Francisco.

Responses to three of these measures of risk avoidance covaried in consistent fashion. At the neighborhood level (N = 10) all four were correlated an average of +.60, and driving and walking with an escort were correlated +.87. Precautionary behavior was a highly neighborhood-related phenomenon. At the individual level, however, responses to the question concerning "taking something with you" were not strongly related to the remainder, and did not vary much. Positive answers to this question could indicate any of a range of reactions to crime, from carrying a whistle to walking a dog or packing a gun, and it is conceptually distinct from the other items as well. A positive response indicates an aggressive stance in the face of attack, not one which avoids or evades a confrontation in the first place. Consider the notes of a field interviewer who talked to three older Black men in Woodlawn about this issue:

> I then asked them . . . what type of precautions do they hopefully take to prevent their victimization. Two of the men said they carry guns. I asked if they feel secure about carrying guns. They told me yes, that the way things are nowadays, the way how people are desperate, that you'd be crazy not to carry some type of gun. . . . Nobody cares about nobody. You care about yourself and if you plan to walk the streets at night you should have some type of protection. . . . So he said he carried a gun because he didn't want nobody ripping him off and he had no intention of letting anybody get to him [Woodlawn, August 1977].

One-third of the survey respondents indicated that they did "take something" at least on occasion, but we do not know what that was. We will not analyze responses to this question in detail, except to note that in every case they follow the pattern of relationships suggested by our remaining measures of behavior. When we excluded responses to this item, and rescored a few respondents who insisted that they did not take precautions because they "never went out," responses to the remainder of these questions formed an additive scale with a reliability of .67. A factor analysis indicated that responses to the three items were unidimensional. This indicates that the bulk of our respondents replied consistently to the items, and that a summary score can be used to represent the precautions they reported taking. The mean score of this scale was 1.8, meaning that the average respondent took precaution against personal attack slightly less frequently than "sometimes." This summary measure will be used below to explore the behavioral consequences of fear of crime.

Fear, Local Conditions, and Personal Precaution

Research on personal precautionary behavior suggests that fear of crime, perceptions of crime problems, and experiences with victimization all should be strongly associated with those activities. Surveys in several cities have shown a strong positive correlation between measures of fear and indicators of risk avoidance tactics (Savitz et al., 1977; Maxfield, 1977; Hindelang et al., 1978). Reporting carrying a gun is positively related to fear and perceived risk of victimization (Frisbie et al., 1977), despite the fact that higher rates of gun ownership are reported by upper-income groups, who generally are less fearful (Wright and Marston, 1975).

This analysis focuses upon attitudes, perceptions, and self-reports of behavior in a neighborhood context. The measure of fear refers specifically to being "afraid to walk in the neighborhood at night," and the measure of risk avoidance is based upon reports of things people do to protect themselves from crime in their neighborhoods. These are conceptually distinct and behavior is presumed to be causally dependent upon assessments of things that could occur. Hindelang et al. (1978: 205-206) argue that fear is strongly related to behavior because fear and behavior indicators actually are both measures of fear of crime: "the question about how safe respondents feel about being alone in their neighborhood at night is an affective indicator of fear, while the personal limiting of activity item can be construed . . . as a behavioral indicator of fear." We prefer to maintain a conceptual distinction between fear and behavior, in part because some features of people's lives affect their behavior independently of their assessments of risk, and despite their fears.

Table 11.2 presents the relationship between our indicators of fear and local crime conditions and two measures of behavioral responses to the threat of personal attack. Fear is substantially related to limiting exposure to risk (a correlation of $-.36$ with the number of times respondents went out after dark during the previous week) and reports of precautionary risk-avoidance tactics (.50). As expected, assessments of local conditions were less strongly related to reports of behavior but all were linked in the expected fashion. In our general operating model, neighborhood conditions were hypothesized to affect behavior through their effect upon fear. This expectation implies that the zero-order relationships should be lower for these causally more distant indicators.

TABLE 11.2   Fear, Local Conditions, and Caution

Fear and Local Conditions	Correlation With:		
	Exposure to Risk	Personal Caution	(N)
Fear	−.36	.50	(1318)
Neighborhood crime conditions	−.13	.23	(1337)
Local order problems	−.05	.16	(1343)

NOTE: Correlations are Pearson's r. All are significant (p < .05). Number of cases varies slightly; averages are given here.

SOURCE: Computed from combined citywide surveys.

Inspection of the data in detail suggests that these relationships all were relatively linear, except in the highest categories. Fear and assessments of the extent of major crime problems were more strongly related to behavior in the "highest fear" and "biggest problem" categories. In the case of exposure to risk, mobility dropped from an average of 4.8 trips to 1.4 trips after dark between the highest and the lowest fear groups, while the average precaution score nearly doubled.

A multivariate regression analysis (not shown) indicates that all of the effects of our measures of neighborhood conditions were mediated by fear. Assessments of neighborhood crime and social-order problems all affected individual precaution through their impact upon personal assessments of danger. When people felt that events and conditions in their communities could affect them, they responded by reducing their exposure to those threats and moving more circumspectly through their environments.

Personal Vulnerability and Precaution

Every analysis of crime-related behavior indicates that women and the elderly are more likely to avoid exposure to risk and to take numerous measures to reduce their chances of being victimized (Biderman et al., 1967; Kleinman and David, 1973; Rifai, 1976; Garofalo, 1977b). In both cases, inability to ward off attacks by young males and potentially severe consequences of victimization seem to lead them to take more extreme measures to avoid criminal confrontations. And, in each case, these factors are used to explain why they apparently experience low rates of actual victimizations (Cook et al., forthcoming; Riger and Gordon, 1979).

Earlier chapters have argued that race and income are useful indicators of propinquity to high crime areas and objectively high

TABLE 11.3   Vulnerability and Precautionary Behavior

| Vulnerability | Correlation With: | | |
	Exposure to Risk	Personal Caution	(N)
Physical			
Female	−.29	.41	(1348)
Old age	−.31	.25	(1256)
Social			
Low Income	−.18	.19	(1040)
Black	−.09	.17	(1238)

NOTE: Correlations are Pearson's r, which is employed because the dependent measures are not categorical. All correlations are significant (p < .05). Number of cases varies somewhat; averages are given here.

SOURCE: Computed from combined citywide surveys.

risks of victimization in American cities. Blacks and the poor are more likely to be victimized by personal theft and aggravated assault in two of these cities, and in the nation as a whole. Age and sex reflect differences in physical vulnerability to attack and in the consequences of victimizatoin.

The relationship between each of these indicators of vulnerability and reports of exposure to risk and risk avoidance is presented in Table 11.3. Those correlations all are significant, and most are substantial. The survey reports on which they are based indicate that men went out after dark an average of 1.8 times per week more often than women (an average total for men of 4.4 trips during the week before the interview). Those over 50 years old reported 2.2 fewer trips per week than did their younger counterparts. Similar differences could be observed in the magnitude of age and sex differences in the adoption of risk-avoidance tactics.

A major feature of these indicators is that by and large they are unrelated to one another. There was a slight tendency for women to be older than men and to report lower family incomes, and Blacks reported lower incomes. Thus the effects of social and physical vulnerability could be cumulative, predicting ever higher levels of precautionary behavior among successively more vulnerable groups. An examination of the data suggested that this was the case. For example, the least vulnerable group — young, white, middle-income males — reported going out after dark an average of 4.6 times during the previous week, while older, poor, Black women recalled an average of only three-tenths of one trip. A multivariate regression analysis (not shown) indicated that sex, age, and (to a lesser extent) race each played an important role in shaping exposure to risk and precaution-

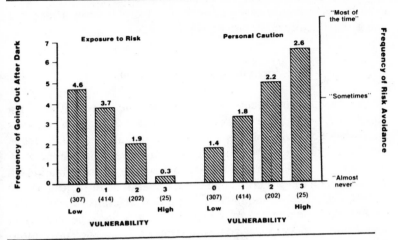

Figure 11.1   Vulnerability and Precautionary Behavior
SOURCE: Computed from combined citywide surveys.

ary tactics, but that once these had been taken into account the effects of income were insignificant. If both race and income truly reflect neighborhood differences in crime-adaptive behavior, one would expect this to occur.

As a result, we will explore in more detail only the age, sex, and race correlates of precautionary behavior. That regression analysis indicated that they were related to each of the specific tactics examined here in somewhat different ways. The strongest determinant of exposure to risk was age, with the elderly being the least likely to report going out after dark. Women reported going out somewhat more frequently, but were much more likely than even the elderly to report high levels of caution in public places. Race was the least important of these factors, and was more substantially related to personal caution than to sheer exposure to risk. In general, physical vulnerability was more important than social vulnerability in determining what steps people took to protect themselves. This is, of course, consistent with our earlier findings regarding fear.

The "stair-step," cumulative effect of vulnerability on personal precaution is illustrated in Figure 11.1. There each respondent was scored in terms of their vulnerability, based upon age, sex, and race. At the low end of the vulnerability continuum (with a score of three) are older black females. Figure 11.1 graphs the relation between group vulnerability rankings and their exposure to risk (the average number of times they went out after dark in the previous week), and their average reported frequency of taking personal precautionary measures. In each case successively more vulnerable groups reported taking significantly more preventive actions.

Victimization and Precaution

Research on the effects of victimization suggests that personal experience with crime and close association with crime victims should have considerable impact upon individual behavior. LeJeune and Alex (1973) describe dramatic behavioral changes among mugging victims, changes which are accompanied by transformations in their attitudes toward crime and their perceptions of it. Rifai (1976) reports a decrease in mobility among elderly victims of crime, and HEW's Safe Schools study concluded that school-age victims of assault and robbery avoided dangerous places within such institutions following their victimization. Skogan (1977b) found moderate but consistent relationships between measures of victimization and crime-related behavior in the National Crime Survey's city studies. In contrast, studies in Philadelphia and Baltimore uncovered no relationship between victimization and reports of subsequent behavior even when serious crimes were involved (Savitz et al., 1977; Furstenberg, 1972). Conklin (1975) found that the relation between fear and risk avoidance was stronger when people identified with those whom they believed to be the victims of crime.

In these cities there is a persistent relationship between criminal victimization and personal precaution. Victims are more likely than nonvictims to report doing something about crime, and those who know neighborhood victims or believe that "people like them" are being attacked in their communities are more likely to report taking steps to reduce their chances of being victimized.

The effects of direct experience with crime can be documented using the victimization data gathered by the Census Bureau in these three cities. In those surveys they asked respondents sixteen years of age and older if they "had limited or changed your activities because of crime in the last few years." This is a very general indicator of the consequences of crime for individuals, but it is related in consistent fashion to a number of their personal attributes and to their past experiences with victimization.

In these analyses we limited our focus to the effects of burglary and robbery, two crimes which are substantial correlates of reports of behavior change (Skogan, 1977b) and which are fairly frequent. Contrasting victims with nonvictims, 62% of robbery victims indicated

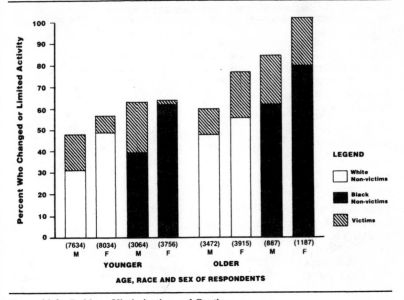

Figure 11.2   Robbery Victimization and Caution
SOURCE: Computed from combined 10% random samples of Census Bureau city victimization surveys.

they had changed their activity because of crime, as compared to only 47% of nonvictims. In the case of burglary the differences were slim — 52% and 47%, respectively. Victimization, by both robbery and burglary, is also related to other characteristics of individuals and households which affect behavior (as described in Chapter 2), but controlling for these revealed that the apparent effect of both types of victimization on behavior remained strong, or even increased. Figure 11.2 illustrates the added "behavioral increment" that might be attributed to robbery victimization in several population groups. For example, among younger white males, 31% of nonvictims but 47% of victims reported changing their activity patterns. In each subcategory victims reported doing something "because of crime" more often than did nonvictims. There was very little effect of victimization apparent among young Black women, perhaps because levels of caution among that group as a whole were already high. Among the 1187 Black women in these surveys who were sixty years of age and older, 100% of those who had been victimized (and 78% of nonvictims) reported limiting their activities due to crime.

While the impact of victimization on the subsequent behavior of those unfortunate enough to have had that experience may be sub-

TABLE 11.4   Indirect Crime Experience and Caution

Measures of Proximity of Crime Victims	Average Value Exposure to Risk (Average Times Went Out)	Personal Caution (Scale Score)	(N)
Number of local crime victims known			
0	3.3	1.8	(597)
1	3.3	1.8	(433)
2	3.6	1.9	(199)
3	3.2	2.0	(107)
4	3.3	2.1	(15)
	(r = .00)	(r = .11)	
Profile match with perceptions of local victims			
None	3.6	1.7	(773)
Age or sex	3.2	1.9	(411)
Age and sex	2.7	2.1	(163)
	(r = −.10)	(r = +.20)	

NOTE: Number of cases varies somewhat for each measure; averages are given here.

SOURCE: Computed from combined citywide surveys.

stantial, relatively few people are victimized by serious personal crimes during the course of a year. However, many more residents of big cities have indirectly experienced crime, through their personal contacts with crime victims. This vicarious experience affects their assessments of the risks they face in their communities, and its net impact on fear proved to be considerable because of the substantial proportion of people who have such contacts. Likewise, four out of every ten city residents that were interviewed resembled in some way the image (by sex and age) they held of the profile of typical victims in their community, and those who did were more fearful. In each case "victim proximity" should affect the caution that they displayed vis-à-vis crime.

The relation between indicators of these forms of "vicarious victimization" and reports of precautionary behavior is described in Table 11.4. It reports average scores on measures of exposure to risk (number of times went out after dark) and risk management (scale score) activity for various degrees of victimization. Generally, the data indicate that geographical and social proximity to victimization had only a moderate effect on the adoption of precautionary tactics, and had little effect on levels of exposure to risk. Three of four relationships were consistent, with those believing that people like them were being victimized also adopting protective measures more frequently, and going out less, and with contact with local victims being associated with more caution when out at night. As we shall see, upon controlling for fear and other important determinants of precautionary behavior, these minor effects persist. People who know of victims in their neighborhoods, or who believe that people like themselves are being victimized there, lead more circumspect lives.

Constraints on Individual Action

This discussion of precautionary activity has advanced a highly volitional model of human behavior. This volume has followed a line of empirical inquiry which assumes that people assess their environments, weigh their risks, and act on the basis of an individual calculus which accounts for those risks, discounting them by the personal costs of sacrificing autonomy. However, it is clear that people do some things, and do not do others, regardless of their intentions. Those who work the night shift must go out even if they perceive that after-dark risks in their neighborhoods are high. People who do not own a car or cannot drive must use public transportation. Any model of behavior true to social processes must account for the tendency of individuals to act on occasion in the face of fear, and must reflect the constraints which shape their behavior regardless of their fear.

These factors are exogenous to the model of crime-linked behavior outlined in Chapter 1. They are constraints because they are "outside" factors unrelated to local crime conditions and other internal, "endogenous" factors sketched in the model. In a sense these factors represent the impact of "the rest of the world" in this analysis, although we will examine only two of them.

Hindelang et al. (1978) point to two general constraints on routine daily activity. The first is that of role expectations that people hold for one another, based on their positions in the social and economic system. People in various status categories are expected to act in particular ways, and there are a host of formal and informal mechanisms which channel activity in "appropriate" directions. The second source of behavior constraint is structural; these are limits on our options which derive from the operation of institutions. Structural factors limit the range of real choices open to most people, including where they will live and work. Together, the authors argue, institutional constraints and the expectations of others shape to a considerable degree how we spend our days.

Many of these forces influence the behavior of people in distinctive social and economic strata. One reason for the powerful predictive utility of measures of age, sex, race, and income is that these descriptive dimensions reflect a host of social and economic adaptations by people in status categories to the reality of life around them. Thus older people are often retired, while younger persons are expected to be in school. Gender is related to differences in people's socialization experiences and to strongly held definitions of appropriate behavior. Income and race shape the range of residential and educational options open to one. One could reread — by inference — much of the analysis presented above in terms of constraints on the behavior of people in various social and economic categories.

This section will examine directly the impact of two major factors which organize people's lives, their work roles and the composition of their households. Both of these factors affect how people spend their time, and where.

> The demands of lifestyle influence where an individual spends time. Those who work have a large portion of their daily activities structured in and around the workplace; those who raise children have a large portion of their time structured in and around the home [Hindelang et al., 1978: 254].

Vocation should be a particularly important determinant of behavior. The issue is one of how much discretion people exercise in the use of their time. Those who have more control over their day-to-day activities can go out during the day rather than at night to run errands, can linger in safe spots while hurrying through risky ones, and can exercise the option to stay at home when that seems to be the safest course. On the other hand, people whose lives are disciplined by the time clock or the school bell are less able to insulate themselves from risk. The effect of vocation on behavior should be greatest for our measure of exposure to risk, for even those who work late hours or must run errands and pursue their social lives after dark are still free to take many precautions.

This section also examines the impact of having children on the behavior of adults in those households. Like the clock and the bell, children impose demands which should shape adult behavior regardless of other calculations. In particular they should affect their parents' exposure to risk, the "going out" behavior which we often employ to explain patterns of victimization. This effect should be largely confined to women, for they traditionally have borne the greatest responsibility for child rearing in our culture.

The measures of these factors are uncomplicated. Near the conclusion of the interviews respondents were asked:

Are you presently employed somewhere or are you unemployed, retired, (a student), (a housewife) or what?[1]

Responses to this question were coded into eight categories. This analysis will use a dichotomous coding of these categories that combines people who have little discretionary control over the use of their time (those working and in school) and those who have more control over their daily routines (including the unemployed, retired, those "keeping house," and so on). In addition, respondents were asked, "How many children under the age of 18 are currently living with you?"

Even though vocation was linked to many other separate social and economic correlates of behavior, those roles were still independently influential. Among those working outside the home (remember that this includes students), 83% recalled going out after dark at least once during the preceding week; for those not in this group the comparable figure was 60%. After statistically adjusting exposure-to-risk rates for demographic factors, students and those regularly going to work still were significantly above the overall mean, and others below. Those in the "keeping house" category reported the fewest trips outside, even controlling for sex and age, followed by the retired and the unemployed. Having a structured vocational role also was significantly related to taking fewer precautionary actions, with workers and students scoring below the mean and retired persons and home managers recalling adopting those *tactics* more often. Sex and age were the most important factors to take into account in examining the role of vocation in shaping behavior, and an analysis which controls for both of them is presented in Table 11.5. It documents the still significant, if somewhat attenuated, relation between vocational role constraints and behavior, in our overall model.

Table 11.5 also documents the linear effect of having children who live at home on self-reports of behavior. In both cases the relation between household composition and measures of exposure to risk and personal caution is significant, if very weak. A close examination of the data indicates that the bulk of this effect is indeed due to the impact of children on the activity patterns of women. Among women under sixty years of age, those who had no children living at home went out an average of 3.4 times during the week before our interview, while those with children at home went out an average of 2.6 times.

TABLE 11.5   Role Constraints and Precautionary Behavior

Attributes	Exposure to Risk			Personal Caution		
	Simple	Multivariate		Simple	Multivariate	
		Beta	(Significance)		Beta	(Significance)
Old age	−.31	−.23	(.01+)	+.26	.18	(.01+)
Female	−.29	−.22	(.01+)	+.42	.36	(.01+)
Vocational constraint	+.32	.16	(.01+)	−.29	−.12	(.01+)
Children at home	−.02	−.07	(.01)	+.03	.05	(.05)
		$R^2 = .19$			$R^2 = .24$	
		N = 1193			N = 1193	

SOURCE: Computed from combined citywide surveys.

While that difference was significant, the difference between men in the same categories (4.6 as opposed to 4.4 trips) was not. Elderly respondents who had children living with them also reported quite low levels of exposure to risk. Through its impact on women, having children at home serves to reduce exposure to risk and to encourage (for both sexes) more circumspect behavior in public places.

This brief examination of constraints on autonomous action suggests the importance of such factors in understanding crime-related behavior. Those who had more flexibility in the timing and manner of their exposure to risk acted more cautiously. Family responsibilities both reduced their nocturnal mobility and encouraged more cautious behavior. As we shall see in the next section, these effects persisted even when we control for fear of crime. Given their level of fear, those who had to go out did so, and those who did not stayed home. A more detailed examination of the role of opportunity and constraints in shaping individual behavior, drawing upon a richer set of data on those factors, would not only be theoretically significant, but would help pinpoint groups in the population who face special problems with respect to crime because of their inability to respond effectively.

Summary

This chapter has described how the fundamental concepts in this analysis, including fear of crime, personal vulnerability, victimization, and the forces which constrain individual freedom of action, all conspire to shape individual precautionary behavior. Fear effectively

TABLE 11.6 Summary Analysis of Precautionary Behavior

Summary Concept Index	Exposure to Risk			Personal Caution		
	Simple	Multivariate		Simple	Multivariate	
		Beta	(Significance)		Beta	(Significance)
Fear	−.35	−.25	(.01+)	.50	.36	(.01+)
Personal vulnerability	−.38	−.28	(.01+)	.46	.32	(.01+)
Indirect victimization	−.07	−.06	(.03)	.23	.07	(.01)
Behavior constraints	.16	.05	(.05)	−.13	.03	(.33-ns)
		$R^2 = .20$			$R^2 = .34$	
		$N = 1128$			$N = 1128$	

NOTE: Summary indices are summed standard scores of larger sets of individual measures.
SOURCE: Computed from combined citywide surveys.

summarized these city dwellers' assessments of conditions in their communities, and was strongly related to their reports of the adoption of precautionary tactics. Women, the elderly, and Black residents of these cities all reported more circumspect behavior with regard to crime. Those who knew victims from their neighborhoods seemed to translate that knowledge into action, and people were more cautious in exposing themselves to possible attack when they believed that people in their social categories are likely victims. Finally, those we surveyed maneuvered through their environments in response to the constraints of social roles.

It is clear, however, that many of these factors are related to one another as well. One must examine their joint as well as individual effects before accepting their importance as determinants of behavior. To do this most clearly, we created summary indicators of the standing of each respondent on these basic dimensions. To measure personal vulnerability we standardized,[2] then summed the values representing age, race, and sex, creating a single measure that increased in value with vulnerability. We did the same with our two indicators of role constraints, and with two measures of indirect victimization. Fear continued to be measured by a single item. These summary measures were employed in a multiple regression analysis of our behavior measures. The explanatory power of these analyses dropped only very slightly when these summary indices were used rather than the eight original indicators (the overall R^2s declined only two percentage points in each case), and the substantive results of the analyses are more readily interpretable. The results of the statistical analyses are reported in Table 11.6.

These data indicate the great significance (in both a substantive and statistical sense) of fear on crime and personal vulnerability in shaping behavior. In contrast, the indirect victimization experiences of the respondents had only marginal consequences for their levels of caution, and role and economic constraints on their behavior (as they were measured) in the end were not very important.

NOTES

1. The interviewer supplied response cues appropriate to each respondent.
2. These are "Z-scores," which standardize the means and variances of measures. This gives them equal value in an index when they are added together. This is the same procedure that was employed in Chapter 7.

Chapter 12

HOUSEHOLD PROTECTION

Introduction

While routine precautionary habits were very common in these three cities, our surveys discovered that efforts by people to protect their households against property crime were even more frequent. The frequency of these activities ranged from 82% (leaving a light on at night) to 11% (asking the police for special patrols). While 60% of those who were interviewed indicated that they had adopted at least one tactic to reduce their chances of being victimized by violent crime, more than 95% reported taking at least one step against burglary. These measures can be very simple and effective. As one resident of a low-rise housing project in San Francisco told a field interviewer:

> We were told by all of our neighbors to rip off our upstairs outside window boxes because that's how a lot of them were getting into the houses [Visitacion Valley, August 1977].

Like several of the precautions examined in the previous chapter, some of these efforts involve only slight variations in people's daily routines. Others require that members of the household make special purchases of equipment, or participate in organized community activities. On the whole, easier and cheaper measures were taken more frequently than difficult or costly ones. We expected that generally these measures would be adopted more often by those who faced serious neighborhood crime problems, and by those who were vulnerable to victimization. Further, because several of these efforts involve mobilizing the support or assistance of neighbors, or participating in programs, they also should be related to the extent to which respondents were integrated into their communities. These efforts were not directly relevant to our measure of fear of crime, which is linked to concern about personal victimization. Rather, the key elements of the general model guiding this research which should have been operative here were the vulnerability of households to burglary, people's assessments of crime conditions in their neighborhoods, their personal and indirect experience with burglary, and their integration into community affairs. Only some of these expectations were fulfilled. It is clear that household protection is better understood in economic and social terms, and not as a direct reaction to the threat of crime.

Protective Measures

Target-hardening efforts are aimed at making it more difficult for potential intruders to break into one's home. Window bars, special locks, steel or solid-core doors, and other equipment often are employed to prevent theft. While in principle it is probably impossible to prevent a skilled burglar from breaking into virtually any home, relatively simple measures like these can ward off amateur or opportunistic offenders (but perhaps only to send them next door). Even professionals may be deterred by physical modifications which increase the length of time it will take them to break in — the "intrusion time" — for this is a period during which they are vulnerable to detection. Researchers have investigated the adoption of target-hardening tactics with some care, for they generally involve some financial outlay and presumably are reliably reported. A review of many of these studies (DuBow, 1979) revealed that about 40% of households report having made some purchase for home protection in the recent past.

Simple target-hardening efforts, such as locking doors, are very widespread. In a survey of Portland over 90% of those questioned indicated that they always locked their doors at night (Maxfield, 1977). Biderman et al. (1967) found that in the mid 1960s 84% of District of Columbia residents always locked their doors. Maxfield's analysis of data for Portland revealed that residents there very often (85%) locked their windows every night as well. Studies of the purchase of special anticrime devices indicate that new door locks are the most frequently chosen items. DuBow (1979) found that the proportion of households which report improving their door locks in "the last few years" ranged from a high of 40% in Detroit (Institute for Social Research, 1975) to a low of 26% in Toronto (Courtis and Dusseyer, 1970). Maxfield (1977) found that in Portland, Kansas City, and Cincinnati, between 34% and 39% of households reported recently installing extra door locks.

This survey as well probed the frequency with which various tactics "that some people do to protect their homes from burglary" were adopted. To gauge target-hardening efforts respondents were asked, "Do you have any bars or special locks on your windows?" Overall, 45% of them indicated that they had. In some neighborhoods window bars could be seen everywhere. One field worker reported this conversation in the Mission district in San Francisco:

(Field Worker): Is there a lot of crime?

(Person 1): There is crime everywhere. There is no place that is safe anymore. You can't walk the streets.

(Person 2): Yeah, look at the bars on the windows. You never used to see that. Now they are everywhere.

(Person 1): Yeah, bars on the windows. That tells you something about what is going on. It's just not safe anymore [Mission, September 1976].

Surveillance activities also are aimed at deterring burglary. These tactics protect households in two ways. When it appears that someone is at home most potential burglars will not enter a building. Watching over the household by being there is perhaps the most effective burglary prevention strategy. In fact, one of the strongest correlates of a household's burglary rate is the number of hours during the day when it is empty (Reppetto, 1974). This suggests to many people that the appearance that someone is at home may be almost as effective. Tactics such as leaving a radio on, stopping the delivery of mail and newspapers, using electric timers to turn lights on and off, and so on, are very often employed to reduce the risk of burglary when people are away from home. Maxfield (1977) found that in Portland 79% of households reported leaving on inside lights at night.

People also frequently mobilize the assistance of others in this enterprise. In this case their goal is to ensure that some intervention takes place in the event of an attempted break in. One can enlist the aid of others by asking neighbors to watch one's house or by calling the police to request a regular inspection while it stands empty. Some related measures, like installing exterior floodlights, are designed to make it easier for neighbors and passers-by to observe suspicious persons. Surveys indicate that surveillance efforts of this type also are very common. In Hartford over one-half of households reported arranging with neighbors to watch their homes while they were away, and 52% used outdoor lights to ward off burglars (Mangione and Noble, 1975).

In one sense these efforts involve two different strategies. Surveillance tactics include both internal, self-sufficient household measures (timers on lights) and attempts to encourage aggressive "protective neighboring" by others. However, they constitute a set of precautions which are often undertaken when people leave their homes unoccupied for a time. They covary in sensible fashion because people think of them as an increasingly extensive set of protective measures surrounding that leave-taking. People are more likely to take simpler measures than to take those which involve extensive effort.

To assess the extent to which surveillance tactics are adopted, respondents were asked:

Now, think of the last time you just went out at night. Did you leave a light on while you were gone?

And:

Now, think of the last time you went away from home for more than a day or so. Did you:

— notify the police so they could keep a special watch?
— stop delivery of things like newspapers or mail, or have someone bring them in?
— have a neighbor watch your house/apartment?

Note that respondents were not asked about general practices, but rather about their behavior the last time they went out. While this may introduce some error in the measures (among those who usually do these things, but did not then), it should increase the validity of the responses (their match with the referent behavior) and control to some extent the likely tendency of people to give answers which they feel they "should" in a crime prevention survey.

This "continuum" view of surveillance measures fits these survey data quite well. These four measures were taken with varying frequency: 82% employed lights at night, 77% asked their neighbors to watch the house, 57% contacted merchants and the post office to stop deliveries, and 11% requested special police patrols. Generally, respondents who reported taking the less frequent steps also took the most common ones (that is, few stopped deliveries and did not leave lights on). These items thus formed an acceptable Guttman Scale, with a coefficient of reproduceability (reflecting how many respondents answered all of the questions consistently) of .92. Of the respondents, 10% did not report taking any of these measures, and 6% took all four; the largest group took three of them. We will use the summary index to represent this class of anticrime effort in the analysis which follows.

Unlike tactics to deter burglary, loss-reduction measures involve minimizing the potential loss that may accrue from property crime, if it should occur. One can "lay off" potential losses from crime by acquiring theft insurance, a strategy which may make it economically rational *not* to invest further in equipment or in efforts to reduce the risk of victimization. Property identification programs also fall in this domain, for they are billed as measures to increase the likelihood that stolen property can be recovered. As a lieutenant in the community crime prevention division of the San Francisco police department put it to a community meeting in the Mission:

> In addition to all these programs we also have Operation ID. What this is is that we loan out free of charge an electric marker. And with that marker you put your driver's license number on all your valuables. The key is to reduce the opportunity for the burglary to happen. And if you are burglarized then at least you could get the property back. If you go down to the Hall of Justice you see all the time property that is not claimed. . . . so with Operation ID you have a better opportunity to get your valuables back [Mission, June 1977).

Many people report having hazard insurance which protects their homes and property against theft, in addition to other misfortunes. A study in Detroit (Institute For Social Research, 1975) and Conklin's (1975) research in two Boston-area communities both indicated that over 75% of respondents had some form of insurance which covered losses due to theft. However, fewer people have what they specifically think of as "theft insurance." Only 10% of respondents in a survey in the District of Columbia reported that they had this kind of protection (Clotfelter, 1977). Of respondents in a Cincinnati survey, 28% said someone in the household had insurance against theft (Maxfield, 1977). These vast differences doubtless reflect confusion or lack of knowledge of the theft-coverage components of various homeowner's and renter's insurance policies, which may be thought of as "fire" insurance. Ironically, having insurance may encourage careless behavior by reducing the direct cost of theft. Becker and Ehrlich (1972) have applied Kenneth Arrow's concept of "moral hazard" to the possible effect of theft insurance in the direction of increasing carelessness.

Property marking projects have been organized in cities all over the country. These programs encourage people to engrave identification numbers on their valuables and to display a special decal in a prominent place which announces their participation in the project. The purpose of the program is twofold: to deter burglary by suggesting to potential intruders that property stolen there will be more difficult to "fence" or otherwise dispose of because of those markings, and to make it easier for police to identify and return stolen goods when they are recovered. Surveys usually indicate that more people mark their property than display the sticker, probably because the latter can be acquired only from some organized program. Schneider (1975) found that 27% of households in Portland had engraved their property and 12% reported displaying a decal announcing that fact. Heller et al., (1975) examined the results of 100 Operation Identification programs throughout the country and found that participation ranged from 25% in the target areas of the most successful programs, to as low as 10%.

This survey gauged the frequency of these loss-reduction strategies with two questions:

> Have you ever engraved your valuables with your name or some sort of identification in case they are stolen?

And:

> Do you carry an insurance policy which covers your household goods against loss from theft or vandalism?

This wording of the "insurance" question elicited a 65% "yes" response, while 31% indicated that they had marked their property in some fashion.

The frequency of all of these activities is summarized in Table 12.1 The city differences recorded in Table 12.1 are sometimes significant, but they do not form a consistent pattern. San Franciscans are least likely to have theft insurance and to leave their lights on when out after dark, but they were most likely to stop deliveries. Philadelphians reported the least target-hardening but the most reliance on their neighbors. There also were few striking or consistent patterns of household protection in the study neighborhoods. In fact, of the 21 neighborhood-level correlations describing the distribution across neighborhoods of the measures summarized in Table 12.1, almost one-half were negative. As this suggests, responses to these items could not be combined to form a summary index of household protective behavior. There was a great deal of overlap among some of the actions due simply to the great frequency with which they were adopted. In all only 4% of our respondents reported that their house-

TABLE 12.1 Frequency of Household Protection

| | Target-Hardening | Loss Reduction | | Surveillance | | |
	Locks/Bars	Insurance	Marking	Lights On	Neighbors	Deliveries	Police
City			Percentage Reporting:				
Philadelphia	42	70	30	86	80	52	12
Chicago	49	65	34	84	75	57	8
San Francisco	44	60	29	76	73	60	11
Average	45	65	31	82	77	57	11

SOURCE: Computed from citywide surveys.

hold did none of these things, and only 9% did all of them; most reported doing two or three. One subset of these activities, that comprising surveillance efforts, did provide a coherent description of protective activity. It describes a repertoire of behaviors people perform when "going away," which doubtless lent them this consistency. An index based on these items, along with responses to the other individual questions, will be employed to explore the antecedents of protective behavior.

Vulnerability, Crime Conditions, and Household Protection

If the adoption process for household protective measures paralleled that for personal precautions, all of these things would be done more frequently by people who are concerned about crime, and who are more vulnerable to victimization. Environmental cues and perceptions that crime was a serious problem played a significant role in shaping habitual responses to the threat of personal crime, and those who were physically and socially more vulnerable to crime were more likely to act to reduce their risks as well.

Because we are examining actions for households rather than individuals, this chapter employs a somewhat different set of indicators of vulnerability. This investigation of protective measures will again contrast the strategies adopted by Blacks and the poor with their counterparts, but in addition it will explore the consequences of two new aspects of household vulnerability — building size and home ownership. Renters and residents of larger buildings often exercise little control over their living arrangements. The ability to take extensive target-hardening measures should in particular be largely reserved to owners. Those living in larger buildings should find it more difficult to organize effective surveillance relationships with their neighbors or the police, for residents there exercise less control over the coming and going of strangers, and often may not know their "close" neighbors. Certainly passers-by will be a less effective surveillance force around large, anonymous buildings.

Data from this survey and the results of victimization surveys both indicate that home ownership and building size affect the vulnerability of households to crime. Our respondents were asked if they "usually try to keep an eye on what is going on in the street in front of your house, or do you usually not notice?" Owners and residents of single-family homes were much more likely to report vigilance. They were asked if they have a neighbor watch their home when they go away for more than a day, and renters and large-building dwellers

TABLE 12.2   Vulnerability, Crime, and Household Protection

Vulnerability and Crime Conditions	Correlation with Household Protection Measures:			
	Locks and Bars	Mark Property	Theft Insurance	Surveillance Scale
Vulnerability				
Black	—	—	−.21	−.16
Low income	−.08	−.18	−.35	−.22
Renter	−.22	−.21	−.82	−.20
Multi-unit building	−.14	−.11	−.53	−.17
Crime Conditions				
Burglary a problem	.12	—	—	.07
Know local burglary victim	.18	—	.20	.15
Was burglarized	.14	—	—	.09

NOTE: Number of cases ranges from 1286 to 1337. No entry indicates correlation (gamma) not significant (p > .05).

SOURCE: Computed from citywide surveys.

more often said no. They also were asked if it was easy to recognize strangers in their areas, and 69% of those in single-family homes, but only 37% living in larger buildings, said it was.

Victimization surveys also point to the relative vulnerability of households in rental or large structures, in the figures they report for rates of property crime which affect them. In the case of burglary, in the 1977 national survey renters reported 55% higher rates than owners and those in larger buildings reported 35% higher rates than those in single-family homes. Differences of an only slightly lower magnitude were found between these groups for the incidence of household theft.

Table 12.2 summarizes the relationship between each indicator of vulnerability and the adoption of household protective measures. The results are quite striking. The correlations relating behavior to household vulnerability generally are moderate-to-strong, but they mostly run in the wrong direction. Every one of the 14 significant correlations (only 2 were not significant) reported at the top of Table 12.2 is counter to our operating hypothesis.

The strongest correlate of household protection was home ownership. People who owned their own homes were more inclined to install special locks and bars, reflecting their ability to make such physical modifications. However, they also were more likely to mark their valuables with an identifying number, and to take special precautions when they were away from home. Theft insurance was more common among home owners as well. Less than half of renters reported having theft insurance, while 90% of home owners carried such policies. This may be in part due to the requirement by mortgage companies that borrowers insure their home, for these policies usually include theft coverage. The extremely high correlation (gamma = +.82) between ownership and insurance probably is an attribute of the home-ownership process, more than it is a reaction to crime.

Of all four measures, household protection was more extensive among those with higher incomes. About 26% of those in the lowest income group reported engraving identifying numbers on their valuables, compared to over 40% for those earning $20,000 per year or more. Families with higher incomes were only slightly more likely to report having special locks or bars on their windows. Theft insurance was more popular among upper-income city residents. Some of this was due to their higher rate of home ownership, but even among renters the correlation (gamma) between income and having insurance was +.31. Blacks and people who lived in larger buildings also were less likely to take most of these measures. Newman (1972), Jacobs (1961), and others have explored the difficulties involved in encouraging a sense of responsibility for the immediate environment among residents of large buildings. If residents of single-family homes are more easily integrated into their neighborhoods, we would expect them to be more involved in those cooperative enterprises. While residents of large buildings were expected to make less use of surveillance strategies, the consistently negative correlations reported in Table 12.2 indicate that the dominant theme describing the state of affairs in these three cities is that vulverability and household protection are inversely related.

Most of these findings are at odds with our expectations with regard to the relationship between vulnerability and household protection. In some cases this may be due to the role of resources in the ability of families to adopt these tactics. In Portland, protective devices were purchased more often by upper-income home owners than by lower-income renters. Furstenberg (1972) reported similar findings in Baltimore. He suggested that this is because the well-to-do have more money to invest in locks, bars, and valuable property, and they are more able to purchase insurance. The differences between the rich and the poor in this regard thus may be due not to motive, but to ability to pay. Higher-income, home-owning families seemingly have the wherewithal, knowledge, and ability to control their own lifespace necessary to take advantage of devices, programs, neighbors, public resources, and insurance programs which insulate them from burglary and its consequences. The multivariate analysis presented demonstrates how economic factors dominate almost all other determinants of protective activity, and how some slight but still positive crime-related correlates of household protection all but vanish.

The distribution of these protective measures across the ten study neighborhoods tells the same story. With the exception of the frequency with which locks and bars were installed (which will be examined below), all of the significant neighborhood-level correlations described negative vulnerability-action relationships. For example, the correlation between the proportion of those in an area living in apartment buildings and the frequency of surveillance efforts there was −.56. In places where more households were vulnerable to property crime, fewer did anything about it.

Table 12.2 also describes the relationship between measures of protective effort and the extent to which property crime touched the lives of our respondents. Three indicators reflecting crime conditions and events are employed there: ratings of the seriousness of neighborhood problems, whether or not the respondent knew a local burglary victim, and whether or not the household had been burglarized "in the past two years."

Data from these cities indicate that local crime conditions had a substantial impact on only one form of household protection, the installation of special locks and window bars. Locks and bars also were the only protective measures which were strongly and positively related to the incidence of crime problems and burglary victimization at the neighborhood level. This form of target-hardening was most frequently employed in Woodlawn (61% of households) and least often in the neighborhoods of Philadelphia (43% in each of them). There was a weaker tendency for people in more burglary-plagued communities to report taking surveillance measures when they were away from home. Otherwise, neighborhood-level correlations and the figures in Table 12.2 are most impressive in their documentation of the limited relationship between neighborhood conditions, as experienced by our respondents, and their propensity to take measures to protect their homes.

The most substantial relationships among this set are those between reports of behavior and knowledge of local burglary victims. Such indirect experience with crime was quite common in our three cities, more common even than the perception that burglary was a "big problem" in the community. What is surprising in Table 12.2 is that this factor outshines even personal direct experience with burglary. Table 12.2 shows only weak relationships between reports of being victimized in the last two years and protective behavior. About 7% more victims than nonvictims reported having special protective devices on their windows, and taking certain steps to provide for the protection of their homes while absent was slightly more common among those who had been victimized. Victims of burglary were slightly *less* likely than others to have theft insurance.

It is somewhat surprising that there is not a stronger relationship between past victimization and these types of property protection. Part of the problem may be the quality of the measure of victimization. This survey was not designed to measure victimization with the same precision as those which were undertaken by the Census Bureau. It does not distinguish among types of burglaries or identify attempted rather than successful crime. Respondents answering affirmatively to inquiries about someone trying to break into their homes may be recalling burglaries which were foiled by existing security measures. The survey doubtless picked up cases where burglars broke into a garage and made off with property which would not normally be protected by the measures shown in Table 12.2. Finally, the burglary victimization question asked about a two-year reference period, and thus included events from the past which may not be well-recalled by respondents. They also may refer to burglaries of previous residences.

Neighborhood Integration and Household Protection

There was one additional cluster of factors which facilitated household protective activity in these three cities: the extent to which a person was linked to his or her neighborhood and its social networks. On most measures of household protection those who were more heavily integrated into the local social stream and those who were committed, long-term residents of the area were more involved in anticrime activity.

The effect of this integration can best be seen in neighborhood-level data. Figure 12.1 depicts the relationship between measures of social ties in the community and surveillance activity scores, averaged for each of the ten target neighborhoods. In places where people knew more neighborhood youths, thought it easy to recognize strangers, and felt a part of their communities, they were more likely to score toward the higher reaches of our surveillance scale. The correlation between the two measures was +.63. The graph is anchored at the bottom by San Francisco's Mission district, an extremely heterogeneous transitional area on the very edge of the

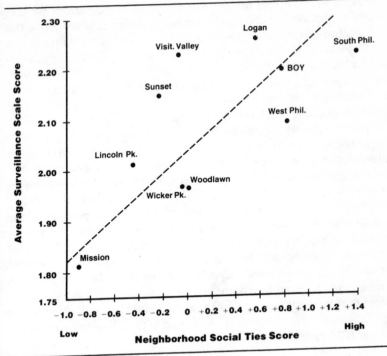

Figure 12.1 Neighborhood Integration and Surveillance
SOURCE: Computed from ten neighborhood surveys.

downtown, made up of large apartment buildings. People in the Mission understood their collective plight. At a block club meeting there our field observer noted the following conversation:

(Person 1): If we all got together then we could make a difference.

(Person 2): Yes, and that's the reason that we have so many problems. We allow ourselves to be bullied around. Crime has been here since Year One. And we allow ourselves to be taken advantage of. That is the reason why there is so much crime. They know that we are not going to get involved. They know that if we see someone walking into our neighbor's garage we will close our shade and say to ourselves, "that is not my business" [Mission, April 1977].

On the other extreme lies South Philadelphia, a stable white ethnic community, a similar area in Chicago (Back-of-the-Yards), and our two most middle-class Black neighborhoods, Logan and West Philadelphia.

The individual-level relationships between those factors are less dramatic. Both social and residential ties were strongly related to the distribution of insurance covering theft or vandalism, with gamma coefficients of .36 and .59, respectively. They were moderately correlated with individual scores on our surveillance scale. People reporting stronger social ties were more likely to have participated in property marking campaigns. Stronger residential ties were linked to property marking and target-hardening.

How neighborhood ties facilitate surveillance activities in particular is of considerable theoretical and policy interest. Surveillance strategies mostly depend upon the cooperation of neighbors and bystanders. It may require some acquaintance and the development of trust before mutual assistance pacts can be worked out between neighbors. Surveillance efforts depend to some degree upon the willingness of neighbors and bystanders to intervene in suspicious situations. Suspiciousness itself depends upon the extent of mutual recognition among neighbors and the development of locally shared norms of appropriate and inappropriate conduct. Because so much crime is perpetrated by youths, recognizing them and being able to identify their positions in the web of local kinship also has important implications for social control. A woman in the Mission noted to one of our field interviewers:

> I know all the kids who steal around here. . . . For instance, they robbed some things from the man next door. I know they did it. And I am going to tell them to give it all back. They shouldn't have done it. He is a nice old man and doesn't hurt anybody. So there was no reason for doing it [Mission, June 1977].

Finally, neighborhood integration has important consequences for the effectiveness of programs and the implementation of crime prevention activities like Operation Identification. Not surprisingly, the extent to which our respondents were integrated into their communities proved to be tenaciously linked to surveillance efforts and participation in property marking programs when we evaluated the joint predictive power of our indicators.

Summary

Thus far this analysis has turned up several quite unexpected findings with regard to the relationship between the extent of household protective measures and indicators of vulnerability to crime and the extent of neighborhood crime problems. The facilitative role of neighborhood integration, on the other hand, is clear and consistent with past research.

As previous chapters have indicated, all of these factors are related to one another as well as to these reports of protective behavior. This complicated any simple interpretation of many of these bivariate correlations. Crime problems tend to be lower for groups (and neighborhoods) where residential and social ties are strong; burglary problems are widespread, striking across all income groups; those who own their own homes tend to report many other ties to their communities as well.

In order to untangle these effects, we turned to regression analysis to evaluate the independent linear effects of each of the clusters of variables considered here. As in previous chapters, this analysis was conducted using summary indicators for each conceptual cluster. Additive scales were created which combined individual measures. In each case the indicators were scored so that they "went together" in cumulative fashion and took equal weight in the summary scales. A comparison of the effects of the aggregated and disaggregated indicators suggested that we did this at little cost to the explanatory power of the data, and that it does not lead us astray in any substantive fashion.

Table 12.3 documents the results of those analyses for each of the protective measures being evaluated here. These figures support the conclusions suggested by the tabulations presented above. In every case, more vulnerable households did less than most in response to the threat of crime. Table 12.3 reports the effects of two measures of vulnerability: household vulnerability (size and ownership) and household status (race and income). Even controlling for other factors, owners, whites, higher-income families, and those who lived in single-family homes did the most to protect themselves from property crime. The most consistently significant effects summarized in Table 12.3 are those of integration. Only our measure of social ties is employed here, for residential integration was too closely allied with home ownership. In every case, persons who were closely tied to the local social system were more likely to do things to protect their homes. Nieghborhood ties were strongly related to surveillance efforts, and were the best (and only significant) predictor of property marking. Property marking generally is a programmatic activity encouraged by group meetings and door-to-door visits, and may even involve neighbors getting together to engrave numbers on their valuables. The weakest and most inconsistent effects here are those attributable to crime conditions, a measure combining ratings of

TABLE 12.3 Correlates of Household Protection

Household Protective Measure	Independent Variables	Standardized Regression Coefficient	(Sig. F.)
Engrave Valuables			
	Household vulnerability	−.03	(.41-ns)
	Household status	.05	(.11-ns)
	Integration (social)	.10	(.01)
	Crime conditions	.00	(.87-ns)
	$R^2 = .02$ (p = .01)		
	N = 866		
Install Locks and Bars			
	Household vulnerability	−.11	(.01+)
	Household status	.01	(.80-ns)
	Integration (social)	.01	(.74-ns)
	Crime conditions	.08	(.02)
	$R^2 = .02$ (p = .01)		
	N = 864		
Carry Theft Insurance			
	Household vulnerability	−.36	(.01+)
	Household status	.18	(.01+)
	Integration (social)	.10	(.01)
	Crime conditions	−.02	(.41-ns)
	$R^2 = .21$ (p < .01)		
	N = 856		
Surveillance Scale			
	Household vulnerability	−.06	(.08-ns)
	Household status	.16	(.01+)
	Integration (social)	.16	(.01+)
	Crime conditions	.04	(.17-ns)
	$R^2 = .07$ (p < .01)		
	N = 873		

NOTE: Regressions use only cases with complete data for all indicators. Summary indices are summed standard scores of sets of individual measures.

SOURCE: Computed from combined citywide surveys.

burglary problems, knowledge of victims, and victimization experience. As in the bivariate case, crime conditions were significant predictors of behavior in only one domain — target-hardening.

This research suggests that an economic and social model of household protection provides a better explanation for how people react to property crime than does an "environmental threat" or "concern about victimization" approach to the problem. Efforts to protect home and property are a function of one's economic investment in the community and depth of social involvement there. Whatever the payoffs of those efforts, they were reaped by the relatively well-to-do and the less vulnerable.

Chapter 13

COMMUNITY INVOLVEMENT

Introduction

Until now we have only examined actions which individuals and households take to reduce their own chances of being victimized. The precautionary strategies we reviewed limited personal risk by putting distance between people and neighborhood toughs. The surveillance and target-hardening measures that respondents to these surveys reported adopting to deter burglars probably would have benefited only themselves. In either case, potential offenders presumably still would have been at large, foraging for other and less wary targets.

As a result, it is useful to think of those as protective as opposed to preventive actions. The issue is not one of the motives of the parties involved, but of the generality of the consequences attendant to their actions. Preventive efforts ideally would have the effect of stopping crime from occurring, or of incapacitating offenders who otherwise would carry on their predations somewhere else. They serve to reduce the overall crime rate. Protective efforts, on the other hand, benefit only those who adopt them. They reduce (perhaps) their chances of victimization, but may simply displace offenses to other locations (see Schneider and Schneider, 1977).

While not all actions taken by individuals have only protective consequences, the principal mechanism for preventive activity is group action. Be they formal or informal, highly organized or spontaneous and amorphous, groups can mount efforts which have general as opposed to particularistic consequences for a community. Many of these involve surveillance activities, including citizen patrols and block watch programs. Other group efforts are designed to facilitate crime reporting and increase the chances that offenders will be apprehended, including Whistlestop and property marking efforts. Perhaps more "fundamental" to the reduction of crime are programs aimed at properly socializing youths and channeling their energies into productive (or at least harmless) activities.

This chapter examines patterns of participation in organizations which do something about crime. Our interest in these activities is that they are done by or through groups, rather than by individuals or families. Some group-based programs have protective outcomes for individual participants, of course. Neighborhood organizations often promote property marking, an effort billed as effective at reducing victimization through the deterrent effects of displaying a sign indicating that one's valuables have been branded. As part of the Citizen Safety Project in San Francisco, block clubs were formed as a vehicle for spreading the gospel about steps individuals could take to protect themselves and their property (Silbert et al., 1978). However, by taking a spatial focus for these organizing efforts, and by channeling their energy into reducing the chances of others being victimized, these were preventive efforts on the part of organizational participants, even if — for their clients — taking these actions had only individual benefits.

This analysis follows lines of earlier research and the general operating model sketched in the first chapter. Thus it dwells on the effects of victimization, personal vulnerability, community conditions, neighborhood integration, and fear of crime. However, there are reasons to suspect that general personal and environmental "pressures" will not go very far toward understanding participation in collective efforts to battle crime. First, those pressures are likely to be contradictory. Chapter 6 documents that neighborhoods where residents share strong residential and social ties enjoy lower levels of crime and disorder, although one would expect each of those factors to be positively related to participation in anticrime efforts. Second, severe crime problems may engender suspicion, distrust, detachment, and even mutual fear among community members, factors that do not seem propitious for organizing them for collective efforts. Finally, an analysis of participation in organizations that have taken on crime as an agenda item enters the world of organizational as well as individual decision making.

In the field interviews conducted in target neighborhoods in these three cities we found that few organizations were exclusively concerned with crime problems, and that few were formed around the crime issue (Podolefsky et al., 1980). Rather, leaders of existing organizations decided to assume a crime-fighting stance of one kind or another, and encouraged involvement among their members on this issue. Because "people join groups," while "groups take on crime," involvement of the sort we will be examining here reflects in large degree "joining" rather than "crime-fighting" predispositions. These often are not congruent with the factors that have been identified as relevant to understanding victimization and fear.

Levels of Participation

DuBow and Podolefsky (1979: 1) offer a useful definition of collective responses to crime:

A collective response to crime is an activity in which unrelated individuals act jointly to "do something about crime." The collective quality of the response may involve a large or small number of people, may be highly organized or spontaneous and informal. Some "collective" responses can only be accomplished in cooperation with others such as neighborhood surveillance programs, while others involve activities that individuals could also undertake on their own, such as engraving property.

This definition focuses upon the collective (multiperson) aspect of activity rather than upon what people in particular do, recognizing the complexity of categorizing activities by some standard regarding whether or not they "could be done" alone as well as in groups. In our surveys it was apparent that what groups did about crime was extremely varied. Some attempted to facilitate property marking, others patrolled their communities watching for infractions, pursued housing programs, and provided recreation, instruction, or employment for local children. Residents quizzed in our surveys reported that a large majority of the groups active in the neighborhoods of these three cities sponsored some activity or program aimed at reducing crime.

In order to assess participation in these organizations we questioned survey respondents about their involvement in local civic life. They were asked first if they knew of any community groups or organizations in their neighborhoods (44% did). Then they were asked if they ever were involved in any of them (47% of that number had been), and, if they had been, we recorded the name of the group. They were asked for these details for up to three groups. About three-quarters of those who mentioned any group named only one group. For each named group they were then asked if it had "ever tried to do anything about crime" in the neighborhood. If any of them had, that respondent was classified as "involved in a neighborhood anticrime group"; in all, 13.5% fell into that category. This is substantially higher than levels of participation uncovered in a statewide survey in Maryland, which revealed that 3% of respondents had joined in a group to help cope with the crime problem in their neighborhoods (Nehnevajsa and Karelitz, 1977). On the other hand, O'Neil's (1977) survey in Chicago revealed a figure quite comparable to ours; about 35% of his respondents reported being involved in a neighborhood group, and 17% were involved in groups that were doing something about crime. Residents of our three cities were moderately differentiated by this measure. Chicagoans scored the highest, with 17% registering some involvement in groups mounting anticrime efforts. Philadelphians were next at 12%, and San Franciscans were at the bottom with 11%. Chicago's long tradition of community organization around issues of every type was reaffirmed here.

There are several substantive implications of the procedure we followed which should be noted. First, "involvement" (not "membership") was defined by the respondent, and doubtless varied in type and intensity. Second, an "organization" was a group with a name; its name affirmed its formal status. Third, residents were asked only about neighborhood organizations, not national or citywide bodies. Their responses thus doubtless underestimate frequency of overall organizational involvement by our respondents. However, in this case neighborhood-based activity may be by far the most significant form of group action. There has been some programmatic activity dealing with the reduction of crime and fear in commercial and industrial sites, central business districts, and work places. Action programs have been combined with a considerable amount of research on the problems of crime and fear in schools and in elderly and public-assistance group housing. But implicit in most of the programs, research, and theory on victimization and fear is that residential neighborhoods are the principal arenas in which the battle against crime must be fought and won. Most people spend a great deal of time in their neighborhoods, and events in those areas threaten themselves, their families, and their friends. Crime also threatens one's economic stake in the community, and one's hopes for its future. In cities plagued by disinvestment, decay, and the flight of those who are able to the suburbs, the sum of these threats can be disaster. Much of the blame for the abandonment of central cities has been laid at the door of criminal disorder. Fear of crime and the inability of citizens to do anything about the problem are numbered among the causes of both more crime and more decay.

On the other side, most ideas about the causes of crime also imply neighborhood-based action. Blocked economic opportunity, the decline of informal mechanisms of social control, the development of disaffected subcultures, and other explanations for the persistence of crime all contain important territorial features. Also, most official data on crime are collected to represent territorial units, and this shapes both the ideas about the genesis of disorder and how we can map our progress in dealing with it.

In the remainder of this chapter we will use this measure of neighborhood civic involvement to probe patterns of collective activity against crime.

Neighborhood Conditions, Fear of Crime, and Participation

It would be easy to assume that participation in collective efforts to combat crime is higher for persons who perceive crime to be a major local problem, or for whom local trends seem to be in the direction of neighborhood deterioration. Surprisingly, evidence concerning this is inconclusive. Kim (1976) found that, in Hartford, people who were worried about property crime were somewhat more likely to ask their neighbors to watch their homes when they were away, and that fears and assessments of many kinds of crime risks were related to attendance at crime prevention meetings there. Yaden (1973) noted that 23% of the respondents in a Portland survey who perceived high risk of being robbed also reported getting together with their neighbors about crime, while the comparable figure for those perceiving low risk was only 9%. In the survey of the Chicago metropolitan area that has been used in previous chapters, Lavrakas and Herz (1979) found that attendance at crime-prevention meetings was positively related to perceptions of significant crime and disorder problems in the area, and to higher levels of perceived risk of personal victimization. However, in an analysis of survey data on participation in neighborhood anticrime programs in Chicago, Baumer and DuBow (1977) found no differences between participants and nonparticipants on a host of measures of perceptions of crime problems. Maxfield (1977) uncovered no differences between attenders and nonattenders of anticrime meetings in Portland and Cincinnati in terms of their assessments of neighborhood safety.

The relationship between neighborhood conditions, fear, and collective involvement appears to be complex. There are fundamentally conflicting theoretical positions regarding the impact of crime upon the ability of neighborhoods to support collective efforts on the issue. One view, that of Durkeim, is that communities faced with crime problems should spawn collective action as a response to that stress. From this perspective crime defines for the community the limits of acceptable social behavior. When people step outside of those limits they clearly are beyond the pale. Crime helps clarify for the community what its central norms are; when those norms are violated it acts to do something about the problem, and by intervening and identifying transgressors community solidarity around legitimate norms is enhanced. For "polite" society, the assessment that crime is a problem serves as a positive inducement for action. Intervention, involving varying levels of formal activity, restores the social balance. This view of collective participation seems to be the "official" one. In a solicitation for proposals to receive grants to organize neighborhoods around the crime issue, the Law Enforcement Assistance Administration (1977: 5-8) noted:

> Fear of crime can motivate citizens to interact with each other and engage in anticrime efforts.

However, it is just as likely that fear and crime problems are divisive forces, destroying the capacity of communities to mount collective efforts around almost any local problem. This is the more "modern" view of community disorganization (Lewis, 1979; Conklin, 1975). From this perspective crime generates suspicion and distrust. Neighborhood residents stay indoors and off the streets, reducing the amount of informal surveillance there. Using our measures, neighborhood social ties would decline. People fall back on webs of kinship for social support, rather than relying upon their relatively unknown neighbors. Crime in their midst undermines people's confidence that there are locally shared norms. When they withdraw from public life, distance themselves from other community members, and lose faith in the moral consensus, public places fall under control of potential predators. In this view, crime begets crime, following a vicious spiral, and fear is incapacitating.

It is also not certain that being personally involved in crime should stimulate victims in collective activities relevant to their experiences. Crime has atomizing effects upon individuals and households. The direct consequences of victimization are felt by individuals, not the collectivity. There may be a tendency by victims to withdraw from public life and to become suspicious and distrustful of others as a result of their experiences (LeJeune and Alex, 1973). There is speculation that other people may shun victims, sensing their "spoiled identities and wishing to disassociate themselves from suffering. Psychologists have uncovered a related phenomenon that they call "blaming the victim." As a result, crime may undermine community cohesion and weaken its surveillance and intervention capacity, creating the conditions for even higher rates of victimization in the future (Conklin, 1975; McIntyre, 1967).

There thus are substantial reasons to expect that victimization and assessments of local conditions either stimulate or depress levels of involvement in neighborhood activities, and it is uncertain which tendency predominates. The issue is further confused by the probable reciprocal effects of participation on these "causal" variables. While fear and local conditions may or may not drive people to action, that action also may have consequences for their fears and perceptions. Again, one's expectations with regard to these effects are contradictory as well. On the one hand, joining with others to take action with regard to community problems may enhance citizens' morale and their sense of efficacy with regard to those problems, but, on the other hand, they may learn enough from that effort to conclude that those problems are more intractable than they previously suspected.

There is suggestive evidence that participation in organizations may promote a sense of efficacy with regard to crime on the part of participants, a positive effect. However, that effect may also reflect the fact that participation is attractive only to those who already think that they can "make a difference," a selection artifact. Meetings may be devoted to presentations about new crime-prevention programs, strategy sessions by project organizers, handbill preparation, and/or envelope stuffing. The sheer sense of activity aimed at the problem may enhance the feeling by participants that something can be done about crime. Cohn et al. (1978) found that people who were involved in community organizations felt more control over crime and reported less fear of crime than did nonparticipants. They also discovered that women who took a self-defense training course gained a greater sense of control over events and reported less fear of crime as a result. This three-city survey found that participants in organizations doing something concerning crime were more likely to believe that groups can make a difference in reducing crime and that the police can reduce crime (the correlation was +.23). Organizational activists generally feel more efficacious about the topic, although the direction of causation remains uncertain.

On the other hand, observations of those meetings suggest that things that happen at them may promote fear and enhance perceptions of crime and disorder. One of the most common features of anticrime meetings is that people spend a great deal of time relating tales about victimization experiences. People report crime stories to others in attendance in order to illustrate the threat of crime in their midst, and the necessity for taking some action. Our field observations illustrate this process. A meeting of neighborhood safety councils with a local block club organized by the Citizens Safety Project in San Frnacisco was cancelled because of a burglary at the meeting site. People arriving to attend that meeting learned firsthand about the crime problem in their neighborhood. A typical incident was related at another block club meeting there:

> *(Person 1):* Two times I got ripped off! The police said they were 95% sure of who did it but they couldn't do anything about it. I was at work when they came in.
>
> *(Person 2):* The same sort of thing happened to me but I was home and the guy across the street saw what was happening. If the neighbors know each other then they can help each other [Mission, January 19, 1977].

The recounting of crime stories is a regular feature of community organization meetings, and may have the effect of enhancing the fears of those in attendance. In the Chicago metropolitan area, people who report involvement in collective crime-prevention efforts are much more likely to know people who have been victimized by street crimes in their neighborhoods (Lavrakas and Herz, 1979). In this area the correlation (gamma) between participation and knowing a local crime victim was +.40. Almost 75% of those active in a group that was doing something about neighborhood crime also knew a local victim.

Based on this three-city data, the relation between perceptions of neighborhood problems or experience with crime and participation in groups attempting to do something about the issue is not very strong. The correlation (gamma) between the extent of crime and social-order problems and reports of such involvement was in the +.10 to +.12 range. The strongest crime-related determinant of organizational participation was victimization: Among those who reported that their households had been broken into within the past two years, 19% were involved with groups, while only 12% of those who did not report being burglarized participated in crime-related organizations. These correlations are presented in Table 13.1.

Fear of crime also was moderately related to participation in local groups, but in the opposite direction. Of those in the "safe" category, 15% reported such involvement, and only 10% in the "unsafe" group. Thus, participation was *lower* among those who felt unsafe in their neighborhoods.

These contradictory findings do not clearly support one or another of the arguments about the consequences of crime. Participation is

TABLE 13.1   Fear, Neighborhood Crime, and Participation

Measures of Fear and Conditions	Correlation (Gamma) With Crime Organization Involvement	(N)
Fear of crime	−.15	(1322)
Major crime problems	.10	(1341)
Social-order problems	.12	(1348)
Burglary victim	.25	(1351)
Neighborhood getting worse	−.14	(1196)

NOTE: All correlations significant ($p < .03$ or better).

SOURCE: Computed from combined citywide surveys.

higher among persons who believe their neighborhoods to be troubled and who have been victimized, which follows Durkheim's analysis. On the other hand, participation is lowest among those that might be classified as (relatively) "incapacitated" by fear or driven from community life by concern about their safety, which follows Conklin. Chapter 7 reported that fear is positively related to assessments of neighborhood crime problems, which compounds the inconsistency of these findings. Below are noted several more important confounded relationships, all of which point to the importance of a multivariate analysis of the data. A multiple regression analysis (not shown) of the fear and crime conditions indicators presented in Table 13.1 indicates that only fear and perceived neighborhood trends were independently related to organizational involvement. Those who were *less* fearful and who thought that conditions in their locale were getting *better* were more likely to report being involved in a group that was doing something concerning crime, while measures of crime-related conditions were otherwise unrelated to participation.

Integration and Participation

One of the most consistent research findings with respect to participation in collective activities is that those with firmly entrenched stakes in a community are most likely to be involved in a variety of local group activities, including those concerned with crime (Emmons, 1979; Wilson and Schneider, 1978; Abt Associates, 1977; Governor's Commission on Crime Prevention and Crime Control, 1976; Washnis, 1976). Some of those linkages are concrete and economic, and involve home ownership and other economic investments.

Others are related to the position of persons in the life cycle, including whether or not they have children enrolled in local schools (DuBow and Podolefsky, 1979). Long-term residents and those with strong social ties to others in the vicinity also are more likely to be participators. These factors tend to be related to the development of what DuBow and Podolefsky dubbed "sentimental attachments" to a community, which also stimulate participation in local affairs.

Further, by bringing together neighbors, local group activities may foster the further development of some of these ties. Thus, even if these activities do not have much direct impact on crime, they may foster morale and increase community cohesion. This is important, for there is considerable evidence that social isolation contributes to fear of crime. In a multivariate analysis of LEAA's city surveys, Antunes et al. (forthcoming) found that living alone was an extremely strong predictor of levels of fear of crime. Collective efforts may help isolated individuals and families rejoin the community, and thus contribute to a reduction in fear. In general, fear of attack in public places is facilitated by a sense that "no one is watching," and that no one will intervene in a risky situation (McIntyre, 1967). By holding meetings and encouraging the development of door-to-door contacts, groups may enhance a sense of informal support among an area's residents, further reducing fear. Schneider and Schneider (1977) investigated what they called "protective neighboring," or the willingness of people (in response to hypothetical questions) to watch one another's houses and to intervene if they observed suspicious circumstances. This turned out to be most strongly related to home ownership and length of residence in the community, two aspects of what they called "stake in the community." Baumer and Hunter (1979) found that in Hartford the ability to recognize strangers in the neighborhood was important in alleviating fear of crime.

Most of these dimensions of community solidarity and economic attachment are captured in our measures of integration. Chapter 9 reported how the strength of social and residential ties shaped patterns of conversation concerning crime in these three cities, and how they served to ameliorate fear. In this case, both social and residential ties were positively and substantially related to greater involvement in crime-focused groups. The correlation (gamma) between this measure of social ties and participation was $+.43$, while for the residential ties measure it was $+.28$ (both are statistically significant). In addition, the correlation between reports of participation and whether or not adult respondents had children living at home was $+.23$. However, in a multiple regression analysis (not shown) only the two integration measures continued to be significantly related to group involvement when the three measures were employed jointly. Those effects were linear, without any significant statistical interaction.

Like our analysis of household protective measures, the findings reported here point to the importance of "investment" in the community (in the largest sense) as a determinant of individual action. This runs counter, of course, to the presumed relation between participation and the extent of crime problems. Individuals who believed that their neighborhoods were troubled were (weakly) more likely to report being involved in a crime-focused group. However, Chapter 6 described how integration and crime problems divided these ten target neighborhoods into two distinct groups, one high on integration and low on perceived crime and the other at the opposite pole. Here community integration and neighborhood crime problems seem to be working to some extent in tandem to stimulate greater organizational involvement. It appears that, as with talk about crime, there may be more than one path to higher levels of organizational involvement. The differences in the strengths of the individual-level correlations suggests that perceptions of troubled conditions should work only at the margins, however, after one controls for differences in the strength of residential and social ties to community life.

Vulnerability and Participation

Finally, patterns of participation in collective anticrime activities should reflect the general distribution of local civic activity. Involvement in these groups does not seem to be a particularly unique effort. Because people join organizations, while it is the organizations which decide to "do something about crime," a profile of general factors which lead people to become involved in community groups should also describe those who are linked to those anticrime efforts.

The irony of this is that patterns of participation in informal organizations are not always congruent with the factors that we have identified as leading to fear of crime, increased vulnerability to crime, or higher rates of victimization. For example, participation in neighborhood activities generally is higher among home owners and those with higher incomes, who also tend to enjoy lower rates of victimization and lower levels of fear of crime. On the other hand, most research indicates that, with controls for social class, Blacks should report higher levels of participation in neighborhood activities than do whites. Those who are long-term residents of the community generally are more active in local affairs, while levels of civic participation (but not interest in those affairs) drop off among the elderly. The relationship between sex and group participation is mixed, but women show a substantial edge among more local, school, and church-oriented bodies.

Measures of social vulnerability produced mixed findings, for Blacks but not lower-income people were significantly more likely than others to report being involved in crime groups. On the other hand, older respondents were more likely to report such participation. Close inspection of the data reveals that this relationship is slightly curvilinear, however. Participation peaked in the 50 to 59 age group, and dropped 4 percentage points among those 60 and older. Levels of involvement among the elderly still were higher than among persons in younger categories, however. There were no significant sex differences in participation. A multivariate analysis of these indicators (not shown) demonstrates that except for sex they all had almost the *same* significant impact on participation; the multivariate standardized regression coefficients were all in the .07 to .10 range. There were no significant interactions among them.

While at odds with our simple "vulnerability" model of who participates, these findings are quite in accord with research on general social participation. Because only central-city residents were interviewed, we have in effect controlled for a great deal of variation in the social classes of our white respondents, yeilding a sample in which Black participation rates should be higher (Verba and Nie, 1972). A host of studies indicate that participation in anticrime activity in particular also is more common among Blacks (Schneider, 1975; Nehnevajsa and Karelitz, 1977; Marx and Archer, 1972; Washnis, 1976). Among our ten target neighborhoods, interestingly, three of the four most participative localities were Black communities: Logan and West Philadelphia, and Woodlawn. Other research points to higher levels of participation by upper-income persons (Wilson and Schneider, 1978; Governor's Commission on Crime Prevention and Crime Control, 1976). Studies of political activity also register a fall-off in participation among the elderly.

The hypothesis that a general "participation" model rather than a crime-specific model is most useful for understanding this form of organizational involvement can also be tested by comparing our respondents who were involved in crime-focused groups with those who were involved in groups that did nothing concerning crime. Using this data, DuBow and Podolefsky (1979) examined differences between these two types of participators on a host of demographic,

TABLE 13.2   Summary Analysis of Participation

Indicator	Beta	(Significance)
Fear of crime	−.03	(.32-ns)
Neighborhood trends — worse	−.04	(.16-ns)
Neighborhood Linkages		
Residential ties	.08	(.02)
Social ties	.17	(.01+)
Personal Attributes		
Black	.08	(.01)
Income	.13	(.01+)
Age	.08	(.02)
$R^2 = .07$		
$N = 1106$		

SOURCE: Computed from combined citywide surveys.

behavioral, and attitudinal measures. They found no significant, meaningful differences between those reporting that they were involved in crime groups and those linked to other groups, although both kinds of participators were different from nonparticipators on a number of dimensions. This again underscored the importance of understanding how it is that groups decide to add crime to their agendas. People chose to participate or not to participate in neighborhood affairs, while leaders of organizations are responsible for guiding those groups in the direction of crime prevention.

Summary

Thus far, this chapter has documented a number of contradictory and sometimes unexpected relationships among the correlates of participation in anticrime organizations. Neighborhood integration and pessimistic assessments of local crime conditions were both positively related to participation, although they generally are negatively related to one another; perceptions of crime problems were positively related to participation but fear was negatively related to the same measure; high-income and Black respondents both claimed higher rates of involvement. People who were involved were much more likely to know of local victims, which generally is related to higher levels of fear.

In order to sort out the unique effect of each of these clusters of factors, we entered them all in a multivariate analysis of participation. The results are presented in Table 13.2.

This analysis points to the central importance of two factors: social linkages with the community, and general patterns of participation. Controlling for all other variables, Blacks, high-income persons, mature adults, and people who enjoyed wide contacts in the community were more likely to participate. Participation was unrelated to fear of crime and perceptions of bad neighborhood trends when those factors were taken into account. Their otherwise negative relationship to participation seems spurious, due largely to their relationship to integration. Controlling for social class and other factors clarified the high rates of participation evidenced by Black residents of these cities. Not surprisingly, participation and local social ties were strongly intertwined, for the relationship between them is doubtless reciprocal.

The overall predictive power of the analysis presented in Table 13.2 is quite low. This is preordained by the dichotomous nature of the dependent variable and its extremely skewed distribution. In these cities involvement in crime-focused groups is in some ways a "rare event," similar in frequency to some forms of victimization. In the simple bivariate analyses we employed a distribution-free measure of correlation, gamma, which is unaffected by the fact that only 13.5% of our respondents were in the "involved" category. However, this multivariate analysis retains parametric assumptions, including normality, and is severely strained by the data. The results are generally consistent with the strength of the simple correlations, and can be observed in complex cross-tabulations as well.

These findings are generally consistent with those concerning patterns of participation across our ten study neighborhoods. Like the individual-level analysis, the factors that have been considered here are only weakly correlated with levels of participation at the neighborhood level. The patterns that are clear, however, also indicate the importance of integration, race, and class as determinants of collective activity concerning crime.

The most consistent correlates of levels of participation in crime-focused groups across these neighborhoods are our aggregated measures of neighborhood social and residential ties. Involvement increases with the extent of integration, albeit in quite scattered fashion. Figure 13.1 depicts this relationship, using our indicator of the strength of residential ties. Neighborhoods that *deviate* from this pattern seem to match the race and class factors that were identified as crucial in understanding participative activity in general. Of the three neighborhoods that evidence substantially "too much" participation on the basis of their levels of integration, two are Black

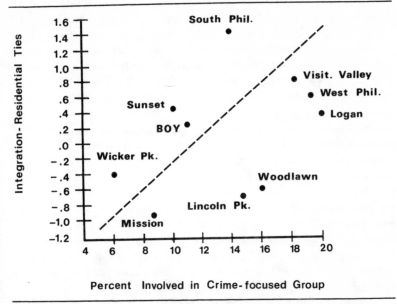

Figure 13.1 Integration and Involvement in Crime-Focused Groups
SOURCE: Computed from ten neighborhood surveys.

communities (Logan and Woodlawn), and one is the highest-income neighborhood that was surveyed, Lincoln Park. As we noted above, there was generally a strong tendency for Black neighborhoods to report high levels of participation in community affairs.

The most distinctive outlier in the direction of evidencing *less* participation than it "should" have had was South Philadelphia. This, too, may be attributable to its social compostion, for South Philadelphia is a white community where residents report distinctively low family incomes and very low levels of education. On the other hand, many have speculated (see Emmons, 1979; Crenson, 1978) that communities enjoying extremely high levels of integration may not require organized group action to handle local problems. Among these study neighborhoods, South Philadelphia alone may fall into this category. On our measure of residential ties South Philadelphia scored 66% above the next most integrated community, Visitacion Valley; on the social ties measure it was 75% higher than the next most integrated (and quite similar) community, Back-of-the-Yards. When participation in local institutions (like churches) and informal social networks achieves very high levels, communities may be able to address many issues involving social control without resort to formal organizations. Those may only be required where people generally do not recognize strangers, know local youths, visit with neighbors frequently, or feel a part of the neighborhood, to the extent to which South Philadelphians report that they do.

These interpretations clearly cannot be confirmed, for in the absence of strong linear effects virtually any pattern can be imposed visually upon observations of ten neighborhoods. These places tend to disconfirm the importance of crime and fear as generators of citizen and organizational involvement in crime. At the neighborhood level, our measures of the extent of crime problems, of social-order problems, and fear of crime all were negatively related to reports of participation in groups doing something about crime. This is quite predictable given the close association between low levels of crime and high levels of integration across these ten sites. Correlations between participation and these measures again were low, but it was impossible to discern any positive "environmental pressure" for the popularity of anticrime activities in these data.

If anything, the fear-and-participation nexus that has been observed in these ten neighborhoods is more supportive of the view that crime is incapacitating. The suspicion, distrust, isolation, and declining community attachment that presumably go hand in hand with high levels of fear may retard rather than stimulate group-based activity focused on the problem. Our findings with regard to participation and "need" for activity to prevent crime parallel those in the previous chapter — they do not go together at all. While Lavrakas et al. (1980) argue that there may be "two paths" to participation in crime-focused groups — a "social path" and a "crime prevention path" — we find only one. Like many forms of household protection, collective involvenment seems to be stimulated most by a vested interest in the community. Ironically, at the neighborhood level participation is highest in places where fear often is lower. With the exception of participation by Blacks, those who are most involved in these activities are those who personally seem the least affected by crime problems.

Chapter 14

FLIGHT TO THE SUBURBS

Introduction

Until now we have only considered actions that people take to protect their persons and property in the face of neighborhood crime. All involved either efforts to prevent crime or actions to reduce the chances of being victimized in their home communities. There is another way in which urban dwellers can deal with crime, however — to flee the city. Socially and politically, this may be the most dramatic and consequential reaction to crime.

Since World War II population growth on the fringes of our greatest cities has been phenomenal. The first great surge of postwar suburban growth can be attributed to the pent-up demand for housing which developed during previous decades. Since then a variety of "push" and "pull" forces have been at work encouraging continuing outmigration from America's central cities. A number of those forces are economic. There have been massive shifts in the location of jobs and concomitant changes in the ratio of services to taxes which favor suburban over inner-city jurisdictions. Other factors stimulating flight are social, including the "pull" of open-space suburban housing styles and the "push" of racial conflict in the central city. One of these social elements may be crime. Surburban crime rates (especially violent crime) are generally lower than those in the central city. High rates of victimization and fear may induce people to leave city neighborhoods, and low suburban rates may influence where those who are moving decide to settle. This chapter explores the role of crime in the suburbanization of the metropolis.

Research on the role of crime in precipitating flight from the inner city is far from definitive in its findings. The issue is complex, for it appears that residential relocation is a two-stage process. Certain factors induce people to change their places of residence, while others shape the direction and distance they migrate. The decision to move is linked to the stage in the life cycle in which a family finds itself. Households move primarily because of changes in marital status, shifts in family size, and changes in family income (Duncan and Newman, 1976). Their choices of destinations when they do move are more affected by social and cultural factors, within a set of relatively stringent economic and racial constraints. It is here that we are most likely to find the effect of crime.

General population surveys indicate that crime usually is not a very important factor in shaping decisions to move. LEAA's city victimization surveys quizzed members of households that reported moving within the past five years about why they left their old neighborhoods. In the eight high-impact cities surveyed in 1973, only 3% of these household informants cited crime as an important reason for moving; adding perceptions that the "neighborhood was deteriorating" or that "bad elements were moving in" to the area raised that figure only to 10%. Most people reported that they moved to find better houses or more convenient neighborhoods (Garofalo, 1977a). Reiss (1967) found the same pattern in his study of high-crime neighborhoods in three cities. In Portland, Rifai (1976) asked elderly residents who had moved within the past ten years why they had done so, and only 5% mentioned crime. Finally, a national Gallup poll (American Institute of Public Opinion, 1978) found that crime was the fourth most frequently mentioned reason that urban residents wanted to move, among those who desired to do so.

Note that except for the Gallup poll these all were retrospective studies, asking people why they had moved. We have no basis for judging the validity of reports of these reconstructed motivations, and no knowledge of how conditions or events since that move may have affected people's interpretations of their past behavior.

Most researchers find that current residents of higher-risk city neighborhoods are more likely to express a strong desire to move somewhere else. Droettboom et al. (1971) found that respondents in a national survey who felt that crime and violence were significant problems in their communities were more dissatisfied with their neighborhoods and were more likely to indicate that they wanted to move. Central-city residents were more likely to be in those categories. Kasl and Harburg (1972) surveyed residents of higher- and lower-status neighborhoods in both Black and white areas of Detroit. They found that residents of higher crime areas were preoccupied with crime, thought their chances of being robbed were high, and

were much more desirous of moving out. This stemmed in part from
their perceptions of crime problems. People who reported feeling
unsafe in their areas also were more threatened by crime and youth
gangs, and were more likely to have been victimized. These crime-
related factors affected their general dissatisfaction with the community and, through that, their willingness to go elsewhere.

Most analyses of patterns of actual city-suburan population flow,
on the other hand, employ aggregate census data on residential location. These consistently show an association between crime and
outward migration. In recent multivariate analyses of 1965-1970 population shifts in large SMSAs, Frey (1979) and Marshall (1979) found
that the impact of crime on the shift of households in the direction of
the suburbs was substantial. The zero-order correlation between
Frey's aggregated measures of suburban relocation and central-city
crime was +.43; in Marshall's study of relocation by whites it was
+.32.

Missing from all of this research are data on relocation which can
be linked to the fears and assessments of risk of the individuals
involved. Most survey studies of inner-city neighborhoods employ
measures of the *desire* of respondents to relocate. This is a serious
flaw, for many more people report a desire or even an intention to
move than actually do so. In one longitudinal study, less than one-half
of those who indicated that they would move within the next three
years did so (Duncan and Newman, 1976). None of these studies
interviewed suburban residents in a way that enables us to compare
them with central-city dwellers in order to discern why some moved
there and others did not. In fact, the LEAA surveys, Reiss's
neighborhood study, and the others all questioned only inner-city
residents. Many who were most likely to actually move to the suburbs
would not be included in the sample — for they would already have
done so. Any study of flight from the central city must have a suburban component.

Aggregate data studies of the problem are useful accounts of
macro-level trends. However, they tend to model a host of complex
hypotheses about the calculations of individuals with a few simple
indicators. For example, while people with children advancing toward school age may be attracted to the suburbs, it is unlikely that
separate measures of "percentage moved" and "percentage under
five years of age" at the SMSA level will capture the microeconomics
of the decisional process. Except for data on jobs and housing, these
studies also focus almost exclusively upon measures of inner-city
conditions, the "push" correlates of relocation, and not on the relative "pull" of attractive suburban alternatives (Marshall, 1979).

Flight in Metropolitan Chicago

In order to investigate the impact of crime upon flight from the city we employed our special survey encompassing the suburbs surrounding Chicago. This survey included many of the measures which we developed for our studies of reactions to crime in central cities. The major difference between the two projects was that this effort included the entire metropolitan region. After appropriate weighting to adjust for the fact that some households had more than one telephone line, the survey had an effective sample size of 1656. Of these, 48% lived in the city of Chicago, and 52% were randomly scattered across 147 suburban municipalities. This matched almost exactly our preliminary estimates of the city-suburban distribution of the area's population.

In this survey the prefix of the telephone number that we dialed identified the present city or suburban location of each sample household. Early in the questionnaire we asked, "Where did you last live before you moved to your present neighborhood?" The responses included central-city locations (49%), suburban places in the Chicago area (27%), places elsewhere in the United States or abroad (16%), and those who indicated that they were lifelong residents of the same area (8%). Our measure of residential relocation is based upon the difference between the last place the respondent lived and his or her current place of residence. Those who continued to live in the city (lifelong residents and people who moved but stayed within the city) we classified as "stayers." Those who previously lived in the central city but currently reside in the suburbs were classified as "movers." All of this analysis of flight from the central city is based on comparisons between these two groups. This excludes two groups from this analysis: those who always lived in the suburbs, and those who previously lived outside of the metropolitan area. While the residential location descisions of these groups are important, they cannot be interpreted as "flight." Together, these groups constituted 51% of our sample. Of the 893 persons included in this analysis, 74% remained city dwellers and 26% left for the suburbs.

This is a far-from-perfect indicator of suburban flight. Most notably, because we could ask only about the *last* places people lived before their current locations, we misclassified those who did flee the city but since then had made one or more intrasuburban moves. Those who moved from the city and left the metropolitan area entirely were lost from our sample area as well. The best evidence is, however, that extra-SMSA migration is precipitated by radical changes in employment or lifestyle preferences, and not by comparative assessments of cities and thier suburbs (Frey, 1979). Empirically, migration seems quite different from relocation, and does not involve the calculations with which we are concerned here (Rossi, 1980).

Comparative profiles of those who left the central city and those who did not reveal some striking differences between the two groups. Those who remained behind were poor. Over 40% of stayers reported family incomes of less than $10,000 per year, while the comparable figure for those who departed was only 16%. Those who moved out were more likely to be married than single, and more who stayed behind did not graduate from high school or attend college. There was a slight tendency for movers to be older than stayers, 28% of whom were under thirty years of age.

By far the most substantial correlate of residential relocation, however, was race. Of those remaining in the inner city, 54% were white, but 94% of those who fled were white. While not all whites have left the city, virtually all of those who have fled are white.

This underscores the irony of the studies of residential dissatisfaction we summarized above. Those studies indicate that Blacks and the poor are far more likely to express discontent with their condition; they cannot, however, find refuge in the suburbs. Kasl and Harburg (1972) found that Blacks were more dissatisfied with their neighborhoods on every dimension, and were more likely to indicate a desire to move. When asked if they actually would move, however, they more realistically reported that probably they would not. Among whites, low-income persons exhibit a similar profile. Droettboom et al. (1971) followed up their survey with a study three years later of actual residential mobility, and found that many who wanted to move could not. The constraints of race and class are among the reasons why survey questions about one's desire to move are not highly related to actual residential relocation.

In short, the problem of flight to the suburbs is a white flight problem. Almost regardless of their income, position in the life cycle, or residential dissatisfaction, Black families are more likely to remain in the central city. Our analysis of the role of crime in precipitating relocation, then, is more appropriately a study of the options open to whites, and which one they choose.

When we reexamine patterns of residential mobility for our metropolitan sample of whites, the dimensions of the flight problem become more apparent: Fully 47% of those who once lived in the city now live in the suburbs. Among Blacks, 7% fled the city and 93% remained there, but whites divided almost evenly among these two groups. Among whites, families and those with the wherewithal to move often did so. Over 50% of movers reported family incomes in excess of $20,000 per year, in contrast with only 36% for those remaining in the city.

There was a modest but consistent effect of life-cycle status on residential location choice as well. Almost two-thirds of those who moved out of the city were married, but only 47% of those who remained behind were in the same category. In order to investigate the effect of potential family formation on relocation, we compared those in prime condition for parenthood — households made up of married couples, one of whom was under 40 — with those who were in some way out of that category. Of those younger married couples, 74% had children living with them when we conducted our interviews. We found that 56% of those currently in the family-formation stage of the life cycle had moved out of the city, as contrasted to 44% of all others.

We also found some evidence of a relationship between place of residence and place of work among whites. Working in the city and staying in the city were only weakly related, but in multivariate analyses this correlation became much stronger. We cannot be sure that the march to the suburbs by this sample was precipitated by the relocation of their jobs, for people may have found suburban jobs after moving there. However, the correlation is consistent with a "pull" effect of growing suburban employment.

Flight and Center-City Crime

In an attempt to explain patterns of white flight, we gathered reports of conditions in the places our respondents lived before and the places where they live now. To assess "push" factors affecting residential relocation we asked them "how much of a problem" various aspects of life presented in their old areas. These problem dimensions included "quality of public schools," "the kind of people who live there," "convenience to work," and "crime and safety." We were interested in the relative importance of crime and other push factors in motivating residential movement. Crime proved to be the most important of these problems. However, none of them seem related to decisions to move out. The data are presented in Table 14.1.

For whites as a whole there were no significant differences between those who stayed in the city and those who reported leaving, on these indicators of community conditions. While 21% of those who fled to the suburbs reported that crime as a "big problem" in their city neighborhoods, 20% of whites who stayed behind made the same assessment. To look at those proportions another way, among whites

TABLE 14.1 Rating of City Neighborhood Problems

Conditions in City Neighborhood	Percentage Rating Condition "A Big Problem" Residential Location	
	Stayed in City	Moved to Suburbs from City
Quality of public schools	14	16
Kind of people living there	18	15
Convenience to work	4	7
Crime and safety	20	21

NOTE: Number of cases approximately 503 for each comparison. None of these differences are significant ($p > .05$).

SOURCE: Computed from metropolitan area survey sample, white respondents only.

who reported that crime was a "big problem," 49% left the city, while among those who said it was "almost no problem," 44% fled. These differences are statistically negligible. This lack of a difference between the two groups characterizes responses about other problems as well. Note that virtually none of our respondents cited accessibility to work as a problem. This is in line with other research on this issue, which suggests that in the era of the automobile work place accessibility is not an important factor in urban residential choice (Granfield, 1975). We also found no "generational" differences in the effect of crime on locational choice. During the 1950s crime rates in the city were fairly stable, while they rose sharply during the 1970s, and stabilized at a high level during the 1980s. However, there were no differences in assessments of inner-city crime conditions between those who moved out of the city and those who moved but stayed within the city during each of those eras.

While among whites as a group there were no discernible effects of community conditions, crime problems (and other factors) did relate to residential relocation by higher-income households. There were no significant differences between lower-income movers and stayers in terms of neighborhood crime problems. However, among white families reporting current incomes in excess of $20,000 per year, more of those recalling crime problems in their areas had fled. The data are presented in Table 14.2.

As we can see, there is an interaction between income and assessments of crime problems; those problems were more likely to precipitate flight to the suburbs among white families that had the wherewithal to make the move. Among those with fewer resources

TABLE 14.2   Income, Crime Problems, and Residential Relocation

Current Income and Extent Crime a Problem in Original Neighborhood	Percentage Moved to Suburbs	(N)	Significance of Difference Between Movers and Stayers
Under $10,000			
Not a problem	38	(79)	ns (p = .17)
Some problem	20	(30)	
Big problem	28	(36)	
$10,000 to $20,000			
Not a problem	47	(106)	ns (p = .89)
Some problem	50	(50)	
Big problem	46	(34)	
More than $20,000			
Not a problem	47	(124)	(p = .01+)
Some problem	66	(76)	
Big problem	67	(48)	

SOURCE: Computed from metropolitan area survey sample, white respondents only.

there was no significant relationship between perceptions of crime problems and movement out of the city. Higher-income city dwellers (who made up 42% of our sample), were responsive to untoward conditions in their old environs — two-thirds of them left. An analysis of variance employing these measures pointed to the same conclusion. There was no significant main effect of perceived crime problems on flight by whites; however, there was a significant crime-income interaction effect on flight, and its joint impact was about one-half as strong as the main effect of income. Note, however, more well-to-do respondents were the least likely to find themselves in troubled neighborhoods, and that a majority of high-income whites in the city of Chicago placed themselves in the "no problems" category.

The fact that moving was related to income and marital status, and (for much of the sample) not to reports of local conditions, is consistent with most research on residential mobility (Quigley and Weinberg, 1977). As we noted above, that research indicates that for most people the decision to move is linked to personal, economic, and life-cycle considerations. Thus Droettboom et al. (1971) found in a three-year follow-up of a survey about moving intentions that earlier perceptions of crime problems were not related to which households actually left the communities they were studying. Those who thought that crime was a serious problem were no more likely to move out of their neighborhoods than those who did not think crime was a problem there. Further, central-city residents who thought that crime was bad in their areas were *less* likely than others to have moved to the suburbs. Overall, less than 2% of their sample evidenced the combination of perceptions of fear and residential relocation that make up the "crime push" hypothesis.

On the other hand, the destination decisions of movers should be more sensitive to conditions characterizing potential places of residence. Crime may be one of several factors affecting the desirability of various residential locations from which (white) city dwellers are relatively free to choose. These are the factors which attract families which have decided to pull up stakes. For example, dissatisfaction with one's home generally is a more important impetus for moving than is unhappiness with neighborhood conditions (Duncan and Newman, 1976). Higher-income persons have more extravagant ambitions with regard to the size, style, and privacy their homes should afford (Kasl and Harburg, 1972). They are, as a result, propelled toward the suburbs in search of more appropriate surroundings. In an aggregate-data study of white relocation patterns, Marshall (1979) found that suburban pull factors rather than center-city push factors predominated.

Our Chicago-area survey indicates that among the pull factors we measured crime was the most important overt consideration consciously shaping residential relocation decisions among whites. We asked respondents who had moved anywhere to rate "how important" the conditions we analyzed in Table 14.1 were when they chose their new neighborhoods. The "quality of public schools" was rated "very important" by 37%, "the kind of people living there" by 48%, "convenience to work" by 49%, and "crime and safety" by 64%. There is little doubt where lower rates of property and (especially) personal crime can generally be found in a metropolitan area. In Chicago, the official robbery rate two years before our survey was 563 per 100,000 in the city and only 65 per 100,000 in the suburbs. The corresponding figures for assault were 328 and 113, and for burglary 1114 and 970, respectively.[1]

The Consequences of Flight

Our last question concerns the outcome of decisions to stay in or leave the central city. If those who fled the city found improved conditions, then exiting the inner city may have been a reasonable response to their concerns — for those who could afford it, and were allowed to do so. From the perspective of those involved, conditions in their current neighborhoods are the consequences of leaving or staying.

TABLE 14.3   Current Neighborhood Ratings of Problems

Conditions in Current Neighborhood	*Percentage Rating Condition "A Big Problem" or "Some Problem" Residential Location*	
	Stayed in City	*Moved to Suburbs*
Buildings or storefronts sitting abandoned or burned out	18	4
Fires being set on purpose	17	5
Vandalism — like kids breaking windows, writing on walls, or things like that	48	37
People breaking in or sneaking into homes to steal something	53	33
Groups of teenagers hanging out on the streets	49	29
People being robbed or having their purses or wallets taken on the street	45	10
People being attacked or beaten up by strangers	28	8

NOTE: Number of cases approximately 585 for each comparison. All differences are significant ($p < .01+$).

SOURCE: Computed from metropolitan area survey sample, white respondents only.

We measured these consequences with respect to crime by asking each of our respondents to assess "how much of a problem" each of seven crime-related conditions was in his or her present neighborhood. These conditions ranged from building abandonment and vandalism to street robbery and arson. Table 14.3 presents the results for whites who either remained in the city or moved to the suburbs.

As we can see, differences in the conditions each group faces as a result of moving or staying are considerable. Building abandonment, street robbery, assault, and arson are three or four times more frequently cited as "big problems" by city residents. Vandalism, burglary, and teenagers often present difficulties for suburbanites, but still are significantly greater problems in the city. By these measures, those who relocated out of the central city achieved a great deal.

We can also read the benefits of suburban flight in our respondents' ratings of crime conditions in their old and new neighborhoods. Among those who moved anywhere (excluding our 60 white city respondents who had always lived in the same neighborhood) we compared separate ratings of the extent to which neighborhood crime was a problem in their old communities and their new locations. For most whites (57%) conditions remained the same, but more improved their lot than worsened it as a result of the move. Whatever their ratings of their original neighborhoods, 27% placed their current residences lower on our crime problems measure, and only 16% placed them higher. Where they moved to made a substantial difference, however. Among those who moved to the suburbs from the city, only 7% came off worse as a result. Those who stayed in the city were only slightly better off as a result of relocation — 31% improved their conditions, but 25% rated their new city neighborhoods as more problem-prone than the ones they left.

The relation between moving to the suburbs and improving the quality of one's life was independent of income. It is not simply that white respondents who fled the city had the money to acquire greater security anywhere. At all income levels, those who fled improved their positions vis-à-vis crime. For example, of those reporting income levels under $10,000 per year who stayed within the confines of the city, 25% gave higher ratings to their new neighborhoods there; among low-income people who moved to the suburbs, 66% fared better there. At all income levels, those who stayed in the city only broke even. Among those reporting earnings under $10,000, 23% gave their new neighborhoods worse ratings; for those in the $20,000-and-above category, 22% were worse off. In other words, the improvement in condition that we have described seems truly to be caused by flight from the city. Flight was greatly encouraged by having the money to afford the move, but anyone who moved out was much more likely to achieve greater security as a result.

Finally, flight seems to have had dramatic consequences for levels of fear among those who previously lived in the city. Comparing those who moved and those who stayed with respect to their current levels of fear illustrates the great gulf between them in terms of neighborhood crime conditions. Among whites, 63% of those who moved to the suburbs now place themselves in the "very safe" category, as contrasted to only 28% of those who did not. Only 13% of those who moved out of the city now feel either "very" or even "somewhat" unsafe. The correlation (gamma) between our measures of fear and flight was +.52. This effect was unshaken when we controlled for the sex, age, and income of our respondents; the partial correlation between flight and fear was lower than the simple correlation between the two only at the second decimal place, and the statistical impact of staying or fleeing was second only to sex in predicting levels of fear.

A Return to the City?

One of the most interesting findings we can report is that our Chicago-area survey did uncover some evidence of a return-to-the-city movement as well as a great deal of suburban flight. Of course, it is much smaller than the reverse flow, but more of it is of recent vintage.

Among our respondents that reported living in the suburbs before their most recent moves (and they were almost exclusively white), 12% now live in the city. They constitute 5% of all the white respondents who moved or stayed in this analysis. These repatriates are distinctive in many ways. They are young (44% are under 30), educated (58% reported "some college"), often unmarried (54% are single), and are renters rather than home owners. On the average, they have lived in the city for only five years.

They had few complaints about their old suburban communities; in fact, their perceptions of neighborhood problems matched those who stayed there. Their distinctive discontent with suburbia was over its inconvenience to work. In this group, 38% indicated that this was "some problem" or a "big problem." In response to questions about employment, 65% reported that they work in the city. Probably because of thier high income and freedom to choose among many residential options, whites who have returned to the city report less troublesome conditions in their new neighborhoods than do those who never left. For example, only 4% of them rated vandalism a "big problem" in their areas, in contrast to 14% of those who continued to live in the city throughout.

What we do not know is whether or not their current residence in the city is a temporary accommodation to their position in the life cycle; as renters and short-term residents, they may be "just passing through." In general, the return-to-the-city movement by the relatively well-to-do has been confined to renters, and this may indivudually limit their stake in core-city revival (Eklund and Williams, 1978). But with sufficient and continuing numbers, even a transitory population can have considerable impact upon a neighborhood or larger community. A neighborhood may be a "stable" place in the sense that the "same kind of people" continue to live there, even if they individually come and go at a relatively rapid pace.

Summary

The irony of flight as a reaction to crime, of course, is that it is most effective when only a few people take advantage of it. The payoff of flight was considerable for our respondents. Movers report better neighborhood conditions than stayers, and those who moved out of the city improved their positions more substantially than did those who moved to other neighborhoods within the city. Some of this advantage doubtless can be laid to the social and economic barriers which limit the scope of relocation. As long as vast demographic chasms divide city from suburb they will retain their distinctiveness with regard to a host of problems and offer greater security for those who blend in. Unlike actual crime prevention efforts, however, the more people flee the less they individually and collectively will gain. If flight becomes more pervasive and heterogeneous in character, and as new cities and employment centers spring up on the metropolitan fringe to provide for that new life, the comparative advantage of suburban relocation will decline.

Our survey of metropolitan Chicago revealed a substantial amount of movement out of the central city. Even based only on information about their most recent moves, it appears that one-quarter of those who previously lived in the city have moved to the suburban fringe. This can fairly be characterized as "white flight." Despite evidence of recent increases in the number of Blacks in Chicago's suburbs, painfully few of those we interviewed had been able to exercise that option. In general, residential relocations by Blacks involve moves of relatively short distances and only marginally upgrade their housing. In one study, Blacks were three times more likely than whites to be involved in involuntary moves, and they faced a tighter and more constrained housing market when they were forced to relocate (MacAllister, 1971). Among whites in our study, on the other hand, almost one-half had left the city.

It appears that decisions about residential relocation among whites involve two sets of calculations; some factors stimulate movement, while others shape its course. The decision to move usually reflects changes in household composition or the position of its members in the life cycle. Where it relocates, on the other hand, may involve the relative strength of various "pull" and "push" forces which shape intrametropolitan migration patterns. Studies of racial residential succession point in the same direction. For example, overt anti-Black attitudes do not generally predict actual movement by whites, which is controlled more by class and income factors. When moving, whites make residential location choices based on their perceptions of what the general future course of neighborhoods will be (Aldrich, 1975). With regard to crime, we found more evidence supporting the pull effect of attractive suburban locations than we found support for explanations of relocation which favor central-city push factors. Neighborhood abandonment and decline may be due less to the flight of area residents than to the fact that few people find good reason to move *into* areas characterized by high levels of crime and other social problems.

Our data document most convincingly the importance of constraints in shaping residential relocation. The option of moving to the suburbs seems largely to be closed to Blacks, and there are relocation hurdles over which relatively few lower-income whites can leap as well. There is ample evidence that Black city dwellers frequently attempt to put some distance between themselves and crime. In a study in Philadelphia, Savitz et al. (1977) found that 39% of Black parents had tried to transfer their children to safer schools, and that 28% were trying to move to safer neighborhoods. The inability of middle-class Blacks to gain access to the metropolitan housing market is frequently cited as an explanation for the fact that they suffer substantially higher rates of victimization than do their white counterparts (Hindelang et al., 1978). In our survey, Blacks were more likely than city-dwelling whites to indicate that they planned to move, but the best evidence indicates that this move will be confined to the inner city.

We found evidence of similar barriers to the relocation of lower-income households as well. Low-income persons were more likley to indicate that they planned to move, but a higher family income was the strongest correlate — following being white — of fleeing rather than remaining in the city. We also found the only evidence of a push effect of crime among those who could most readily afford to relocate in response to deteriorating neighborhood conditions. Class and race barriers may be confounded here, for 63% of the (few) Black respondents who indicated that they had moved out of the city reported yearly family incomes in excess of $15,000. However, when we control for income differences, Black residents of the metropolitan area are underrepresented among those who left the city in every income category.

There is considerable evidence that the growth of the suburbs has had deleterious consequences for the cities they surround (Kasarda, 1972). Housing investment has followed the movement of people, and both white-collar and higher-paying blue-collar occupations have begun to concentrate on the fringes of the metropolis (Kasarda, 1976). With industrial and commercial investment following the construction of new housing, the central-city tax base has begun to decline both proportionally and absolutely. At the same time, the proportion of service-receiving residents in inner-city populations has increased.

This has further accelerated a trend toward even greater central-city/suburban differentiation with respect to the incidence of social problems. In the case of crime, in places where suburbs have grown most extensively there is much more reported crime concentrated in the central city (Skogan, 1977a).

The findings presented here and elsewhere present something of a dilemma in this regard, however. The current comparative advantage of suburbia is great on most quality-of-life dimensions. It seems unlikely that crime (or other neighborhood conditions such as those we probed earlier in this chapter) could be curbed enough in central cities to bring it into the suburban range — in the case of robbery, this would involve reducing reported crime rates by a factor of nine. Moreover, if relocation out of the city is indeed a function of pull more than of push factors, the fate of the central city would seem to lie in the hands of others, elsewhere. The decision to move seems largely independent of the neighborhood-related factors we have discussed here, and is affected rather by shifts in even more fundamental social and economic arrangements. These certainly are beyond the ken of the most ambitious urban administrators. If racial barriers to individual relocation decisions were somehow overcome, this triumph might well exacerbate the problem. Currently those barriers bottle many moderate-income Black families in the city, and opening up housing markets might only extend the flight option to many who would gladly take it.

NOTE

1. The crime data for these figures came from the Chicago Police Department (for city community areas) and the Illinois Law Enforcement Commission (for suburban municipalities). Population estimates used in computing these rates came from the Chicago Department of Planning, the Northern Illinois Planning Commission, and the U.S. Census Bureau.

Chapter 15

CONCLUSION

Introduction

The research reported in this volume sought to understand fear of crime and how people variously cope with the threat of crime. From the outset it was clear the origins of fear and reactions to crime were complex issues. Research in this area had revealed two paradoxes concerning the relationship between crime and fear of crime. The first was that many more people are fearful than report being directly involved with crime; the second was that many of the most fearful urban dwellers are in groups that enjoy the lowest rates of victimization. There also was a seeming paradox in the apparent lack of a clear relation between fear and behavior. On the one hand, commentators indicated big-city residents were virtually "prisoners of fear"; on the other, governments were spending vast sums of money attempting to convince these residents to do things to protect themselves from crime.

The model we pursued to unravel these puzzles was a cognitive and volitional one. The elements in the model reflected the assumption — despite these apparent paradoxes — that people act in response to assessments of risk in their environments and the potential costs of becoming involved in crime. Further, we recognized that in doing so, people could only choose among the alternatives that were open to them. The operating model sketched in Chapter 1 indicated the general concepts which seemed to be important in understanding fear and behavior. In various chapters we then examined patterns of victimization, vulnerability to crime, neighborhood conditions, community integration, and the sources of secondhand information concerning crime. We demonstrated how those factors were related to fear and to the things people do to protect themselves from crime, and explored how far a cognitive and volitional model can go toward explaining attitudes and behavior.

This concluding chapter reviews those findings, and speculates about the long-run implications of what we found.

The Basis of Fear

Four factors proved to be significant correlates of fear: victimization, vulnerability, vicarious experience, and neighborhood conditions. Not all aspects of these elements of the model were equally important, however.

Victimization. Direct, personal experience with crime was directly related to fear. The seemingly obvious connection between the two had been obscured in past studies by the inadequate measurement of victimization and the failure to recognize that some types of crime are more strongly related to fear than are experiences with property crime, and that victimizations involving rape and serious physical injury were the most traumatic. The relation between victimization and fear was clarified by controlling for the sex and age correlates of both, for young males are disproportionately victimized by violent crimes but generally are less fearful.

While victims are more fearful, most people have not been victimized in the recent past. Victimization, especially in its most serious forms, is a "rare event." In other research this has confounded the analysis of the relation between victimization and fear, for experience with crime is infrequent enough to break the mathematical requirements of most statistics. This has sometimes led to the incorrect conclusion that the two were "unrelated." We also found that *among* various forms of victimization those rated by the public as the most serious are the least frequent forms of predation. In any given year the most fear-provoking crimes strike only a small fraction of the population.

The most common serious crime we examined, burglary, had only a modest impact upon fear. On the other hand, because of its frequency, the *aggregate* impact of burglary may be very large. We dubbed the intersection of the frequency of crime and its impact on fear its "net effect."

Many people live in households that recently have been burglarized. Further, unlike most personal crimes, burglary victimization is widely distributed in the population. It is as high in wealthy as in low-income areas, and it strikes whites almost as frequently as it does Blacks. Thus burglary may spread concern about victimization in places that are otherwise insulated from serious crime.

Vulnerability. Vulnerability to victimization also was a useful clue for understanding the fears and actions of potential victims. We examined in detail two forms of vulnerability to crime, physical and social. Physical vulnerability entails powerlessness to resist attack, while social vulnerability reflects frequent exposure to the threat of victimization. There are a number of potential indicators of people's standing on each of these dimensions, and numerous investigations have found those measures are among the strongest and most consistent predictors of fear and crime-related behavior. We found that measures of physical vulnerability had a stronger relation to fear than did those reflecting social vulnerability. This accounts in part for the generally inverse relationship between personal victimization and fear. As we saw, measures of physical vulnerability were among the strongest correlates of reduced exposure to risk of personal attack.

We did not find that persons who are more vulnerable to crime are more attuned to conditions around them, however. It has been argued that groups like women and the elderly, who may suffer more substantial consequences if they are victimized, are more sensitive to variations in the risks of their environment. In every test, the effects of threatening surroundings and vulnerability to attack were cumulative but independent of one another.

Vicarious Experience. Because of the relatively low incidence of direct experience with crime in comparison to the frequency of fear, it is clear that many people are reacting instead to secondhand impressions concerning the threat of crime. We examined in depth two sources of such messages, the media and personal conversation. We could find no discernible impact of the media, but the latter carried news of great significance to those we interviewed.

A content analysis of local media confirmed that the coverage of crime in these cities was ubiquitous. There was extensive coverage of crime in the newspapers and a complementary study indicates that television news is, if anything, more devoted to such events. The media emphasizes violence. In general, media coverage is inversely related to the true frequency of various types of criminal incidents. Newspapers in these cities were so similar in this respect that it did not seem meaningful to attempt to distinguish among them in terms of their impact upon readers, and it seems likely this umbrella could be extended to include television as well.

At the consumer end, our survey revealed widespread attention to crime news. Over three-quarters of our respondents were recently exposed to crime via the media. There were differences among groups in which of the media they were most attentive to, which served to spread crime news throughout the population. Attention to crime in the media was as common in low crime neighborhoods as in high crime neighborhoods, and the same among low- and high-victimization groups. Thus it potentially could account for fear among lower-risk strata.

However, we could discern no impact of media exposure on fear of crime. Controlling for other relevant factors, we found no relation between fear and attentiveness to either television or newspaper coverage of crime. This is in line with some previous research which indicates that media effects are confined to more abstract and general perceptions of crime, and not to close-to-home assessments of risk.

When we asked people what they felt was their best source of information about local crime, they indicated their friends and neighbors. Our analysis found that the crucial linkage between those conversations about crime and fear was the information such talk brought them about local events. When people knew of crime in their areas, they were more afraid. Further, gossip about crime seems to magnify some of its more fear-provoking features. Stories about personal crimes seem to spread further than those concerning property crime, magnifying the relative frequency of violence. Stories about women and elderly victims seem to travel further than those describing more typical victims of personal crimes. Finally, when people hear of victims like themselves, they are even more fearful as a consequence.

Conversation about crime is thus fear-provoking. And unlike direct experience with crime, the secondhand information about crime that flows through networks of interpersonal communication is not a rare event. Talk magnifies the importance of each local incident. Our analysis also documented that talk about crime spreads news widely in low crime neighborhoods as well as in high crime neighborhoods. Thus it accounts in part for the fears of people who live in areas where the actual incidence of personal crime is relatively low. And because talk is as likely to involve low-risk persons as high-risk persons, it serves to stimulate fear among those who enjoy low rates of victimization.

Neighborhood Conditions. In our survey we found significant, if minority, pessimism about neighborhood conditions and future trends. The level of concern was quite similar to the level of fear in these cities. Those who lived in certain neighborhoods were likely to indicate that major crimes were a problem and that the local social order was threatened. Like both fear and most forms of actual victimization, these concerns were more pronounced among Blacks and the poor. Thus it was not surprising that concern about local crime and disorder was strongly related to fear. Assessment that personal crime was a "big problem" in the neighborhood was the strongest predictor of fear. However, more people perceived burglary as a local problem, and as a result the net effect of burglary on fear (the combination of its impact and frequency) was greater.

Problems with crime and disorder were less common where communities were more tightly integrated. We employed two measures of integration, one reflecting the strength of social ties and the other residential ties. Controlling for other factors both were related to lower levels of fear. (One of those other factors was personal conversation about crime which was stimulated by close neighborhood ties.) Much of this effect (but not all) was due to the negative relationship between integration and local problems, however. When concern about crime and disorder was taken into account the impact of integration on fear diminished substantially. We also found little evidence of the presumed "ameliorative" consequences of integration. It has been argued that people who are more attuned to local conditions are less fearful even when the threat of crime around them is substantial. However, we found no such complex relation among crime conditions, integration, and fear.

Reactions to Crime

In our operating model we hypothesized about factors that play a key role in motivating precautionary and protective measures against crime. These included fear of crime and concern about crime-related conditions, vulnerability to victimization, knowledge of local crime, and neighborhood integration. However, many of the crime-reduction actions that we examined were not particularly responsive to these factors. Fear and neighborhood integration were most consistently linked to behavior in the way that we hypothesized. Other "causal" factors proved unrelated to crime-reduction efforts, or were linked to those activities in quite unexpected ways. As a result, the benefits of protective and preventive behavior often accrued to those who already enjoyed lower rates of victimization and lower levels of fear and concern about crime. This outcome was reinforced by suburban flight. That proved to be an act which was not particularly motivated by crime, but which still had implications for the level of crime and fear in America's central cities.

Personal Precaution. The operating model we posited at the outset was most effective in explaining patterns of exposure to personal risk and risk-reduction efforts. All but the "media path" affected the manner in which individuals dealt with the threat of attack. Our measures of personal precaution included walking with others, driving rather than walking after dark, avoiding dangerous places, and simply staying home. Reports of these precautions were related to the extent of crime and disorder problems in the neighborhood and fear, the physical and social proximity of known victims, and social and physical vulnerability. We found only a very limited role for the constraints on "free choice" we hypothesized, following our operating model. However, most of these tactics are simple, cheap, and habitual, and they only need to be employed when people want to go out after dark. Their flexibility mitigates against finding strong constraints on their use.

The personal costs that ensue could weigh heavily upon people who are forced to adopt these tactics often. They may be forced to forgo opportunities for employment, recreation, and even simple social contact. Staying at home — being a true "prisoner of fear" — may be the most significant consequence. The elderly in particular find it difficult to avoid the use of public transportation, and many cannot drive. Even walking to the store may seem threatening in places where senior centers have not organized "buddy systems" to provide them with partners. This is one of the mechanisms by which crime atomizes a community, by raising the costs of ordinary social intercourse.

On the other hand, there may be substantial individual benefits for those who avoid exposure to risk, especially if they are otherwise vulnerable and live in a high crime community. That benefit is their personal safety. One of the principal factors seemingly related to the low levels of victimization reported by many women and most senior citizens is their extremely low exposure to attack by strangers and their reduced vulnerability (by being at home) to burglary. As our model suggests, these tactics may be adopted "for good reason."

The consequences for the community which aggregate from the individual experiences of its citizens all seem to be negative in this regard. While being wary may protect individuals from harm, such wariness probably does not have any preventive payoff for the community as a whole. These precautionary tactics are passive, not aggressive actions against crime. They leave potential offenders untroubled, displacing their attention onto others who are less watchful. Further, the atomizing effects of crime may further undermine the ability of a community to exercise any semblance of order. Where people are suspicious, avoid social contact, and surrender their interest in public facilities, it is impossible to rely upon informal social-control mechanisms to control youths and suspicious persons. Someone must enforce rules governing behavior in a neighborhood. As Clotfelter (1977: 502) has noted:

> It is quite possible that some of the very measures taken by individuals for protection may actually decrease the safety of other households by interfering with routine neighborhood surveillance.

This is the "reciprocal relation" between crime and community that Wilson (1975) noted. The aggregate consequences of individual actions, which may be quite rational from the point of view of those involved, may collectively be highly dysfunctional.

An antidote to the pessimism this may engender is that our surveys did not indicate that these restrictions on personal freedom are inordinately common. The adoption of these risk-reducing tactics was concentrated in certain neighborhoods; for the cities as a whole, many people pursued only one of these tactics, and a full 40% of our respondents reported that they did not do any of them. Even taking into account those who pursued a majority of the actions we investigated, the average score on our summary precautionary measure was somewhat less than "sometimes."

Household Protection. Unlike personal precaution, efforts by households to reduce their risk of loss from property crime were not related in any simple way to the threat of victimization. Rather, we found property marking, target-hardening, surveillance, and the like were a reflection of economic stakes and social ties. Those with more resources did more (although we do not think this was because of the cost, for most of these measures are cheap). Those who were vulnerable to crimes of this sort, on the other hand, did less. Household protection was not significantly linked to the perceived level of neighborhood crime problems. It was facilitated by neighborhood integration, which generally discourages the development of crime and fear.

Thus, whatever the benefits of this sort of action, they accrue to the better-off. Blacks, the poor, renters, and those in more vulnerable dwelling units all remain more open to victimization, which runs directly counter to our simple "threat of crime" model.

There is evidence elsewhere that protective measures may reduce the chances of household victimization from burglary, at least relative to others in the immediate vicinity. Like personal precaution, it may thus encourage a "fortress mentality," multiplying the incidence of watchdogs and alarms and encouraging the installation of more locks and lights. Collectively, it is not completely clear that this is a benefit. Experiments indicate that when the adoption of household protective measures is widespread in a target neighborhood, victimization rates may drop there relative to other, control neighborhoods. The evidence on whether this constitutes true crime prevention, or if crime simply is displaced into other categories or into other neighborhoods, is not persuasive one way or the other. Because a great deal of residential burglary seems to be opportunistic, it is likely there is some true prevention when a large area is successfully saturated with effective measures. However, none of our study neighborhoods was so saturated, making it difficult to expect a strong negative correlation between the adoption of protective measures and burglary rates at the neighborhood level.

Community Involvement. Our analysis indicated that citizen involvement in community organizations which were engaged in some kind of anticrime activity was fairly widespread (14% were so involved). It was difficult to describe this participation as "crime-fighting" in origin, however. The things people did may have had implications for crime and disorder, but they did them because (a) they were "joiners," and (b) the organizations with which they were involved decided to do something about crime.

This was not the view of Durkheim, who argued that community activity concerning crime was sparked by the magnitude of the problem. It comes closer to the position of Conklin, who suggested that the factors related to crime discouraged community organization. We found neighborhood integration was one of the best predictors of participation, and therefore places where participation was highest reported the least fear, the fewest crime problems, and the least disorder. Thus participation in anticrime activities was lowest in places where things were most disorganized (by our measures) and the conditions generally attendant to social disorganization were rampant. This is certainly not evidence for a "problem-solving" view of such involvement, and is more consistent with Conklin's view that fear is incapacitating.

Not much is known of the effectiveness of the kind of involvement we examined here. For individuals, *joining* may be a significant act, leading to enhanced morale, community commitment, and decreased fear. The relationship between membership and morale may in part be a "selection artifact," stemming from a tendency for high-morale people to be joiners. Those who were involved in crime-focused groups were more likely to believe that citizen participation can "make a difference," and that the police can be effective at reducing crime. From what we know about these cities, these beliefs probably did not originate in any great victory against crime, and may rather reflect people's motives for getting involved in the first place. Also, we observed that the spread of information about local events may be facilitated by attending local meetings, and the effect of this knowledge generally is negative. However, it seems likely that on balance the effect of joining is positive, enhancing feelings of mutual support and facilitating mutual surveillance efforts.

At the neighborhood level, extensive citizen involvement in crime-focused activity may facilitate the adoption of both individual and household protective measures. These groups often attempt to get individuals to mark their property, watch their neighbors' houses, and challenge suspicious persons. This involvement may also enhance feelings of security among nonparticipators, if they gain the impression that "someone is watching" and may intervene if they find themselves in difficult situations.

On the other hand, an organized community may take on fortress aspects of its own. Citizen patrols and agressive "protective neighboring" are control mechanisms which may run wild. One of the benefits of urbanity is the tolerance of city residents for diversity and their actual taste for heterogeneity. A certain looseness of social controls, the feeling that "city air makes free," has been an attraction of cities since at least the Middle Ages. In our most integrated neighborhood, South Philadelphia, bands of white toughs actively patrol the boundaries of Black enclaves. While this may serve to keep "strangers" out of the community, and to reduce conflict over appropriate standards of behavior there, this model of crime prevention surely has racist implications. In none of our cities is it entirely clear where social control to prevent crime and social control to stabilize the current distribution of ethnic and racial turf begin and end.

Suburban Flight. The final, and perhaps most significant, reaction to crime we have considered in this volume is flight to the suburbs. Like some others, we found little evidence of a strong "push" effect of neighborhood crime conditions. Rather, people move largely in response to changes in income and household composition. Where they move to, on the other hand, is shaped by the relative attractiveness of various localities and constraints of the housing market. People rate crime as an important consideration when they decide where to move, and crime rates are much lower outside of the central city. However, race and money count for a great deal. Those who live in the worst center-city neighborhoods cannot escape the city, while whites with higher incomes tend not to live in the worst inner-city locations in the first place.

For those involved, moving to the suburbs pays handsome benefits. We contrasted the neighborhoods that those who fled the city had lived in with their ratings of the suburban communities in which they landed. On every dimension things were substantially better in their new places of residence.

For the central city, the consequences of suburban development have been disastrous. The metropolitan area has been segregated on the basis of class and race, concentrating in the city those who can least afford to support the social overhead this entails. The tax base, new investment, and desirable new jobs have fled. While not necessarily *caused* by crime, all of this has implications for inner-city conditions, most of them negative.

Summary

In sum, our findings paint a somewhat gloomy picture of the condition of those whose lives are plagued by serious crime and disorder. Where there is some hope that crime-reduction efforts can play a truly preventive or deterrent function, they are adopted most frequently by upper-status persons in lower crime neighborhoods. The only crime-related efforts we investigated which seemed to be encouraged by crime and adopted most often by those who were more vulnerable to victimization were those which probably simply displaced the efforts of determined offenders on others nearby. Those precautionary tactics, ironically, also are those which may in the aggregate undermine the capacity of the community to control crime and disorder. Actions to protect households and involvement in organized efforts to reduce crime also were concentrated (with a few exceptions in Black neighborhoods) in places where those efforts and services were least needed. Their truly preventive consequences accrue largely to whites and upper-income persons. Finally, while individual decisions to move to the suburbs did not prove to be motivated directly by the threat of crime, other research has dwelled on the criminogenic consequences of flight for the central cities that upper-income whites have left behind. While those who move enjoy tremendous advantages in comparison to the conditions they left behind, those conditions have been made even worse as a result.

Thus while we have solved two of the paradoxes which motivated this research, by demonstrating how crime is "multiplied" into fear and how the vulnerabilities of potential victims serve as powerful psychological and behavioral stimulants, we leave the last of them unresolved. Those who are most affected by crime *do* generally do less about it, and their reactions to crime may in fact have adverse consequences for the communities in which they live.

Our data suggest some avenues for remedying this situation. Household protection seems to be encouraged by home ownership, moderate levels of income, and integration into community life. The latter recommends efforts to encourage the development of neighborhood social networks, and points to potential payoffs from community development programs. Community involvement seems to hinge on decisions by organizational leaders to add crime to the agendas of their groups, and to encourage those who are involved with these groups to participate in those activities. This also recommends a community-organization approach to crime prevention.

Finally, the growth of the suburbs at the expense of central cities has been encouraged and supported by federal and state policies with regard to transportation, home financing, school aid, local taxation, and annexation. There is some sign of a growing understanding of the costs of those policies for society as a whole. In conjunction with the energy crisis, new efforts to restore the traditional vitality of central cities and to plan more carefully the distribution of people and jobs in the metropolis may pay substantial benefits with respect to crime.

REFERENCES

Abt Associates (1977) Seattle Community Crime Prevention Program: Supplementary Report. Cambridge, MA: Abt Associates.

ALDRICH, H. (1975) "Ecological succession in racially changing neighborhoods." Urban Affairs Q. 10 (March): 327-348.

―――― and A. J. REISS, Jr. (1976) "Continuities in the study of ecological succession: changes in the race composition of neighborhoods and their businesses." Amer. J. of Sociology 81 (January): 846-866.

American Institute of Public Opinion (1978) Urban Residents View Their Cities: A National Normative Study, Conducted for the Charles F. Kettering and Charles Mott Foundations. Wilmington, DL: Scholarly Resources.

American Institute of Public Opinion Research (monthly) Gallup Opinion Index.

ANTUNES, G.E., F.L. COOK, T.D. COOK, and W.G. SKOGAN (1977) "Patterns of personal crime against the elderly." Gerontologist 17 (August): 321-327.

ARCHER, D., R. GARTNER, R. AKERT, and T. COCKWOOD (1978) "Cities and homicide: a new look at an old paradox." Comparative Studies in Sociology 1: 73-95.

BALKIN, S. (1979) "Victimization rate, safety, and fear of crime." Social Problems 26: 343-358.

BARD, M. and D. SANGREY (1979) The Crime Victims Book. New York: Basic Books.

BAUMER, T.L. (1980) "Urban crime and personal protective behavior: a comparative analysis." Ph.D. dissertation, Loyola University.

―――― (1979) "The dimensions of fear of crime." Evanston, IL: Center for Urban Affairs, Northwestern University.

―――― (1978) "Research on fear of crime in the United States." Victimology 3, 3-4: 254-264.

―――― and F. DuBOW (1977) "Fear of crime in the polls: what they do and do not tell us." Presented at the annual meeting of the American Association of Public Opinion Research, Buck Hills Falls, Pennsylvania, May 20-22.

―――― and A. HUNTER (1979) "Street traffic, social integration, and fear of crime." Evanston, IL: Center for Urban Affairs, Northwestern University.

BECKER, G. and I. EHRLICH (1972) "Market insurance, self-insurance, and self-protection." J. of Pol. Economy 80 (July/August): 623-648.

BECKER, H.S. (1971) Culture and Civility in San Francisco. New Brunswick, NJ: Transaction.

BIDERMAN, A.D., L.A. JOHNSON, J. McINTYRE, and A.W. WEIR (1967) Report on a Pilot Study in the District of Columbia on Victimization and Attitudes Toward Law Enforcement, Field Surveys I. Washington, DC: Government Printing Office.

BIELBY, W.T. and R.A. BERK (1980) "Sources of error in survey data used in criminal justice evaluations: an analysis of survey respondents reports of 'fear of crime.' " Baltimore, MD: Workshop on Research Methodology and Criminal Justice Program Evaluation, Law Enforcement Assistance Administration.

BLACK, D.J. (1970) "Production of crime rates." Amer. Soc. Rev. 35 (August): 733-747.

BROOKS, S. (1980) Politics of Crime in the 1970s: A Two-City Comparison. Evanston, IL: Center for Urban Affairs, Northwestern University.

BROWN, R.M. (1970) "The American vigilante tradition," in H.D. Graham and T.R. Gurr (eds.) The History of Violence in America. New York: Bantam.

CAMPBELL, D.T. and D.W. FISKE (1959) "Convergent and discriminant validation by the multitrait-multimethod matrix." Psych. Bull. 56 (March): 81-105.

Chicago Police Department (1979) Murder Analysis 1978. Chicago, IL: Chicago Police Department.

CLOTFELTER, C.T. (1977) "Urban crime and household protective measures." Rev. of Economics and Statistics 59 (November): 499-503.

COHN, E.S. (1978) "Fear of crime and feelings of control: reactions to crime in an urban community." Ph.D. dissertation, Temple University.

——— L. KIDDER, and J. HARVEY (1978) "Crime prevention vs. victimization: the psychology of two different reactions." Victimology 3, 3-4: 285-296.

CONKLIN, J.E. (1976) "Robbery, the elderly, and fear: an urban problem in search of solution," pp. 99-110 in J. Goldsmith and S. Goldsmith (eds.) Crime and the Elderly. Lexington, MA: D.C. Heath.

——— (1975) The Impact of Crime. New York: Macmillan.

——— (1972) Robbery and the Criminal Justice System. Philadelphia: J.B. Lippincott.

——— (1971) "Dimensions of community response to the crime problem." Social Problems 18: 373-385.

COOK, F.L., W.G. SKOGAN, T.D. COOK, and G.E. ANTUNES (forthcoming) Criminal Victimization of the Elderly. New York: Oxford Univ. Press.

CORRADO, R.R., R. ROESCH, and W. GLACKMAN (1980) "Lifestyles and victimization: a comparison of Canadian and American survey data." Burnaby, British Columbia: Department of Criminology, Simon Fraser University.

COURTIS, M. and I. DUSSEYER (1970) "Attitudes toward crime and the police in Toronto: a report on some survey findings." Toronto: Centre of Criminology, University of Toronto.

CRENSON, M.A. (1978) "Social networks and political process in urban neighborhoods." Amer. J. of Pol. Sci. 11 (August): 578-594.

DAVIS, F.J. (1951) "Crime news in Colorado newspapers." Amer. J. of Sociology 57 (November): 325-330.

Department of Housing and Urban Development (1973) Abandoned Housing Research: A Compendium. Washington, DC: HUD.

DOMINICK, J. (1973) "Crime and law enforcement on prime-time television." Public Opinion Q. 37 (summer): 241-250.

DOOB, A.N. and G.E. MACDONALD (1979) "Television viewing and fear of victimization: is the relationship causal?" J. of Personality and Social Psychology 37, 2: 170-179.

DROETTBOOM, T., R.J. McALLISTER, E.J. KAISER, and E.W. BUTLER (1971) "Urban violence and residential mobility." J. of the Amer. Institute of Planners 37 (September): 319-325.

DuBOW, F. (1979) Reactions to Crime: A Critical Review of the Literature. Washington, DC: Government Printing Office.

—— and A. PODOLEFSKY (1979) "Participation in collective responses to crime." Evanston, IL: Center for Urban Affairs, Northwestern University.

DUNCAN, G. and S. NEWMAN (1976) "Expected and actual residential moves." J. of the Amer. Institute of Planners 42 (April): 174-186.

DUSSICH, J. and C.J. EICHMAN (1976) "The elderly victim: vulnerability to the criminal act," pp. 91-98 in J. Goldsmith and S. Goldsmith (eds.) Crime and the Elderly. Lexington, MA: D.C. Heath.

EKLUND, D.E. and O.P. WILLIAMS (1978) "The changing spatial distribution of social classes in a metropolitan area." Urban Affairs Q. 13 (March): 313-338.

EMMONS, D. (1979) "Neighborhood activists and community organizations: a critical review of the literature." Evanston, IL: Center for Urban Affairs, Northwestern University.

ENNIS, P.H. (1967) Criminal Victimization in the United States: A Report of a National Survey, Field Surveys II. Washington, DC: Government Printing Office.

EPSTEIN, E.J. (1973) News from Nowhere: Television and the News. New York: Random House.

Federal Bureau of Investigation (yearly) Uniform Crime Report. Washington, DC: Government Printing Office.

FISHMAN, M. (1978) "Crime waves as ideology." Social Problems 29 (June): 531-543.

FOX, J.A. (1978) Forecasting Crime Data: An Econometric Analysis. Lexington, MA: D.C. Heath.

FREY, W.H. (1979) "Central city white flight: racial and non-racial causes." Amer. Soc. Rev. 44 (June): 425-448.

FRISBIE, D.W., G. FISHBINE, R. HINTZ, M. JOELSON, and J.B. NUTTER (1977) Crime in Minneapolis: Proposals for Prevention. St. Paul, MN: Community Crime Prevention Project, Governor's Commission on Crime Prevention and Control.

FUNKHOUSER, G.R. (1973) "The issues of the sixties: an exploratory study in the dynamics of public opinion." Public Opinion Q. 37 (spring): 62-75.

FURSTENBERG, F.F., Jr. (1972) "Fear of crime and its effects on citizen behavior," in A. Biderman (ed.) Crime and Justice: A Symposium. New York: Nailburg.

—— (1971) "Public reactions to crime in the streets." Amer. Scholar 40 (autumn): 601-610.

GAROFALO. J.A. (1977a) Public Opinion About Crime. Washington, DC: National Criminal Justice Information and Statistics Service, Law Enforcement Assistance Administration.

—— (1977b) "Victimization and the fear of crime in major American cities." Presented at the annual meeting of the American Association for Public Opinion Research, Buck Hills Falls, Pennsylvania, May 20-22.

—— and M.J. HINDELANG (1977) An Introduction to the National Crime Survey. Washington, DC: National Criminal Justice Information and Statistics Service, Law Enforcement Assistance Administration.

GAROFALO, J.A. and J. LAUB (1978) "The fear of crime: broadening our perspective." Victimology 3, 3-4: 242-253.

GERBNER, G. and L. GROSS (1976) "Living with television: the violence profile." J. of Communication 26: 172-199.

——— (1975) "Television as enculturation — a new research approach." Philadelphia: Annenberg School of Communication, University of Pennsylvania.

GOODWIN, C. (1979) The Oak Park Strategy: Community Control of Racial Change. Chicago: Univ. of Chicago Press.

GORDON, M.T., L. HEATH, and R. LeBAILLY (1979) "Some costs of easy news: crime reports and fear." Evanston, IL: Center for Urban Affairs, Northwestern University.

——— J. REISS, and T. TYLER (1979) Crime in the Newspapers and Fear in the Neighborhoods: Some Unintended Consequences. Evanston, IL: Center for Urban Affairs, Northwestern University.

GORDON, M.T., S. RIGER, R.K. LeBAILLY, and L. HEATH (1980) "Crime, women, and the quality of urban life." Signs 5 (spring): 144-160.

Governor's Commission on Crime Prevention and Crime Control (1976) Minnesota Crime Watch. St. Paul: State of Minnesota.

GRABER, D. (1977) "Ideological components in the perceptions of crime and crime news." Presented at the annual meeting of the Society for the Study of Social Problems, Chicago.

GRANFIELD, M. (1975) An Econometric Model of Residential Location. Cambridge, MA: Ballinger.

GREER, S. (1962) The Emerging City. New York: Macmillan.

GUBRIUM, J.F. (1974) "Victimization in old age: available evidence and three hypotheses." Crime and Delinquency 20 (July): 245-250.

GURR, T.R. (1977a) "Contemporary crime in historical perspective: a comparative study of London, Stockholm, and Sydney." Annals of the Amer. Academy of Pol. and Social Sci. 434 (November): 114-136.

——— (1977b) "Crime trends in modern democracies since 1945." Evanston, IL: Center for Urban Affairs, Northwestern University.

HALBERSTAM, D. (1979) The Powers That Be. New York: Knopf.

HANSEN, R.D. and J.M. DONOGHUE (1977) "The power of consensus: information derived from one's own and other's behavior." J. of Personality and Social Psychology 35: 294-302.

HARTNAGEL, T.F. (1979) "The perception and fear of crime: implications for neighborhood cohesion, social activity, and community effect." Social Forces 37: 176-193.

HELLER, N.B., W.W. STENZEL, A.D. GILL, R.A. KOLDE, and S.R. SCHIMERMAN (1975) Operation Identification Projects: Assessment of Effectiveness. Washington, DC: National Institute of Law Enforcement and Administration of Justice, Law Enforcement Assistance Administration.

HENIG, J. and M.G. MAXFIELD (1978) "Reducing fear of crime: strategies for intervention." Victimology 3, 3-4: 297-313.

HINDELANG, M.J. (1978) "Race and involvement in crimes." Amer. Soc. Rev. 43 (February): 93-109.

——— M. GOTTFREDSON, and J. GAROFALO (1978) The Victims of Personal Crime. Cambridge, MA: Ballinger.

HOFSTETTER, C.R. (1976) Bias in the News. Columbus: Ohio State Univ. Press.

HUNTER, A. (1978a) "Persistence of local sentiments in mass society," pp. 133-162 in D. Street (ed.) Handbook of Contemporary Urban Life. San Francisco: Jossey-Bass.

——— (1978b) "Symbols of incivility: social disorder and fear of crime in urban neighborhoods." Presented at the annual meeting of the American Society of Criminology, Dallas, Texas, November 8-12.

——— (1974) Symbolic Communities. Chicago: Univ. of Chicago Press.

HURLEY, P. and G.E. ANTUNES (1977) "The representation of criminal events in Houston's two daily newspapers." Journ. Q. 54: 756-760.

Institute for Social Research (1975) Public Safety: Quality of Life in the Detroit Metropolitan Area. Ann Arbor: University of Michigan.

JACOBS, J. (1961) The Death and Life of Great American Cities. New York: Vintage.

JANOWITZ, M. (1978) The Last Half-Century: Societal Change and Politics in America. Chicago: Univ. of Chicago Press.

JAYCOX, V.H. (1978) "The elderly's fear of crime: rational or irrational." Victimology 3, 3-4: 329-333.

JONES, E.T. (1976) "The press as metropolitan monitor." Public Opinion Q. 40 (summer): 239-244.

KASARDA, J.D. (1976) "The changing occupational structure of the American metropolis," pp. 113-136 in B. Schwartz (ed.) The Changing Face of the Metropolis. Chicago: Univ. of Chicago Press.

——— (1972) "The impact of suburban population growth on central-city service functions." Amer. J. of Sociology 77 (May): 1111-1124.

KASL, S.V. and E. HARBURG (1972) "Perceptions of the neighborhood and the desire to move out." J. of the Amer. Institute of Planners 38 (September): 318-324.

KELLER, S. (1968) The Urban Neighborhood: A Sociological Perspective. New York: Random House.

KIM, Y. J. (1976) "The social correlates of perceptions of neighborhood crime problems and fear of victimization." Evanston, IL: Center for Urban Affairs, Northwestern University.

KLECKA, W.R. and G.F. BISHOP (1978) "Neighborhood profiles of senior citizens in four American cities: a report of findings to the National Council of Senior Citizens." Washington, DC: National Council of Senior Citizens.

KLEINMAN, P. and D. DAVID (1973) "Victimization and perception of crime in a ghetto community." Criminology 13 (November): 307-343.

LALLI, M. and L.D. SAVITZ (1976) "The fear of crime in the school enterprise and its consequences." Education and Urban Society 8 (August): 401-416.

LAVRAKAS, P. J. and E. J. HERZ (1979) "An investigation of citizen participation in crime prevention meetings and other anti-crime activities." Evanston, IL: Center for Urban Affairs, Northwestern University.

LAVRAKAS, P. J., J. NORMOYLE, W.G. SKOGAN, E.J. HERZ, G. SALEM, and D.A. LEWIS (1980) Citizen Participation and Community Crime Prevention: An Exploration. (Draft Report). Evanston, IL: Center for Urban Affairs, Northwestern University.

Law Enforcement Assistance Administration (1977) Guidelines Manual: Guide to Discretionary Grant Programs. Washington, DC: LEAA.

LAWTON, M.P., L. NAHEMOW, S. YAFFE, and S. FELDMAN (1976) "Psychological aspects of crime and fear of crime," in J. Goldsmith and S. Goldsmith (eds.) Crime and the Elderly. Lexington, MA: D.C. Heath.

LeJEUNE, R. and N. ALEX (1973) "On being mugged: the event and its after-math." Urban Life and Culture 2 (October): 259-287.

LEMERT, E.M. (1951) Social Pathology. New York: McGraw-Hill.

LEWIS, D.A. (1980) "Sociological theory and the production of a social problem: the case of fear of crime." Ph.D. dissertation, University of California — Santa Cruz.

——— (1979) "Design problems in public policy development: the case of the community anti-crime program." Criminology 17 (August): 172-183.

——— R. SZOC, G. SALEM, and R. LEVIN (1980) Crime and Community: Understanding Fear of Crime in Urban America. Evanston IL: Center for Urban Affairs, Northwestern University.

MACALLISTER, R.J., E.J. KAISER, and E. BUTLER (1971) "Residential mobility of blacks and whites: a national longitudinal study." Amer. J. of Sociology (November): 445-456.

Malt Associates (1971) An Analysis of Public Safety as Related to the Incidence of Crime in Parks and Recreation Areas in Central Cities, Phase I. Washington, DC: HUD.

MANGIONE, T.W. and C. NOBLE (1975) Baseline Survey Measures Including Update Survey Information for the Evaluation of a Crime Control Model. Boston: Survey Research Program, University of Massachusetts.

MARSHALL, H. (1979) "White movement to the suburbs." Amer. Soc. Rev. 44 (December): 975-994.

MARX, G.T. and D. ARCHER (1976) "Community police patrols and vigilantism," in H.J. Rosenberg and P.C. Sederberg (eds.) Vigilante Politics. Philadelphia: Univ. of Pennsylvania Press.

——— (1972) Community Police Patrols: An Exploratory Inquiry. Cambridge: Harvard and MIT Joint Center for Urban Studies.

MAXFIELD, M.G. (1979) "Discretion and the delivery of police services." Ph.D. dissertation, Northwestern University.

——— (1977) "Reactions to fear." Evanston, IL: Center for Urban Affairs, Northwestern University.

——— and A. HUNTER (1980) Methodological Overview of the Reactions to Crime Project. Evanston, IL: Center for Urban Affairs, Northwestern University.

McINTYRE, J. (1967) "Public attitudes toward crime and law enforcement." Annals of the Amer. Academy of Pol. and Social Sci. 374 (November): 34-46.

McPHERSON, M. (1978) "Realities and perceptions of crime at the neighborhood level." Victimology 3, 3-4: 319-328.

National Council on Aging (1978) Fact Book on Aging. Washington, DC: National Council on Aging.

National Opinion Research Center (1978) National Data Program for the Social Sciences: General Social Survey Cumulative Codebook 1972-1977. Chicago: University of Chicago.

NEHNEVAJSA, J. and A.P. KARELITZ (1977) The Nation Looks at Crime: Crime as a National, Community, and Neighborhood Problem. Pittsburgh: University Center for Urban Research, University of Pittsburgh.

NEWMAN. O. (1972) Defensible Space: Crime Prevention Through Urban Design. New York: Macmillan.

——— and K. FRANCK (1979) Factors Influencing Crime and Instability in Urban Housing Developments. New York: Institute for Community Design Analysis.

O'NEIL, M.J. (1977) "Calling the cops: responses of witness to criminal incidents." Ph. D. dissertation, Northwestern University.

PODOLEFSKY, A., F. DuBOW, G. SALEM, and J. LIEBERMAN (1980) Collective Responses: Approaches to Reducing Crime in the Neighborhood. Evanston, IL: Center for Urban Affairs, Northwestern University.

President's Commission on Law Enforcement and Administration of Justice (1967) The Challenge of Crime in a Free Society. Washington, DC: Government Printing Office.

QUIGLEY, J.M. and D.H. WEINBERG (1977) "Intra-urban residential mobility: review and synthesis." Int. Regional Sci. Rev. 2.

RAINWATER. L. (1966) "Fear and the house-as-haven in the lower class." J. of the Amer. Institute of Planners 32 (January): 23-31.

Reactions to Crime Project (1978) The Results of the Preliminary Analysis: Findings and New Directions. Evanston, IL: Center for Urban Affairs, Northwestern University.

REISS, A. J., Jr. (1967) Public Perceptions and Recollections About Crime, Law Enforcement, and Criminal Justice, Volume 1, Section 2 of Studies in Crime and Law Enforcement in Major Metropolitan Areas. Washington, DC: Government Printing Office.

REPPETTO, T. (1974) Residential Crime. Cambridge, MA: Ballinger.

RIFAI, M.A. (1976) Older Americans Crime Prevention Research Project. Portland, OR: Multnomah County Division of Public Safety.

RIGER, S. and M.T. GORDON (1979) "Fear of rape project interim report." Evanston, IL: Center for Urban Affairs, Northwestern University.

——— and R. LeBAILLY (1978) "Women's fear of crime: from blaming to restricting the victim." Victimology 3, 3-4: 274-284.

ROSENCRANZ, A. (1977) "Interviews with San Francisco city officials." Evanston, IL: Center for Urban Affairs, Northwestern University.

ROSENTHAL, J. (1969) "The cage of fear in cities beset by crime." Life 67 (July 11).

ROSHIER, B. (1973) "The selection of crime news by the press," in S. Cohen and J. Young (eds.) The Manufacture of News. Beverly Hills, CA: Sage.

ROSSI, P.H. (1980) Why Families Move. Beverly Hills, CA: Sage.

RUBINSTEIN, J. (1973) City Police. New York: Farrar, Straus and Giroux.

SAVITZ, L.D., M. LALLI, and L. ROSEN (1977) City Life and Delinquency — Victimization, Fear of Crime and Gang Membership. Washington, DC: Office of Juvenile Justice and Delinquency Prevention, Law Enforcement Assistance Administration.

SCARR, H., J. PINSKY, and D. WYATT (1973) Patterns of Burglary. Washington, DC: Human Sciences Research, Inc.

SCHNEIDER, A.L. (1978) The Portland Forward Records Check of Crime Victims: Final Report. Washington, DC: National Institute of Law Enforcement and Criminal Justice, Law Enforcement Assistance Administration.

——— (1975) Evaluation of the Portland Neighborhood-Based Anti-Burglary Program. Eugene, OR: Oregon Research Institute.

——— and P.B. SCHNEIDER (1977) "Private and public-minded citizen responses to a neighborhood-based crime prevention strategy." Eugene, OR: Institute of Policy Analysis.

SEIDMAN, D. and M. COUZENS (1974) "Getting the crime rate down: political pressures and crime reporting." Law and Society Rev. 8 (spring): 457-493.

SHAW, C.R. and H.D. McKAY (1942) Juvenile Delinquency and Urban Areas. Chicago: Univ. of Chicago Press.

SHOTLAND, R.L., S. HAYWARD, C. YOUNG, M. SIGNORELLA, K. MIN-DINGALL, J. KENNEDY, M. ROVINE, and E. DANOWITZ (1979) "Fear of crime in residential communities." Criminology 17 (May): 34-45.

SILBERMAN, C.E. (1978) Criminal Violence, Criminal Justice. New York: Random House.

SILBERT, M., H. SCHECHTER, and D. BOATRIGHT (1978) Final Evaluation Report on the SAFE Project. Oakland, CA: Approach Associates.

SINGER, S.L. (1977) "The concept of vulnerability and the elderly victim in an urban environment," pp. 75-80 in J.E. Scott and S. Dinitz (eds.) Criminal Justice Planning. New York: Praeger.

SKOGAN, W.G. (1979a) "Crime in contemporary America," ch. 14 in H. Graham and T.R. Gurr (eds.) Violence in America. Beverly Hills, CA: Sage.

———— (1979b) "Citizen satisfaction with police services," pp. 29-42 in R. Baker and F.A. Meyer, Jr. (eds.) Evaluating Alternative Law Enforcement Policies. Lexington, MA: D.C. Heath.

———— (1978a) The Center for Urban Affairs Random Digit Dialing Telephone Survey. Evanston, IL: Center for Urban Affairs, Northwestern University.

———— (1978b) Victimization Surveys and Criminal Justice Planning. Washington, DC: National Institute of Law Enforcement and Criminal Justice, Law Enforcement Assistance Administration.

———— (1977a) "The changing distribution of crime: a multi-city time-series analysis." Urban Affairs Q. 13 (September): 33-48.

———— (1977b) "Public policy and fear of crime in large American cities," pp. 1-18 in J.A. Gardiner (ed.) Public Law and Public Policy. New York: Praeger.

———— (1976a) "Citizen reporting of crime: some national panel data." Criminology 13 (February): 535-549.

———— (1976b) "Crime and crime rates," pp. 105-120 in W. Skogan (ed.) Sample Surveys of the Victims of Crime. Cambridge, MA: Ballinger.

———— (1975) "Public policy and public evaluations of criminal justice system performance," pp. 43-62 in J.A. Gardiner and M.A. Mulkey (eds.) Crime and Criminal Justice. Lexington, MA: D.C. Heath.

———— (n.d.) "Notes on the cumulative probability of being victimized in a life-time" (with the assistance of R.A. Linster). Northwestern University. (unpublished)

———— and W.R. KLECKA (1977) The Fear of Crime. Washington, DC: American Political Science Association.

SMITH, T.W. (1979) "America's most important problem: a trend analysis 1946-1976." Presented at the annual meeting of the American Association for Public Opinion Research, June.

SPARKS, R.F., H. GENN, and D.J. DODD (1977) Surveying Victims. New York: John Wiley.

SPRINGER, L. (1974) "Crime perception and response behavior." Ph.D. dissertation, Pennsylvania State University.

STINCHCOMBE, A., C. HEIMER, R.A. ILIFF, K. SCHEPPELE, T.W. SMITH, and D.G. TAYLOR (1978) Crime and Punishment in Public Opinion: 1948-1974. Chicago: National Opinion Research Center.

SUDMAN, S. and N. BRADBURN (1974) Response Effects in Surveys. Chicago: Aldine.

SUNDEEN, R.A. and J.T. MATHIEU (1976a) "The fear of crime and its consequences among elderly in three urban communities." Gerontologist 16 (June): 211-219.

―――― (1976b) "The urban elderly, environments of fear," pp. 51-66 in J. Goldsmith and S. Goldsmith (eds.) Crime and the Elderly. Lexington, MA: D.C. Heath.

SUTTLES, G.D. (1972) The Social Construction of Communities. Chicago: Univ. of Chicago Press.

―――― (1968) The Social Order of the Slum. Chicago: Univ. of Chicago Press.

TAUB, R. and D.G. TAYLOR (1979) Memo from National Opinion Research Center, Chicago, to the National Institute of Justice. (unpublished)

TUCHFARBER, A. and W.R. KLECKA (1976) Random Digit Dialing: Lowering the Cost of Victimization Surveys. Washington, DC: Police Foundation.

TURNER, A.G. (1972) San Jose Methods Test of Known Crime Victims. Washington, DC: National Information and Statistics Service, Law Enforcement Assistance Administration.

TYLER, T.R. (1978) "The effects of directly and indirectly experienced events: the origin of crime-related judgements and behavior." Northwestern University. (unpublished)

U.S. Bureau of the Census (1978a) Indicators of Housing and Neighborhood Quality. Current Housing Report H-150-76, Part B. Washington, DC: Government Printing Office.

―――― (1978b) "Population profile of the United States 1977." Current Population Reports, series p-20, no. 324 (April). Washington, DC: Government Printing Office.

U.S. Department of Justice (1979) The Cost of Negligence: Losses from Preventable Household Burglaries. Washington, DC: National Criminal Justice Information and Statistics Service, Law Enforcement Assistance Administration.

―――― (1978a) Criminal Victimization in the United States: A Comparison of 1976 and 1977 Findings (Advance Report). Washington, DC: National Criminal Justice Information and Statistics Service, Law Enforcement Assistance Administration.

―――― (1978b) Sourcebook of Criminal Justice Statistics — 1977. Washington, DC: Government Printing Office.

―――― (1977a) Criminal Victimization Survey in San Francisco. Washington, DC: National Criminal Justice Information and Statistics Service, Law Enforcement Assistance Administration.

―――― (1977b) Criminal Victimization in the United States 1974. Washington, DC: National Criminal Justice Information and Statistics Service, Law Enforcement Assistance Administration.

―――― (1977c) Criminal Victimization in the United States: A Comparison of 1975 and 1976 Findings. Washington, DC: National Criminal Justice Information and Statistics Service, Law Enforcement Assistance Administration.

―――― (1976) Criminal Victimization Surveys in Chicago, Detroit, Los Angeles, New York and Philadelphia. Washington, DC: National Criminal Justice Information and Statistics Service, Law Enforcement Assistance Administration.

―――― (1975) Criminal Victimization Surveys in 13 American Cities. Washington, DC: National Criminal Justice Information and Statistics Service, Law Enforcement Assistance Administration.

VAN DIJK, J.J. (1978) "Public attitudes toward crime in the Netherlands." Victimology 3, 3-4: 265-273.

VERBA, S. and N.H. NIE (1972) Participation in America: Political Democracy and Social Equality. New York: Harper & Row.

WASHNIS, G.J. (1976) Citizen Involvement in Crime Prevention. Lexington, MA: D.C. Heath.

WILSON, J.Q. (1975) Thinking About Crime. New York: Basic Books.

——— (1968a) Varieties of Police Behavior. New York: Atheneum.

——— (1968b) "The urban unease: community versus the city." Public Interest 12 (summer): 25-39.

WILSON, L.A., II (1976) "Private and collective choice behavior in the provision of personal security from criminal victimization." Ph.D. dissertation, University of Oregon.

——— and A.L. SCHNEIDER (1978) "Investigating the efficacy and equity of public initiatives in the provision of private safety." Eugene, OR: Institute of Policy Analysis.

WIRTH, L. (1938) "Urbanism as a way of life." Amer. J. of Sociology 44, 1: 1-24.

WOLFGANG, M.E. (1978) "National survey of crime severity." Report to the National Information and Statistics Service, Law Enforcement Assistance Administration.

——— (1957) "Victim precipitated criminal homicide." J. of Criminal Law, Criminology and Police Sci. 48 (May/June): 1-11.

WRIGHT, J.D. and L.I. MARSTON (1975) "The ownership of the means of destruction: weapons in the United States." Social Problems 23 (October): 93-107.

YADEN, D., S. FOLKSTAND, and P. GLAZER (1973) The Impact of Crime in Selected Neighborhoods: A Study of Public Attitudes in Four Portland Census Tracts. Portland, OR: Campaign Information Counselors.

YANCEY, W.L. and E.P. ERICKSEN (1979) "The antecedents of community: the economic and institutional structure of urban neighbors." Amer. Soc. Rev. 44 (April): 253-261.

ZION, R.J. (1978) "Reducing crime and fear of crime in downtown Cleveland." Victimology 3, 3-4: 341-344.

INDEX